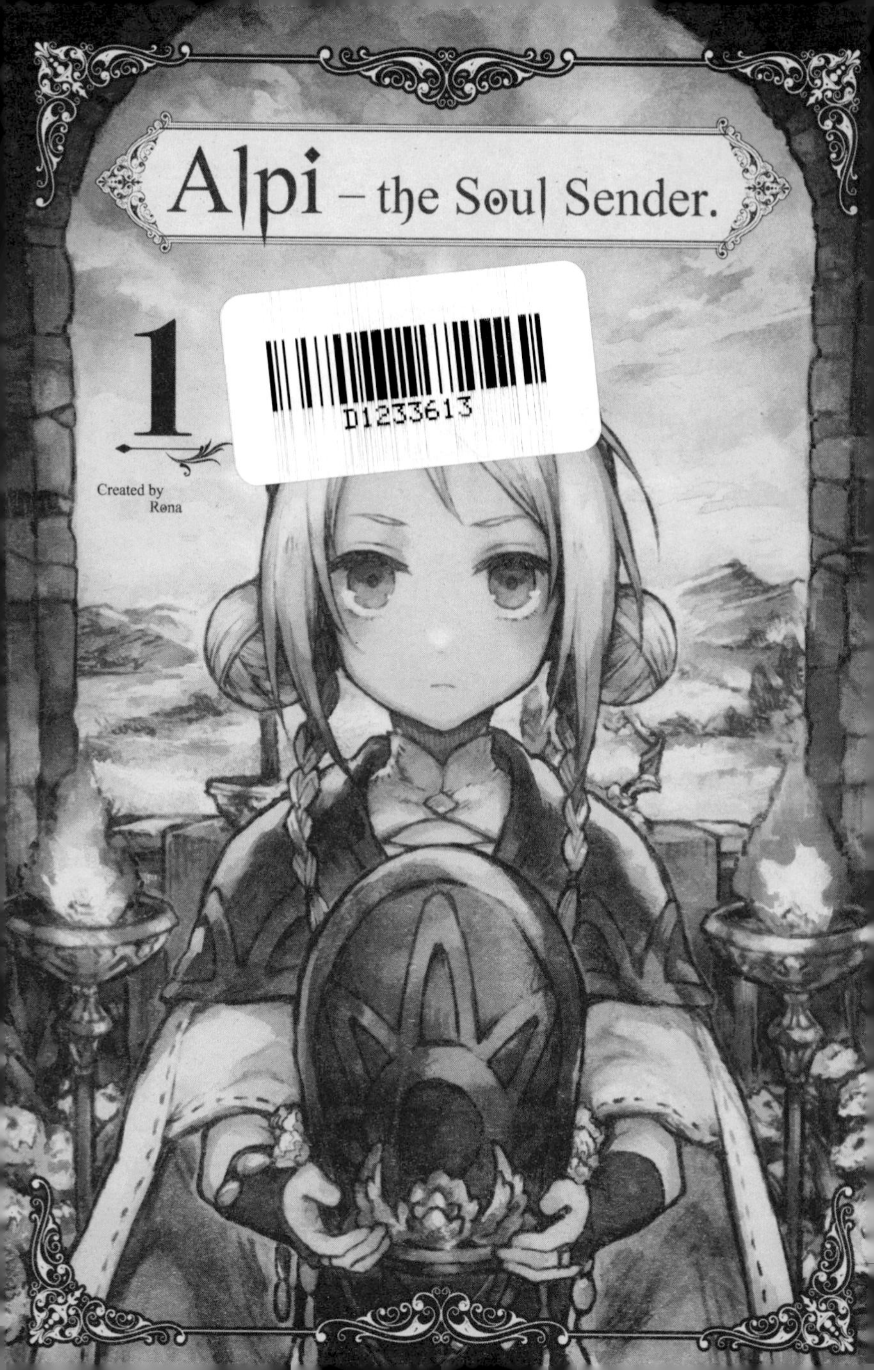
Alpi – the Soul Sender.
1
Created by
Rona

Contents

Alpi – the Soul Sender.

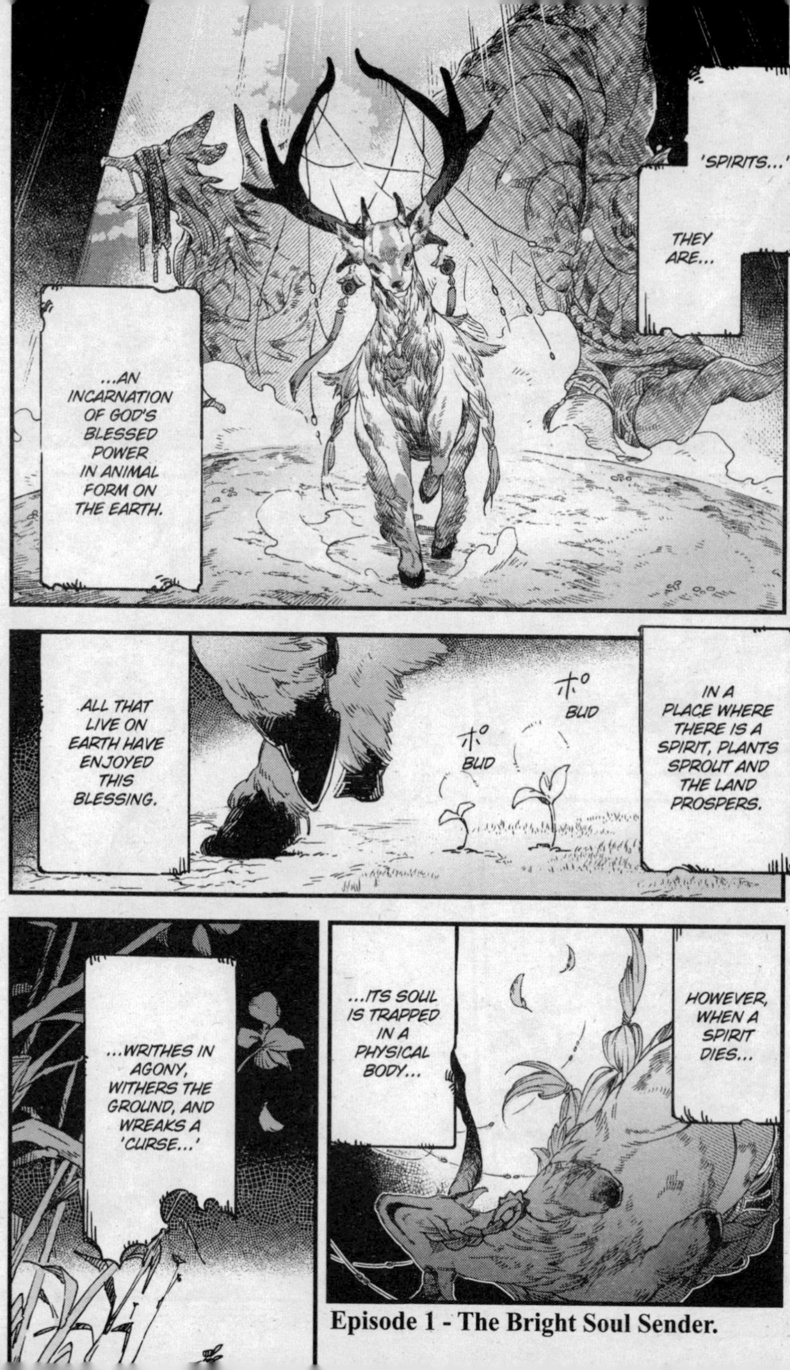
'SPIRITS...'
THEY ARE...
...AN INCARNATION OF GOD'S BLESSED POWER IN ANIMAL FORM ON THE EARTH.
IN A PLACE WHERE THERE IS A SPIRIT, PLANTS SPROUT AND THE LAND PROSPERS.
ポ BUD
ポ BUD
ALL THAT LIVE ON EARTH HAVE ENJOYED THIS BLESSING.
HOWEVER, WHEN A SPIRIT DIES...
...ITS SOUL IS TRAPPED IN A PHYSICAL BODY...
...WRITHES IN AGONY, WITHERS THE GROUND, AND WREAKS A 'CURSE...'

Episode 1 - The Bright Soul Sender.

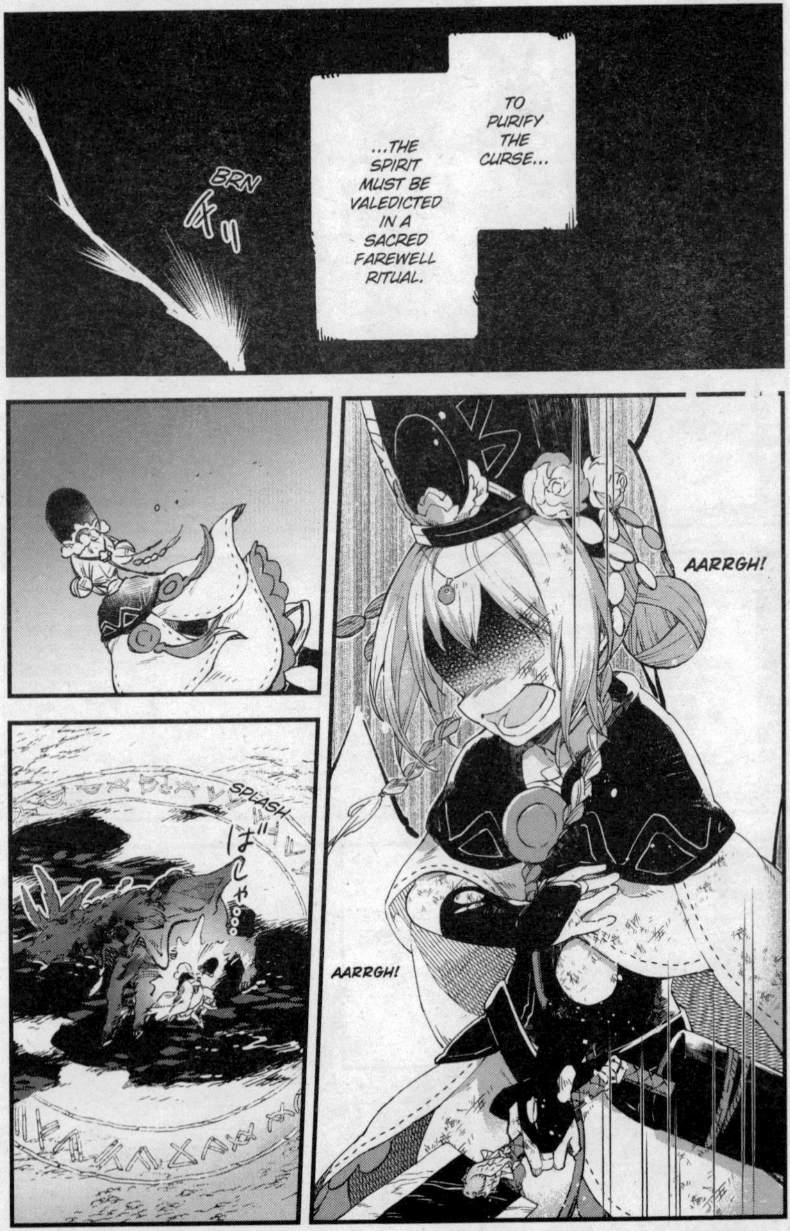
TO PURIFY THE CURSE...
...THE SPIRIT MUST BE VALEDICTED IN A SACRED FAREWELL RITUAL.
BRN
ギリ
AARRGH!
AARRGH!
SPLASH
ばしゃ

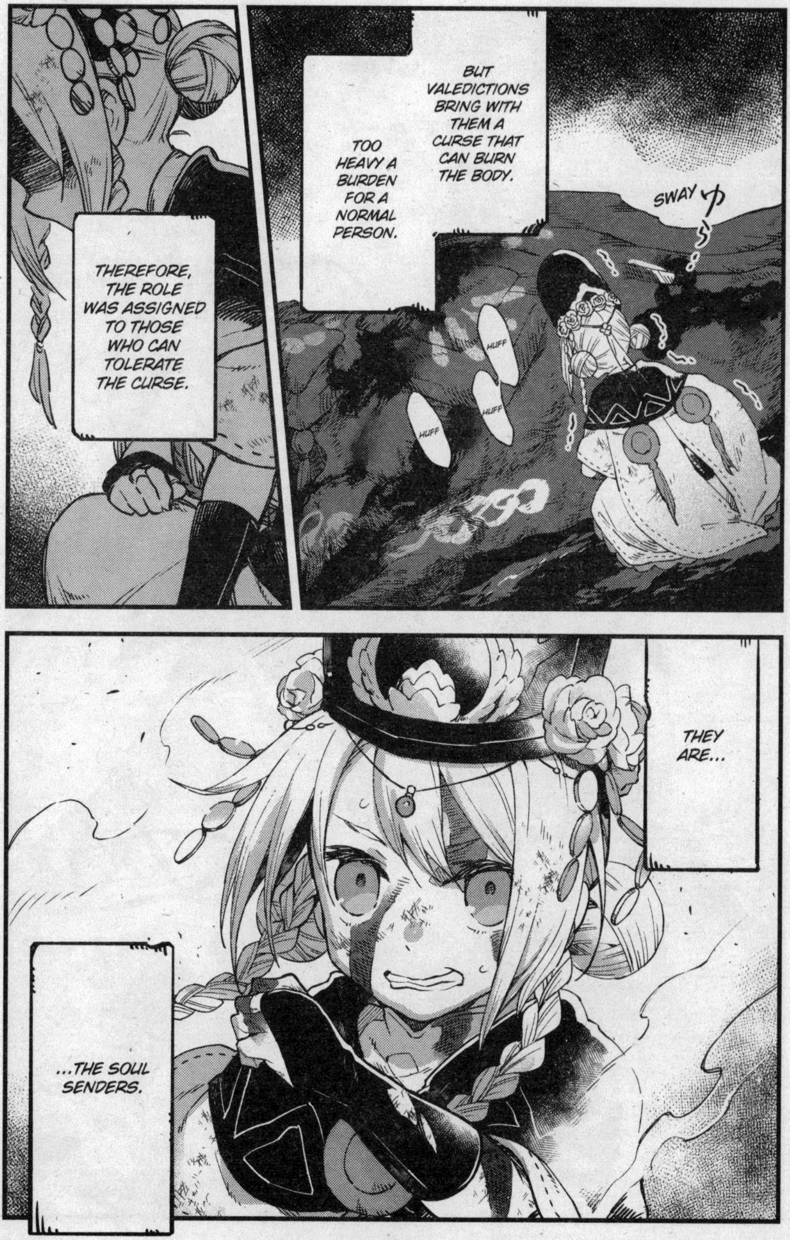
BUT VALEDICTIONS BRING WITH THEM A CURSE THAT CAN BURN THE BODY.
TOO HEAVY A BURDEN FOR A NORMAL PERSON.
SWAY
HUFF
HUFF
HUFF
THEREFORE, THE ROLE WAS ASSIGNED TO THOSE WHO CAN TOLERATE THE CURSE.
THEY ARE...
...THE SOUL SENDERS.

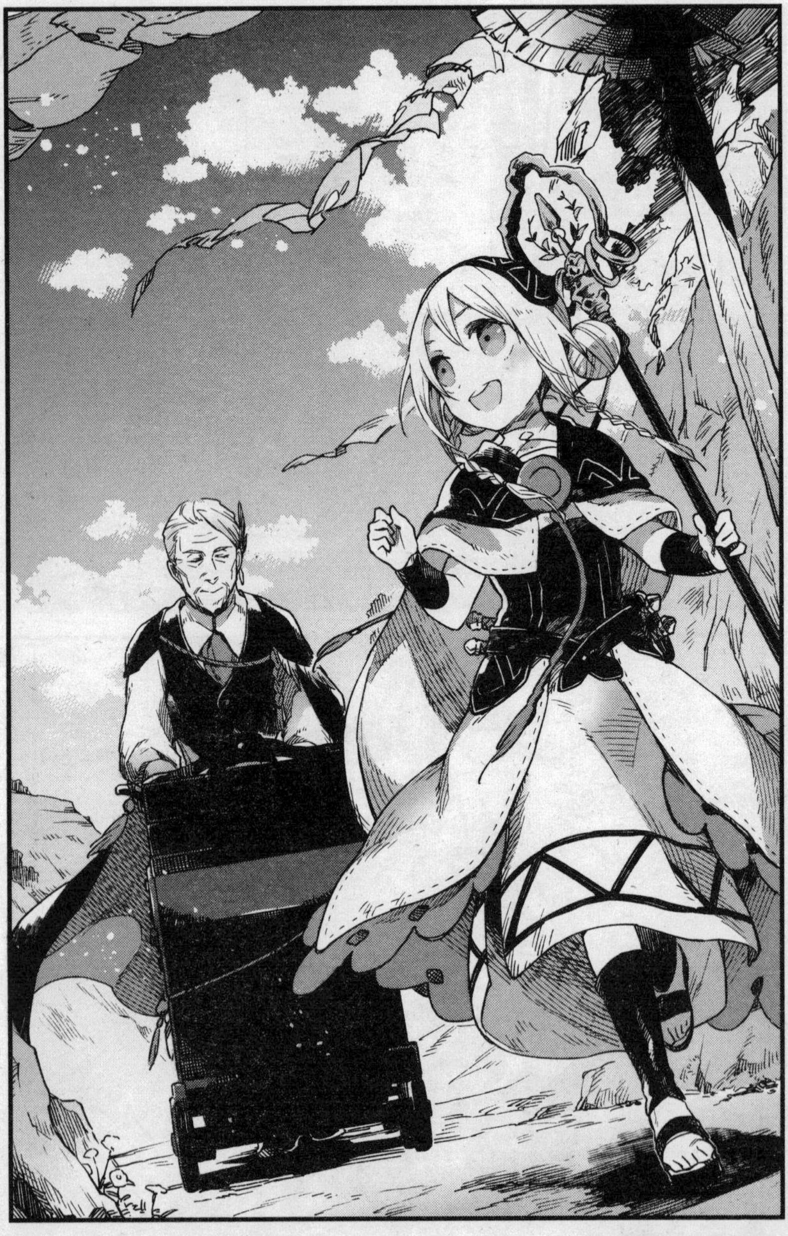

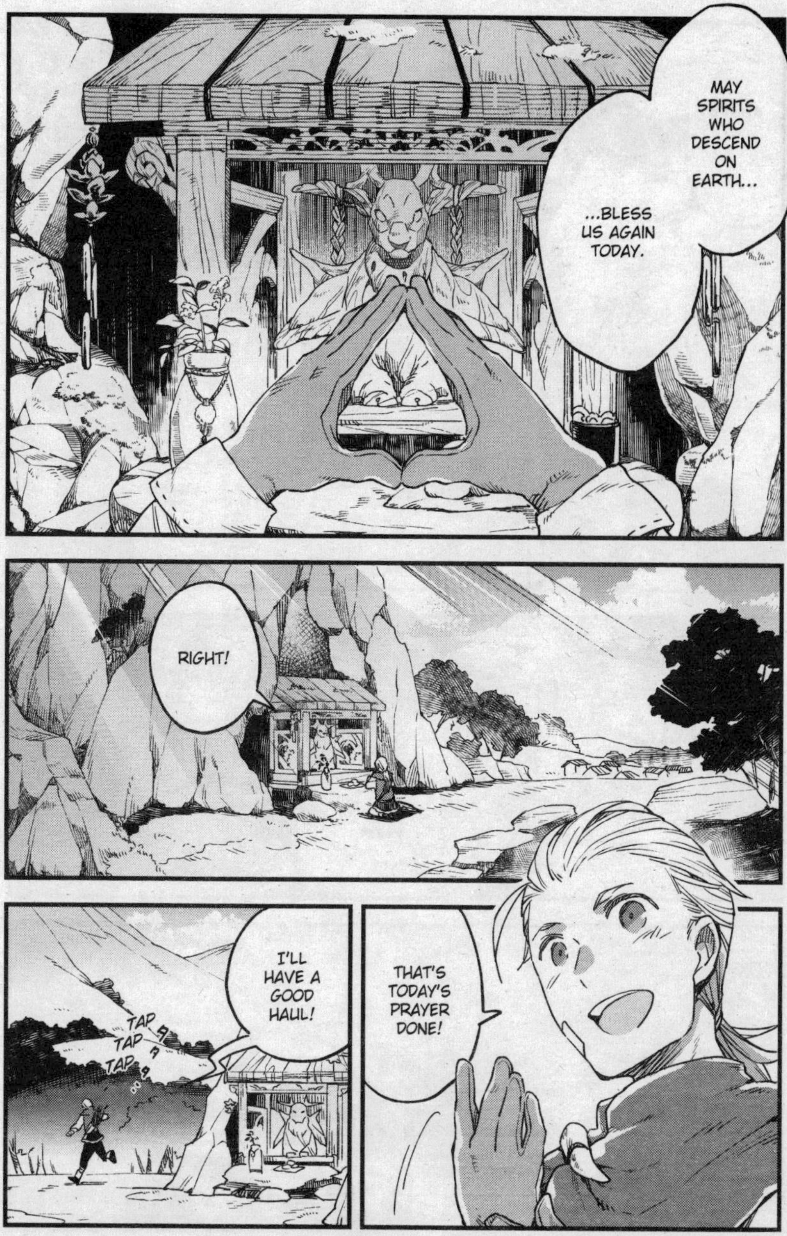
MAY SPIRITS WHO DESCEND ON EARTH...
...BLESS US AGAIN TODAY.
RIGHT!
THAT'S TODAY'S PRAYER DONE!
I'LL HAVE A GOOD HAUL!
TAP TAP TAP

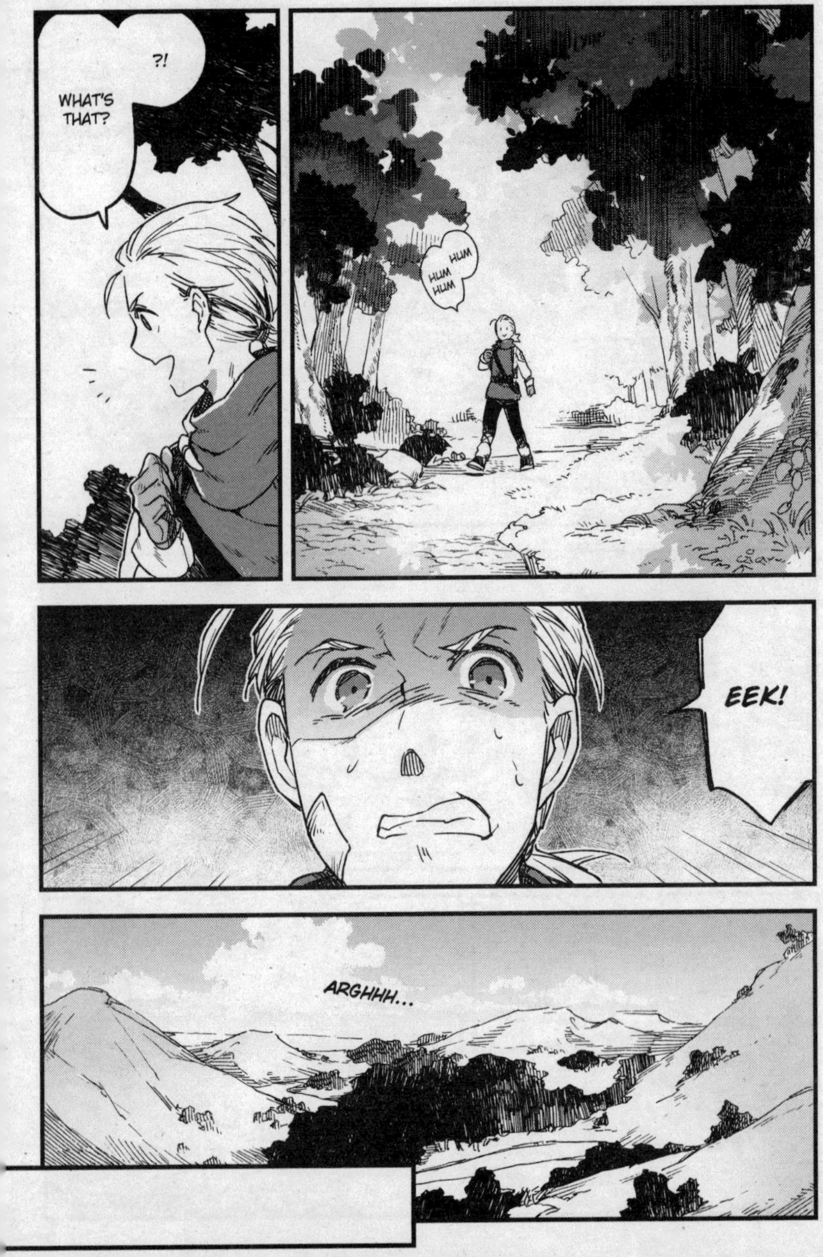
HUM HUM HUM
?!
WHAT'S THAT?
EEK!
ARGHHH...

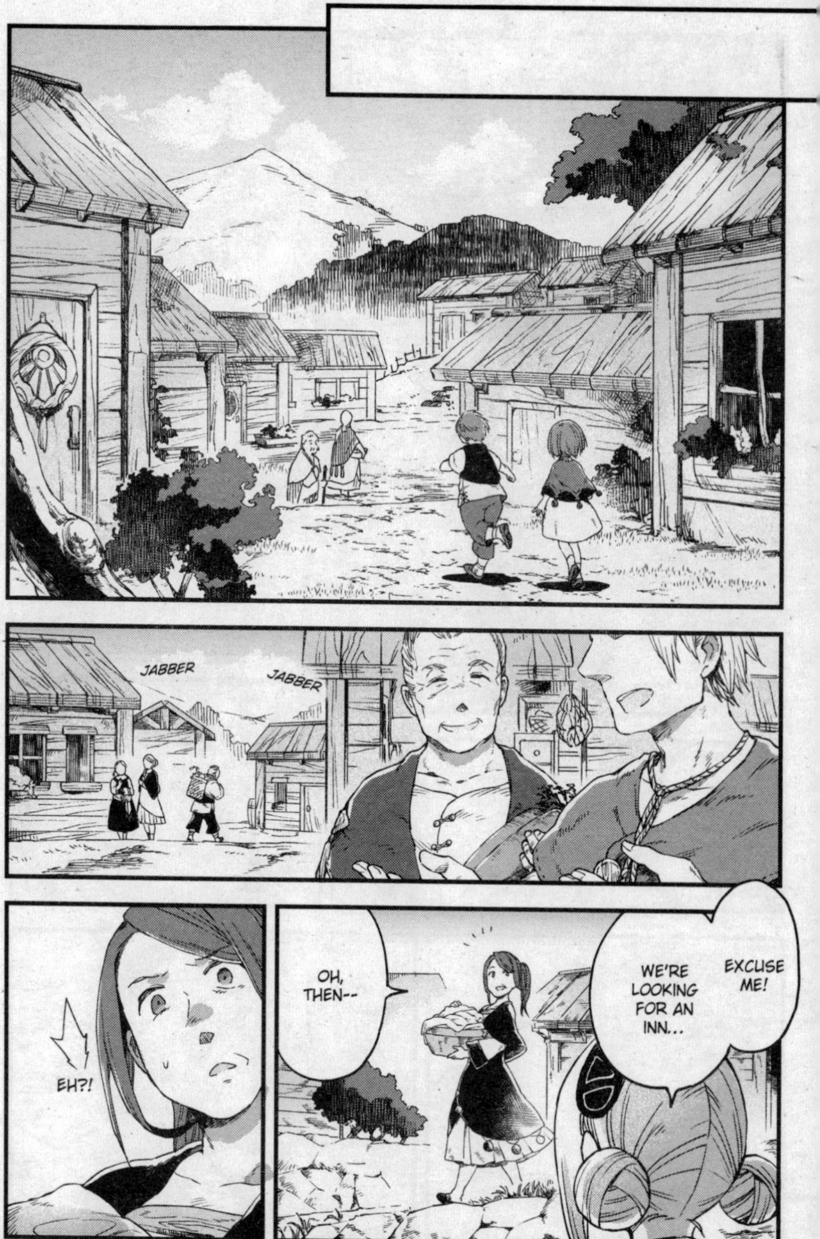
JABBER
JABBER
EXCUSE ME!
WE'RE LOOKING FOR AN INN...
OH, THEN--
EH?!

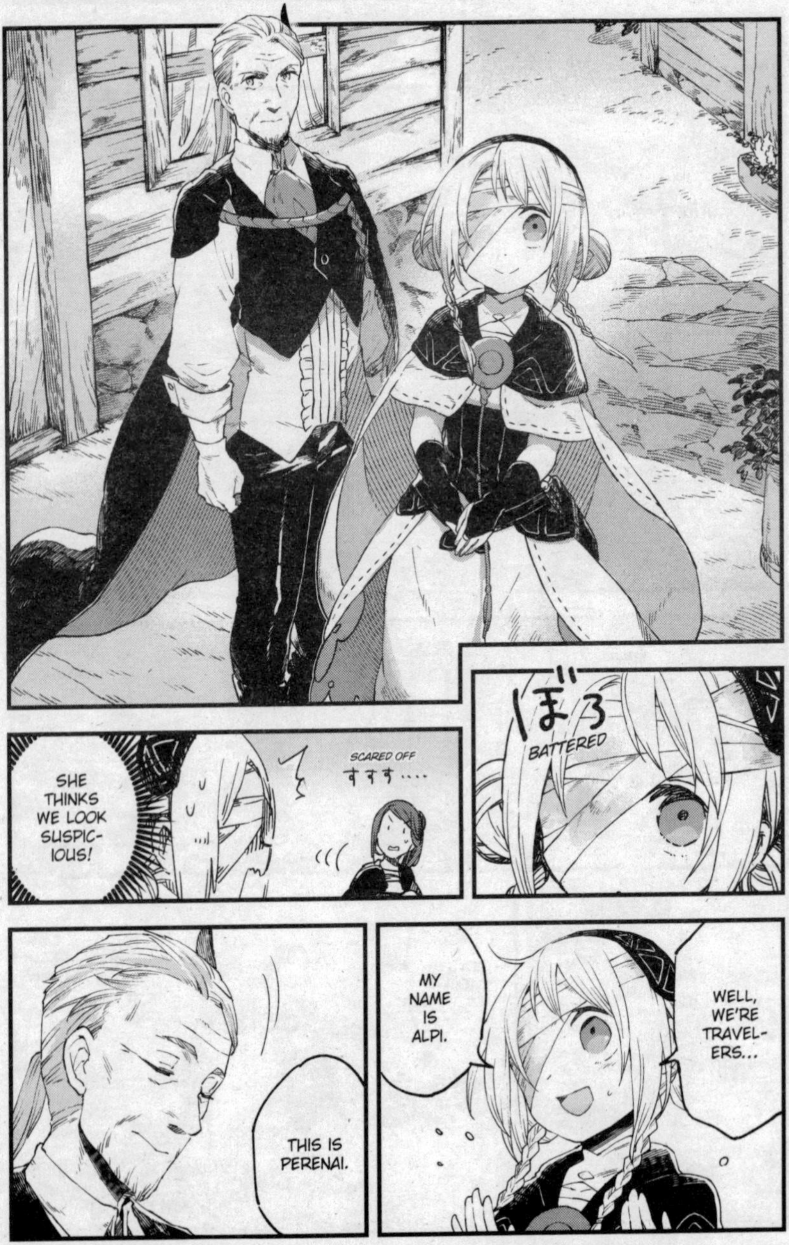
ぼろ
BATTERED
SCARED OFF
すすす....
SHE THINKS WE LOOK SUSPICIOUS!
WELL, WE'RE TRAVELERS...
MY NAME IS ALPI.
THIS IS PERENAI.

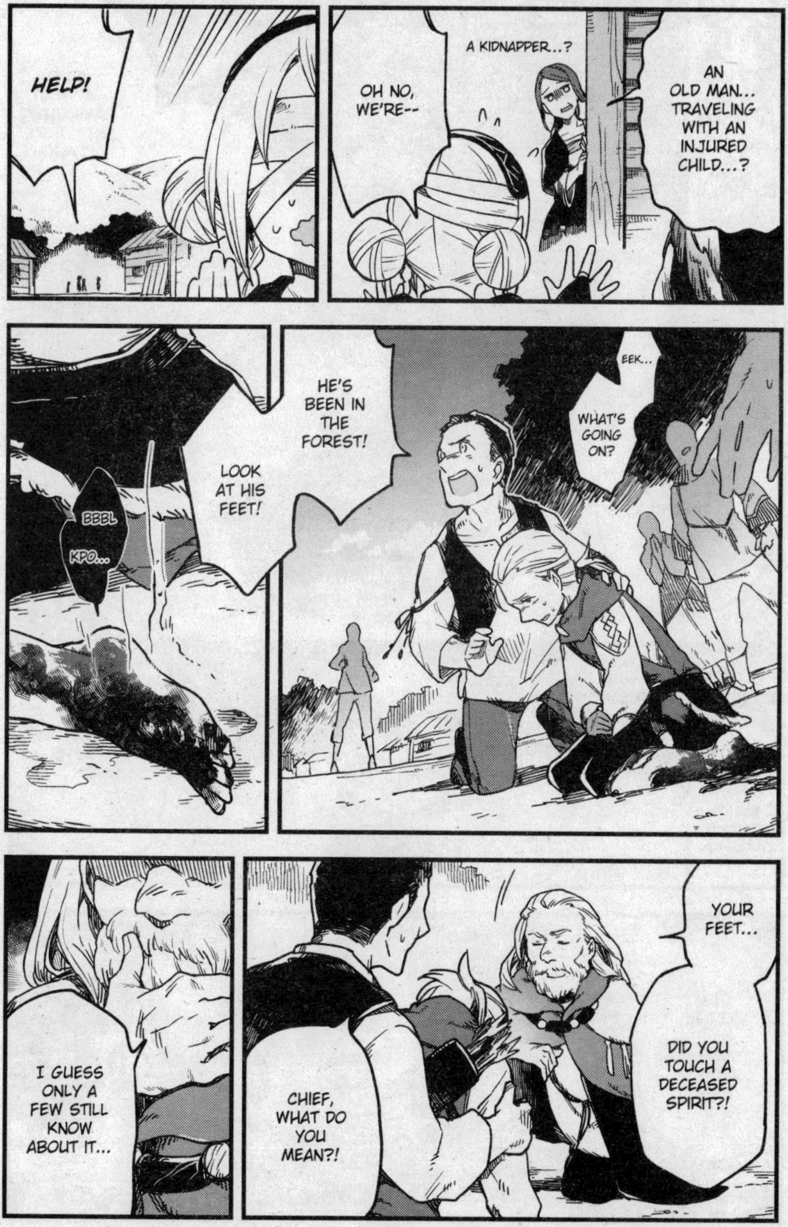
AN OLD MAN... TRAVELING WITH AN INJURED CHILD...?
A KIDNAPPER...?
OH NO, WE'RE--
HELP!
EEK...
WHAT'S GOING ON?
HE'S BEEN IN THE FOREST!
LOOK AT HIS FEET!
BBBL
KPO...
YOUR FEET...
DID YOU TOUCH A DECEASED SPIRIT?!
CHIEF, WHAT DO YOU MEAN?!
I GUESS ONLY A FEW STILL KNOW ABOUT IT...

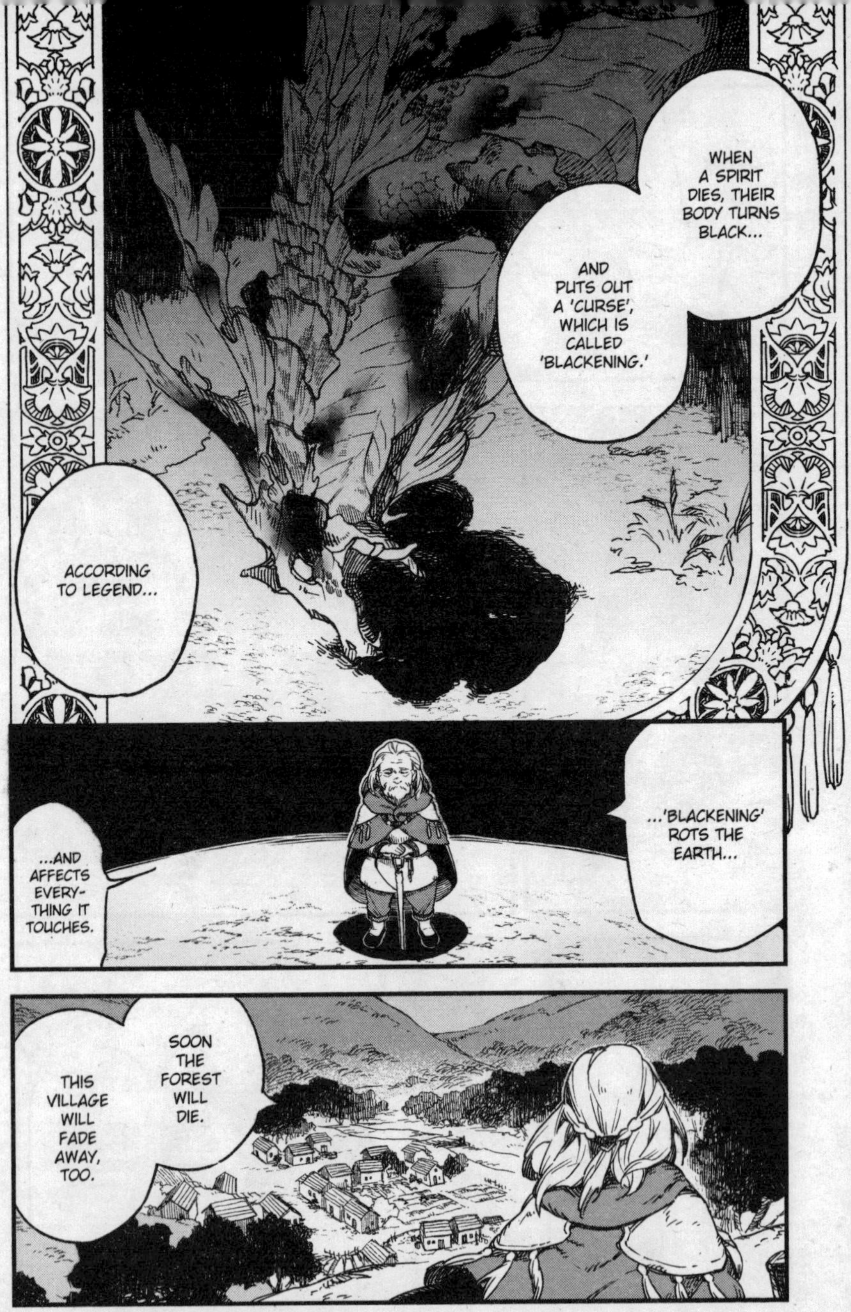
WHEN A SPIRIT DIES, THEIR BODY TURNS BLACK...
AND PUTS OUT A 'CURSE', WHICH IS CALLED 'BLACKENING.'
ACCORDING TO LEGEND...
...'BLACKENING' ROTS THE EARTH...
...AND AFFECTS EVERY-THING IT TOUCHES.
SOON THE FOREST WILL DIE.
THIS VILLAGE WILL FADE AWAY, TOO.

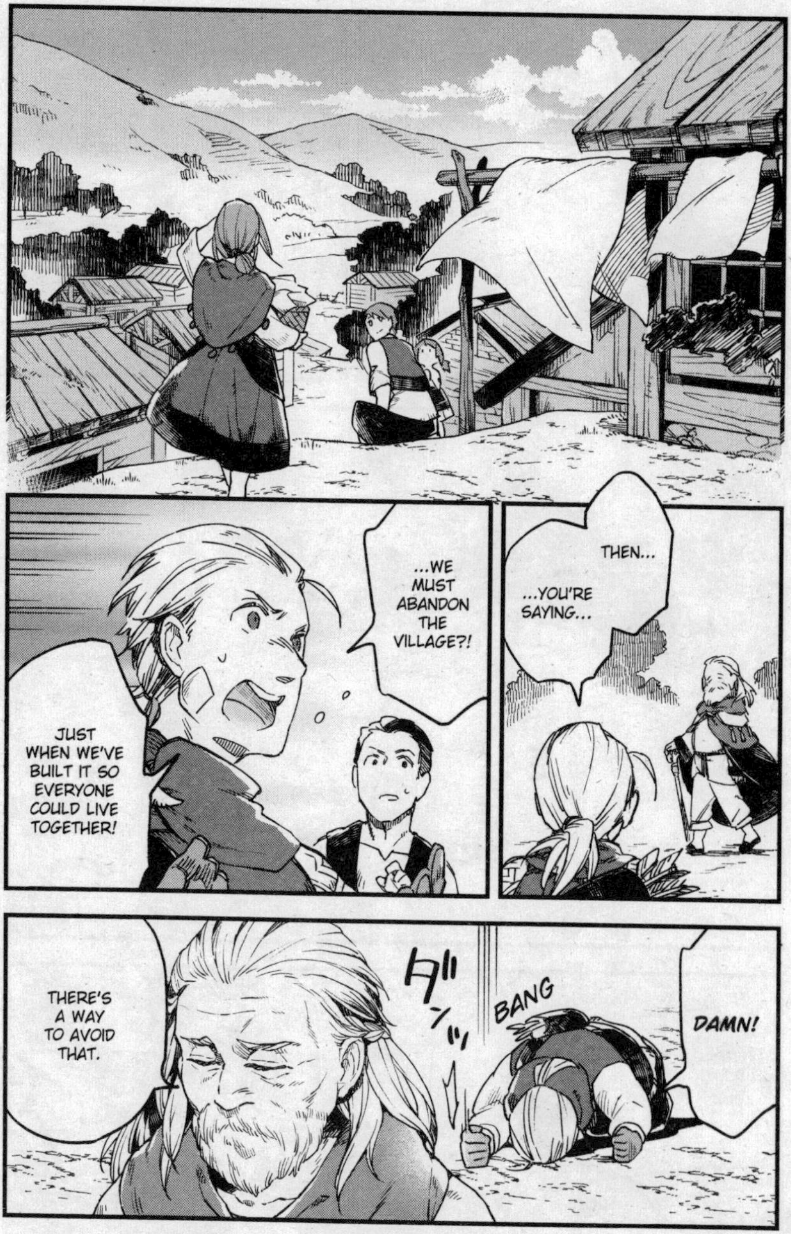
THEN...
...YOU'RE SAYING...
...WE MUST ABANDON THE VILLAGE?!
JUST WHEN WE'VE BUILT IT SO EVERYONE COULD LIVE TOGETHER!
DAMN!
BANG
THERE'S A WAY TO AVOID THAT.

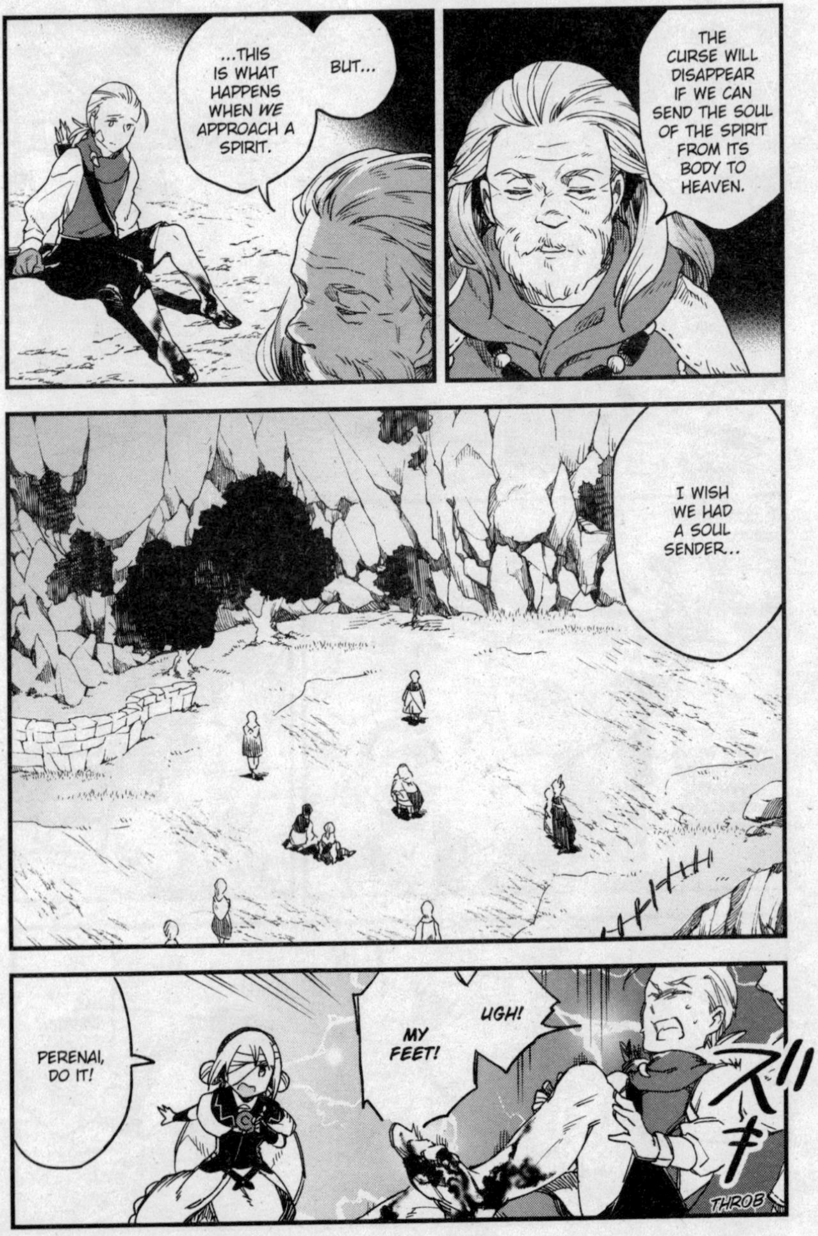
THE CURSE WILL DISAPPEAR IF WE CAN SEND THE SOUL OF THE SPIRIT FROM ITS BODY TO HEAVEN.
BUT...
...THIS IS WHAT HAPPENS WHEN *WE* APPROACH A SPIRIT.
I WISH WE HAD A SOUL SENDER..
ズキ
THROB
UGH!
MY FEET!
PERENAI, DO IT!

シャッ
SWISH

きゃぽ
CUPO

ガラ
RATTLE

YES,
M'LADY.

コポポ
CLIK.
CLIK...

JUST
TO MAKE
YOU FEEL
BETTER.

WOW!

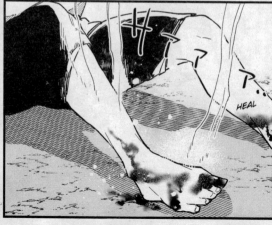
サーア
ア...
HEAL

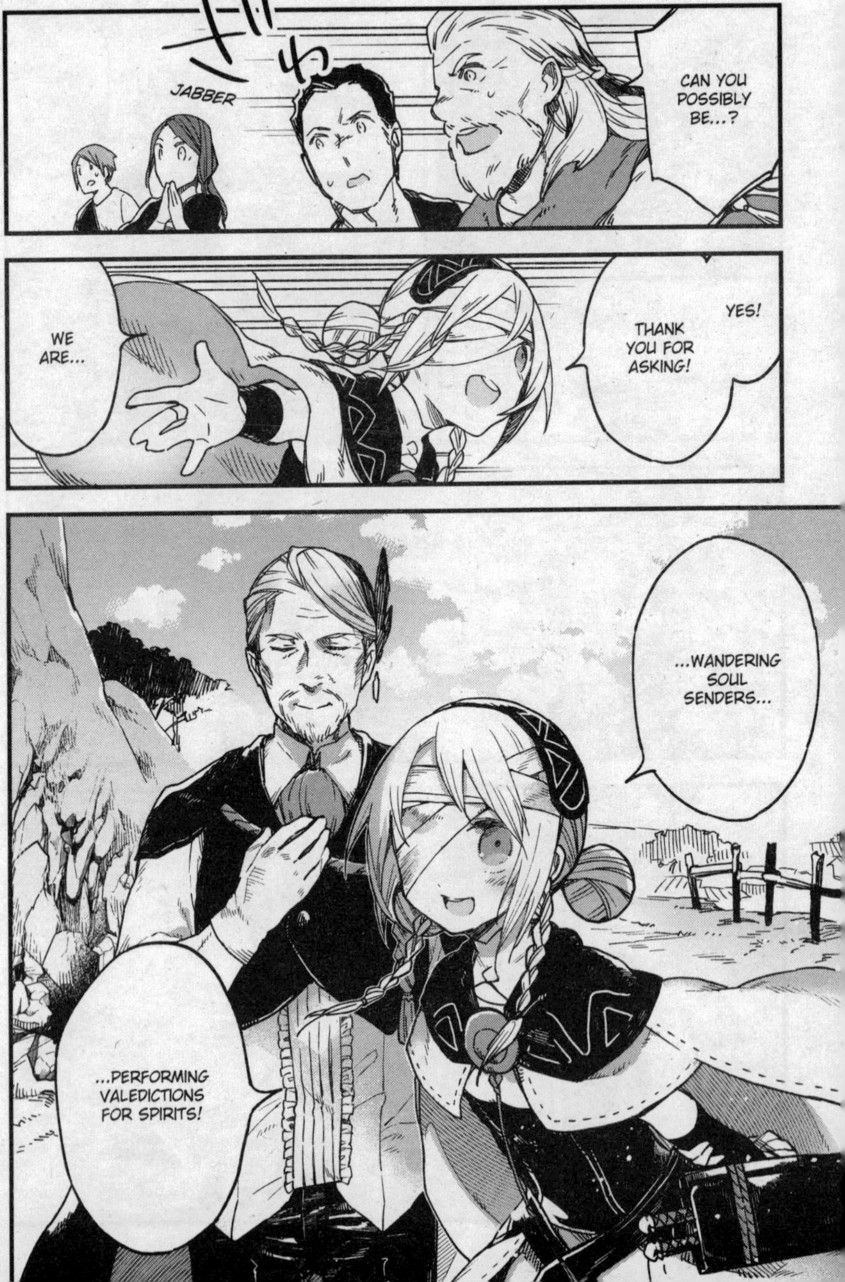
CAN YOU POSSIBLY BE...?
ざわ
JABBER
YES!
THANK YOU FOR ASKING!
WE ARE...
...WANDERING SOUL SENDERS...
...PERFORMING VALEDICTIONS FOR SPIRITS!

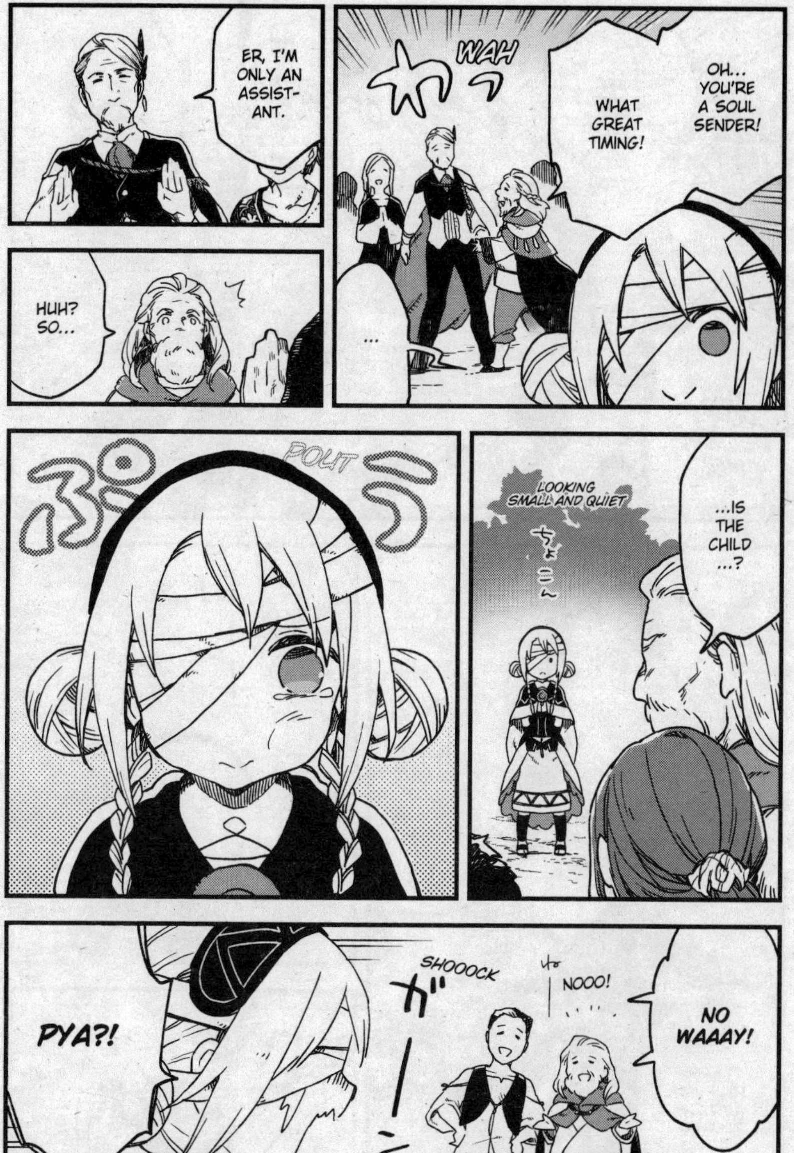
OH... YOU'RE A SOUL SENDER!
WHAT GREAT TIMING!
WAH
...
ER, I'M ONLY AN ASSIST-ANT.
HUH? SO...
...IS THE CHILD ...?
LOOKING SMALL AND QUIET
ちょこん
POUT
NO WAAAY!
NOOO!
SHOOOCK
PYA?!

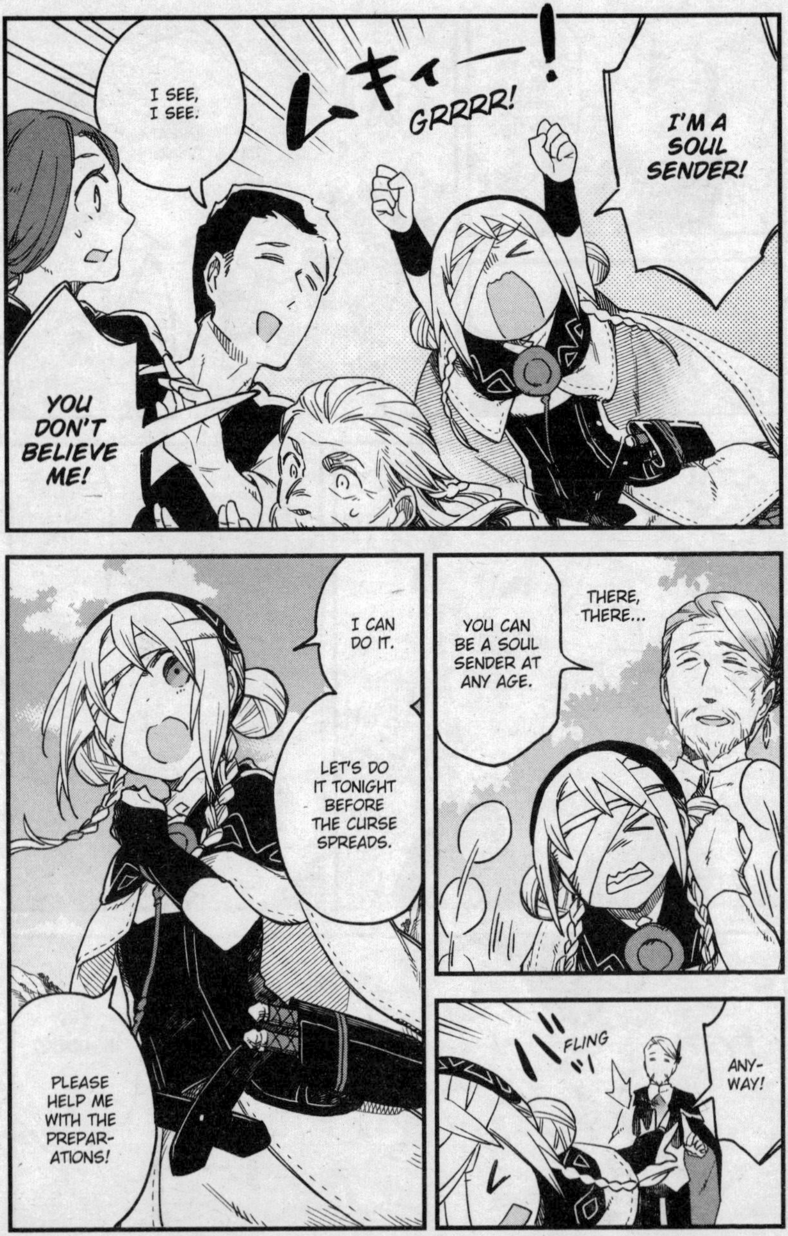

I'M A SOUL SENDER!
ムキィー!
GRRRR!
I SEE, I SEE.
YOU DON'T BELIEVE ME!
THERE, THERE...
YOU CAN BE A SOUL SENDER AT ANY AGE.
ANY-WAY!
バッ
FLING
I CAN DO IT.
LET'S DO IT TONIGHT BEFORE THE CURSE SPREADS.
PLEASE HELP ME WITH THE PREPARATIONS!

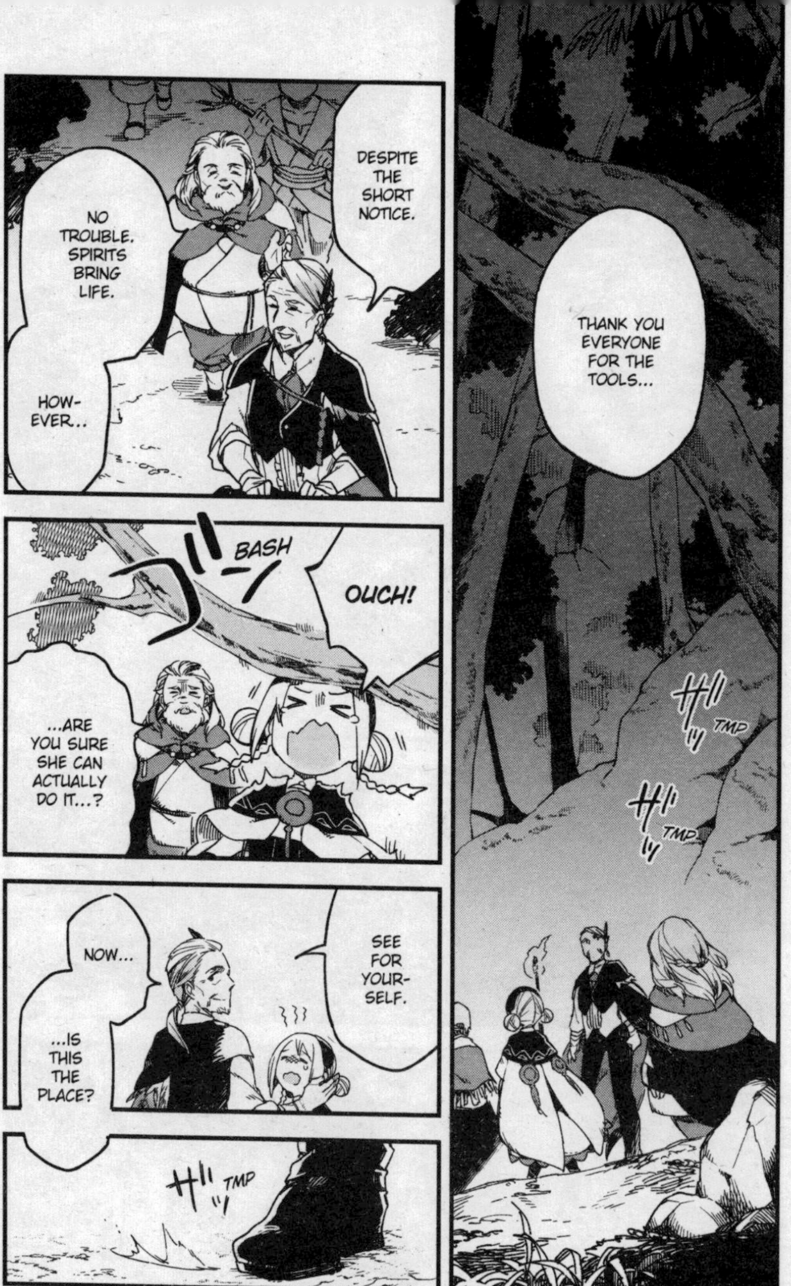
THANK YOU EVERYONE FOR THE TOOLS...
TMP
TMP
DESPITE THE SHORT NOTICE.
NO TROUBLE. SPIRITS BRING LIFE.
HOW-EVER...
BASH
OUCH!
...ARE YOU SURE SHE CAN ACTUALLY DO IT...?
SEE FOR YOUR-SELF.
NOW...
...IS THIS THE PLACE?
TMP

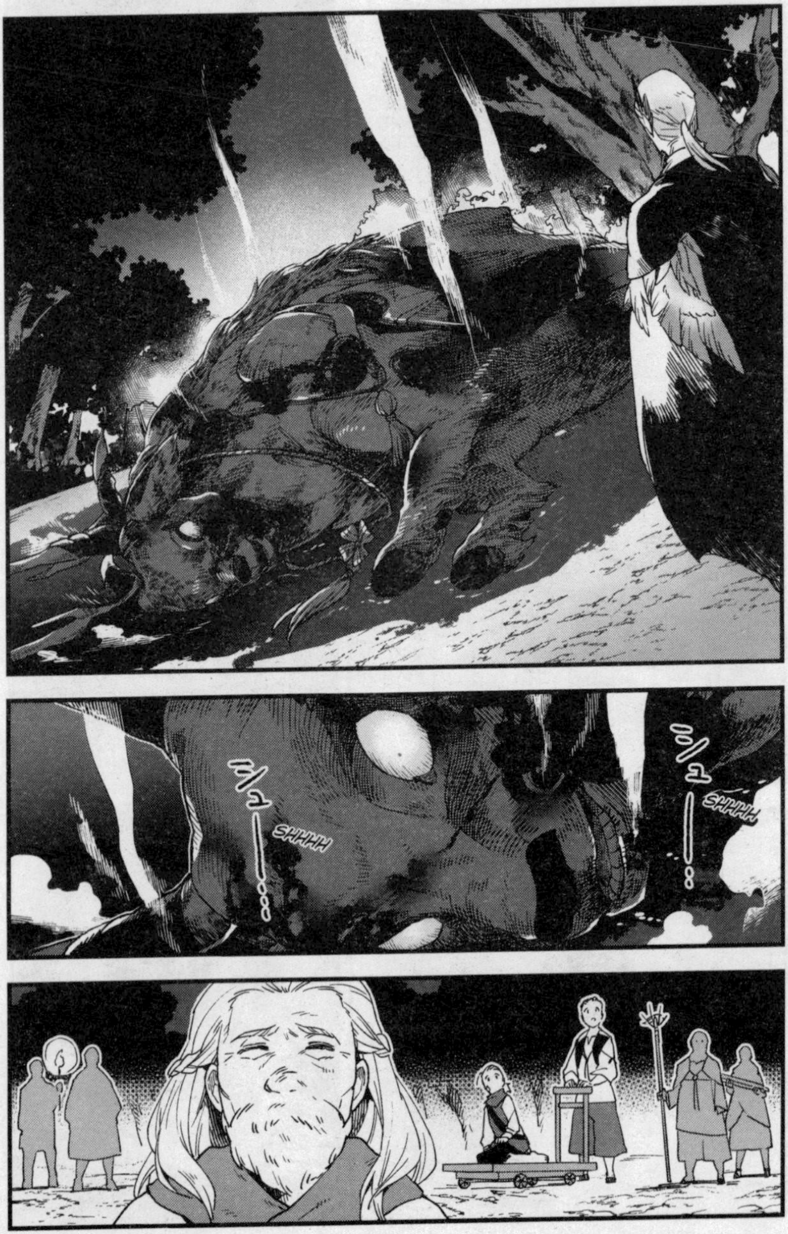
シューー…
SHHHH
シューー…
SHHHH

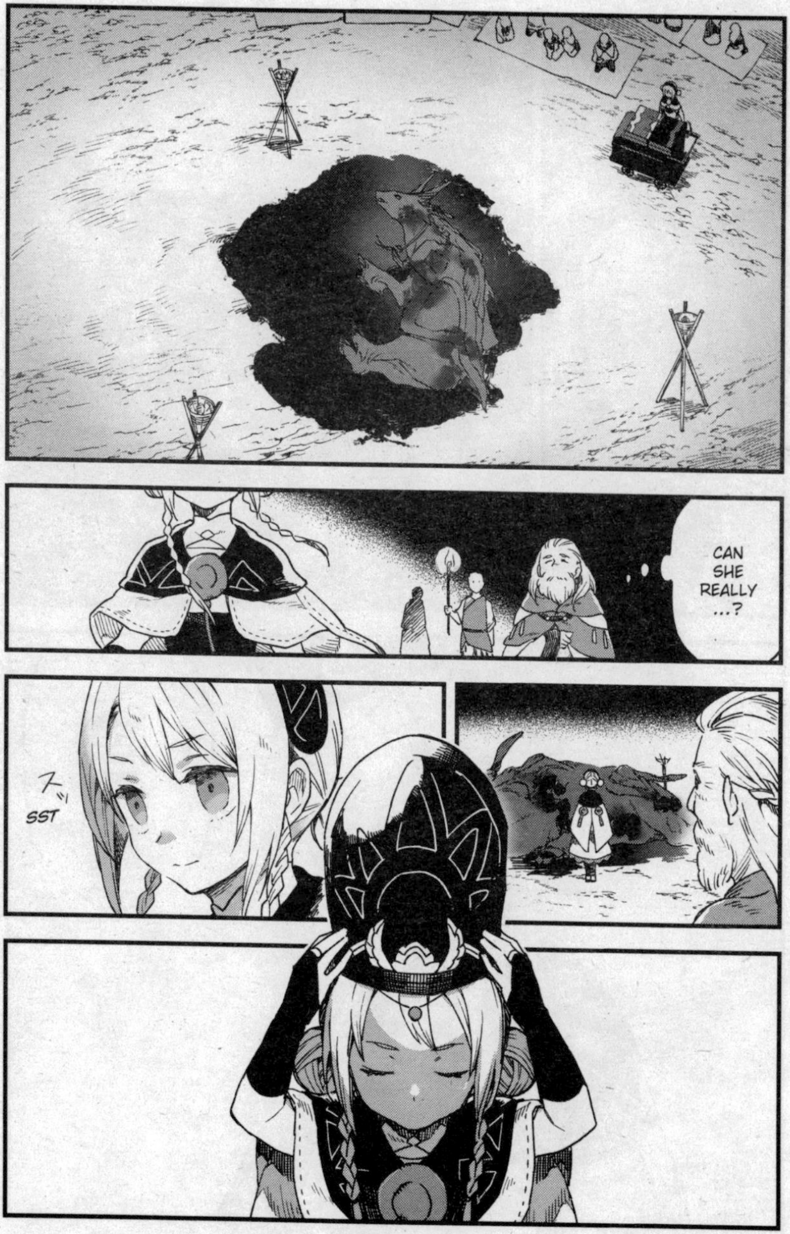
CAN SHE REALLY ...?
スッ
SST

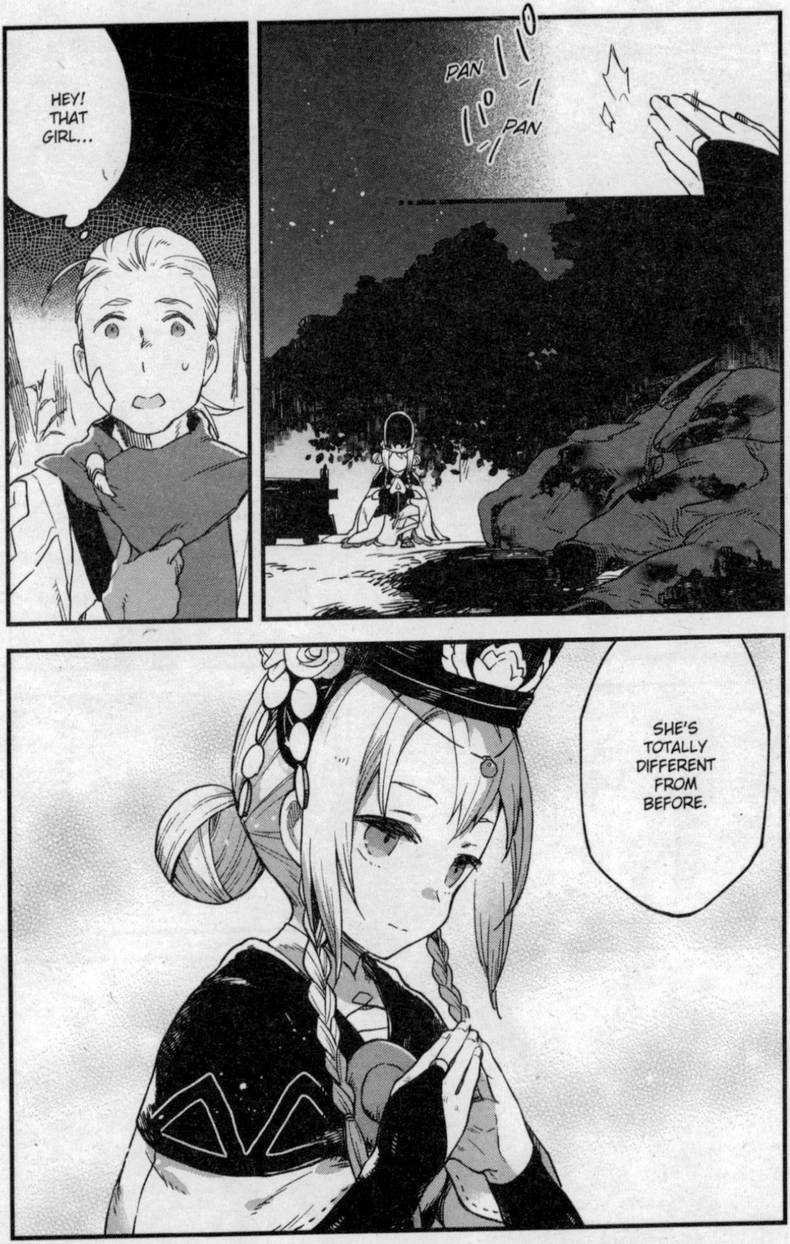
PAN
PAN
HEY! THAT GIRL...
SHE'S TOTALLY DIFFERENT FROM BEFORE.

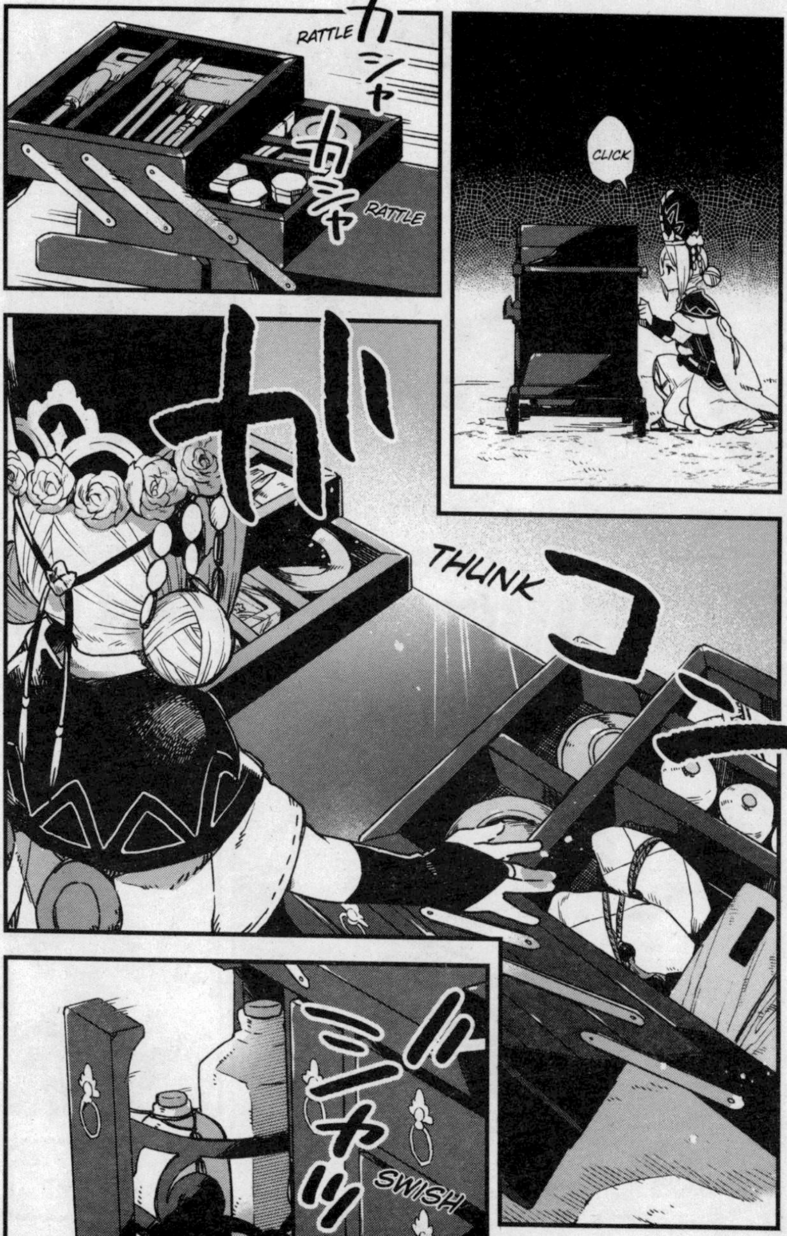
CLICK
RATTLE
カシャ
カシャ
RATTLE
THUNK
SWISH

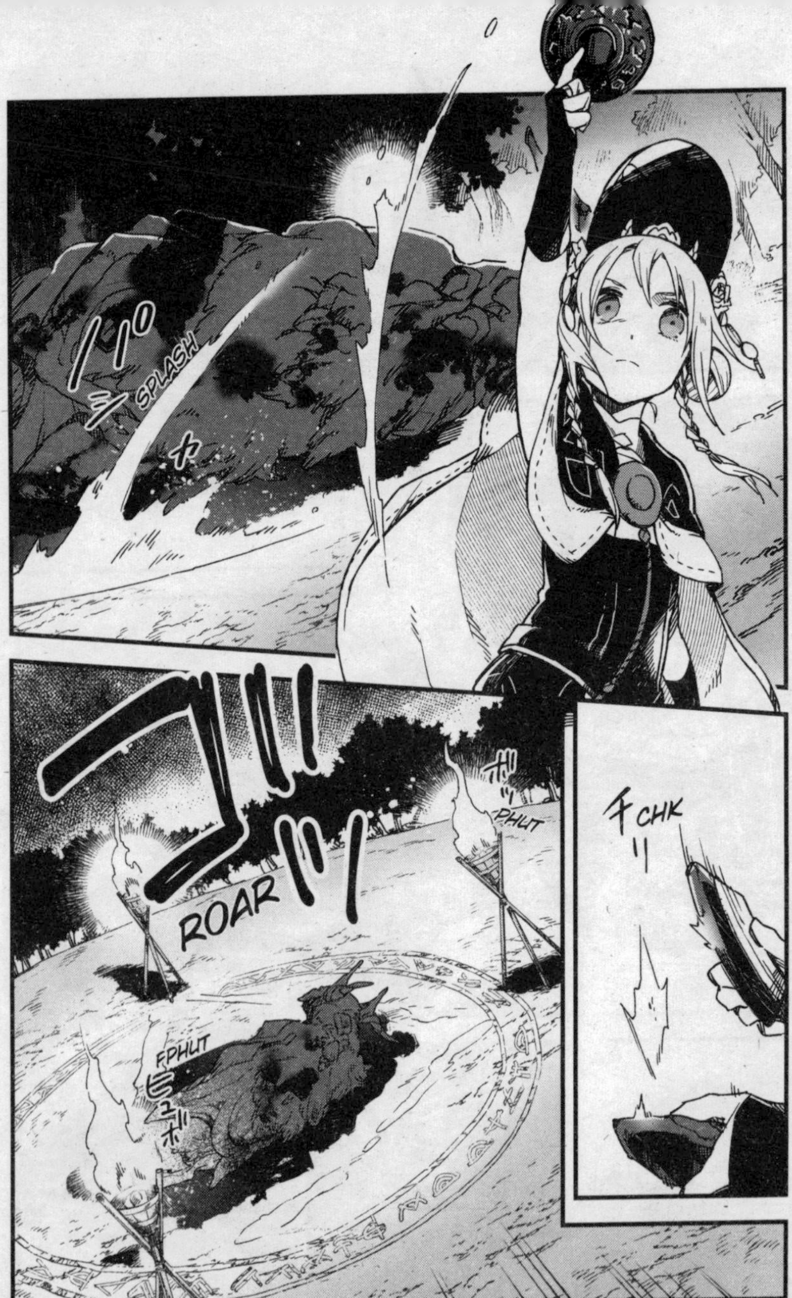
SPLASH
CHK
ROAR
PHUT
FPHUT

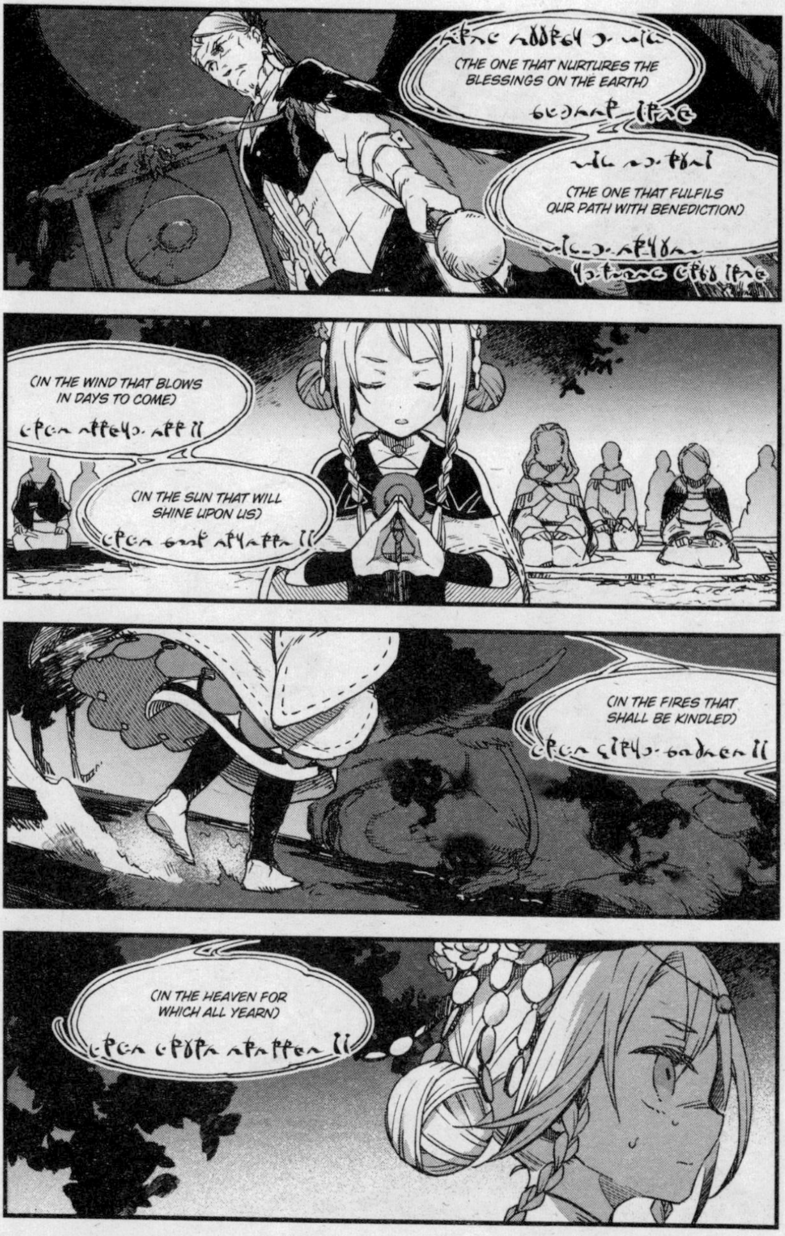

(THE ONE THAT NURTURES THE BLESSINGS ON THE EARTH)
(THE ONE THAT FULFILS OUR PATH WITH BENEDICTION)
(IN THE WIND THAT BLOWS IN DAYS TO COME)
(IN THE SUN THAT WILL SHINE UPON US)
(IN THE FIRES THAT SHALL BE KINDLED)
(IN THE HEAVEN FOR WHICH ALL YEARN)

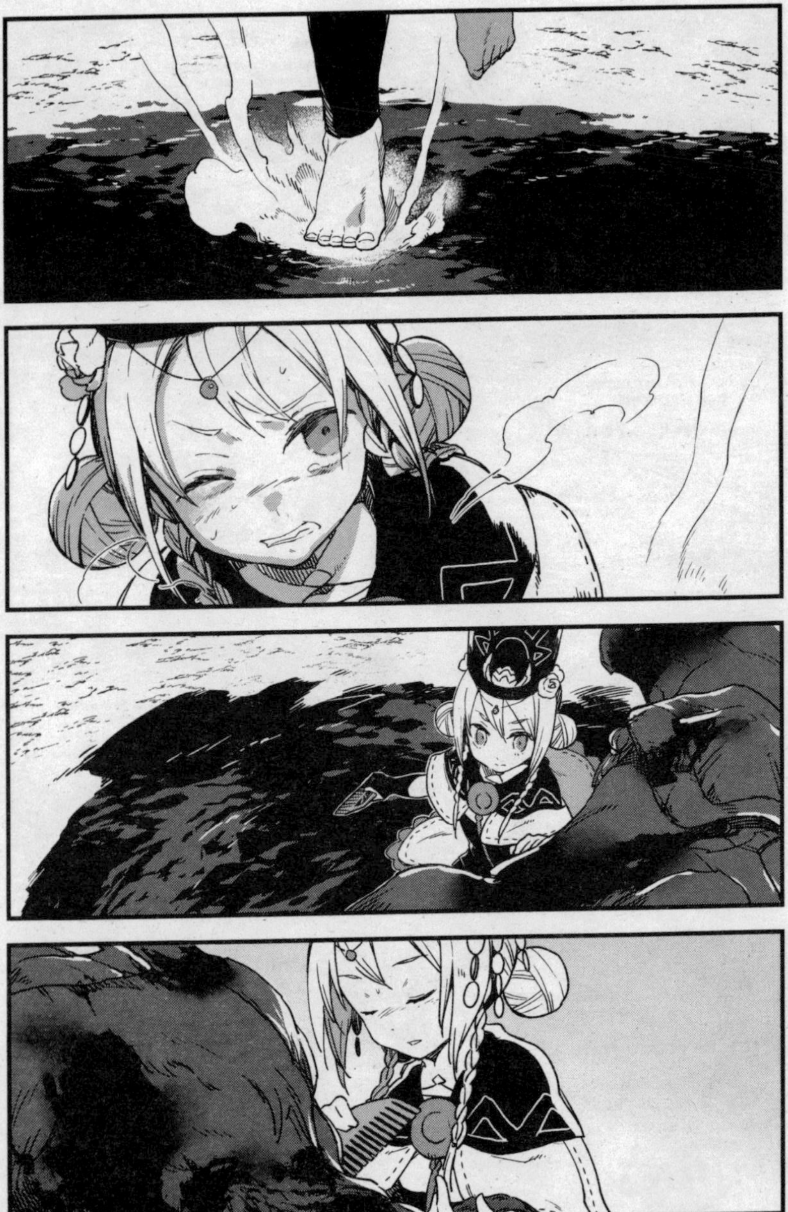

...THE CURSE SO MUCH, BUT...

SHE'S TOUCHED...

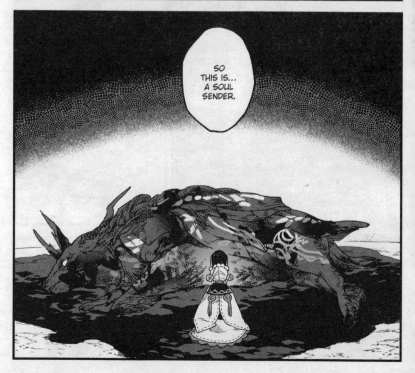

SO THIS IS... A SOUL SENDER.

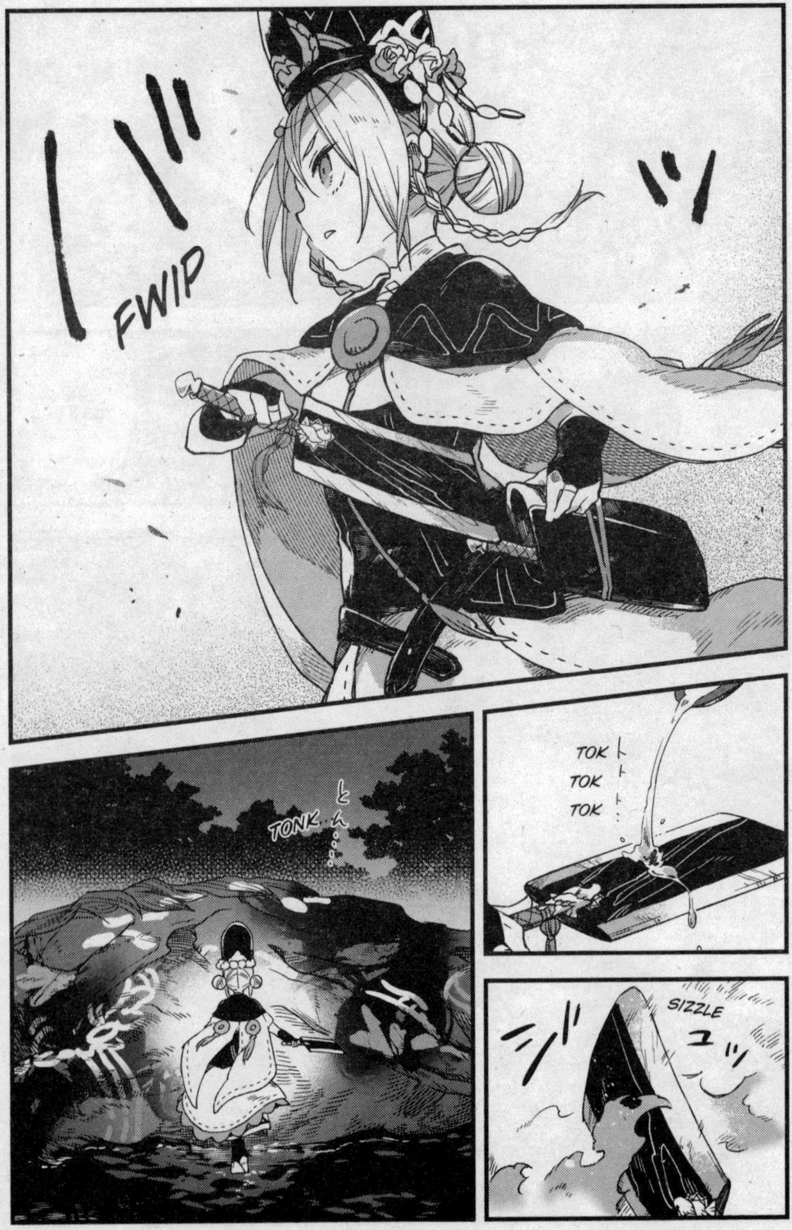
バッ
FWIP
トトト…
TOK
TOK
TOK
ジュッ
SIZZLE
とん……
TONK

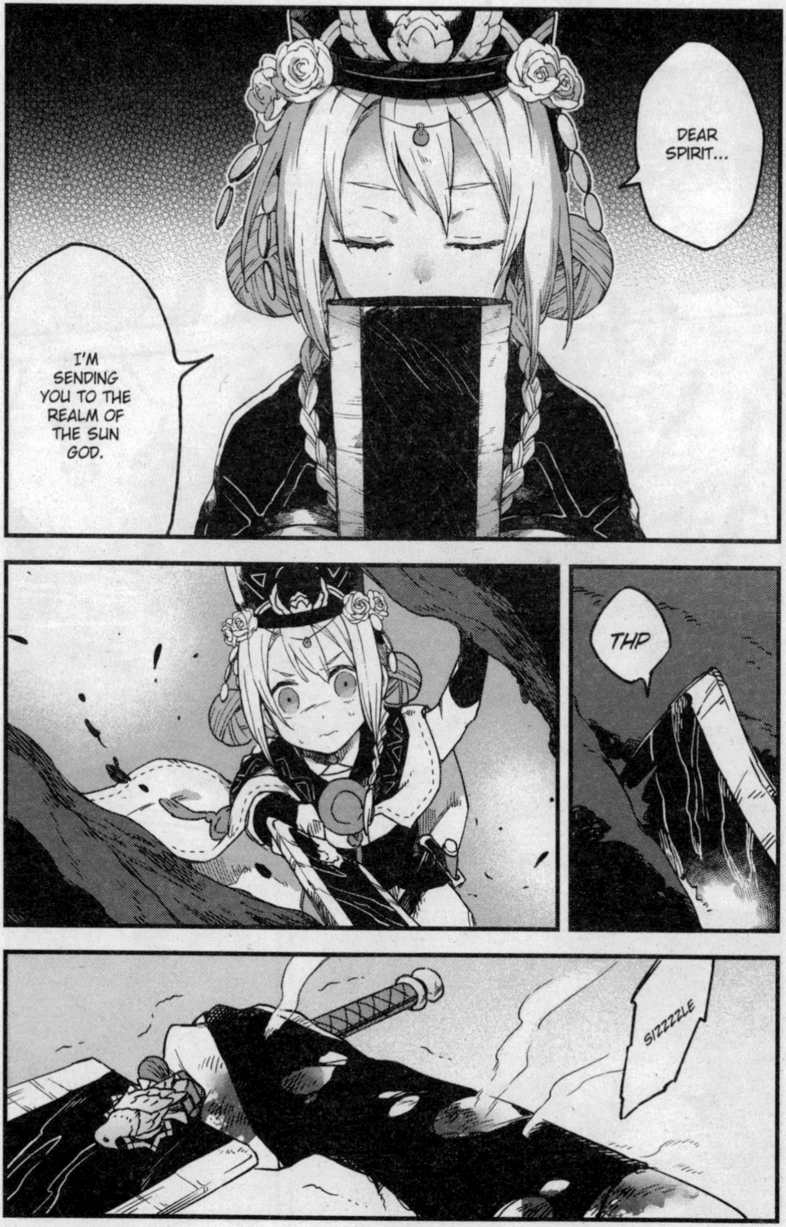
DEAR SPIRIT...
I'M SENDING YOU TO THE REALM OF THE SUN GOD.
THP
SIZZZZLE

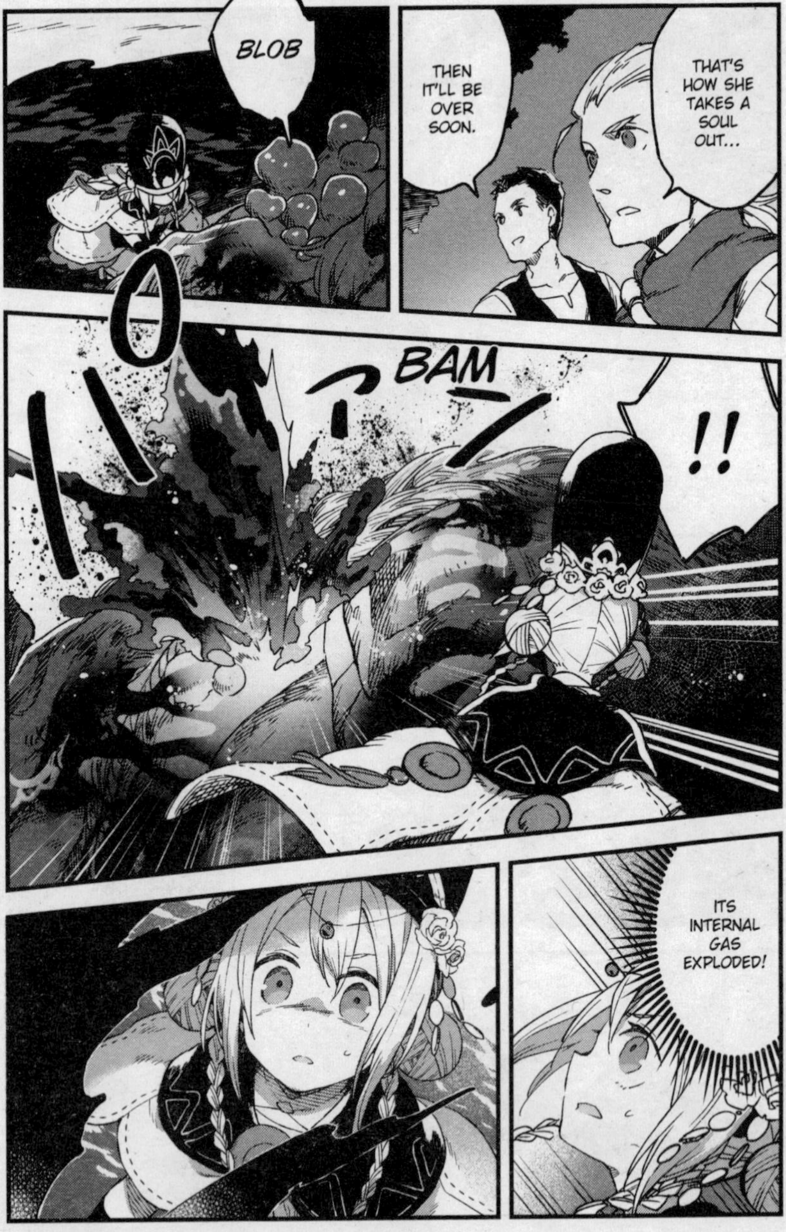
THAT'S HOW SHE TAKES A SOUL OUT...
THEN IT'LL BE OVER SOON.
BLOB
!!
BAM
ITS INTERNAL GAS EXPLODED!

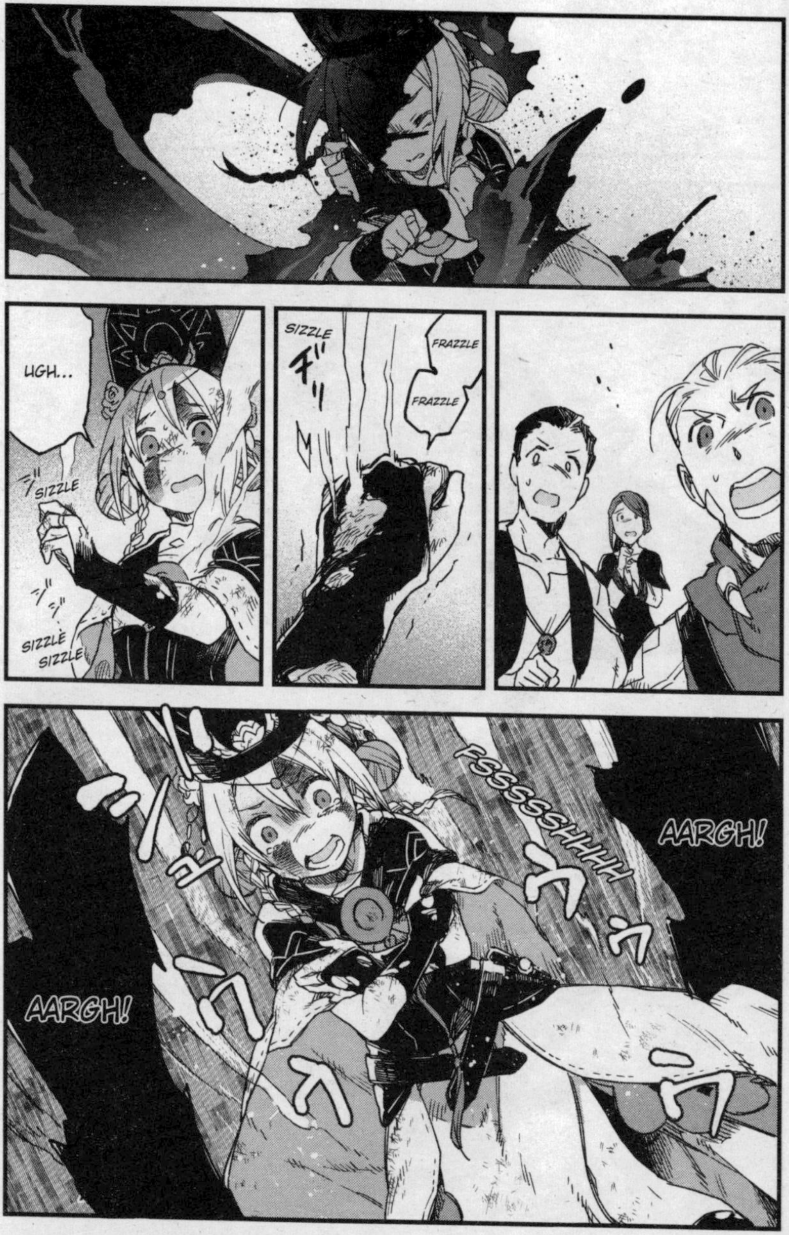
FRAZZLE
FRAZZLE
SIZZLE
UGH...
SIZZLE
SIZZLE
SIZZLE
AARGH!
FSSSSSHHHH
AARGH!

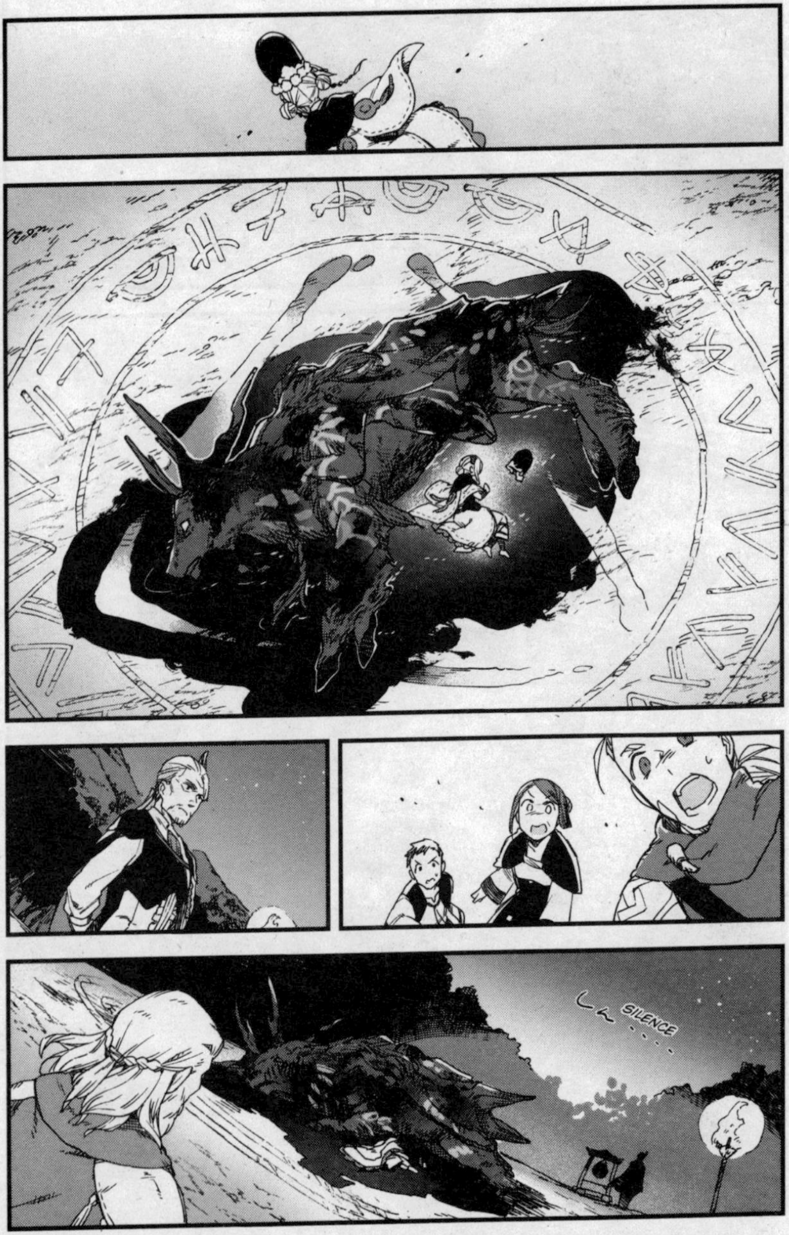
しん
SILENCE

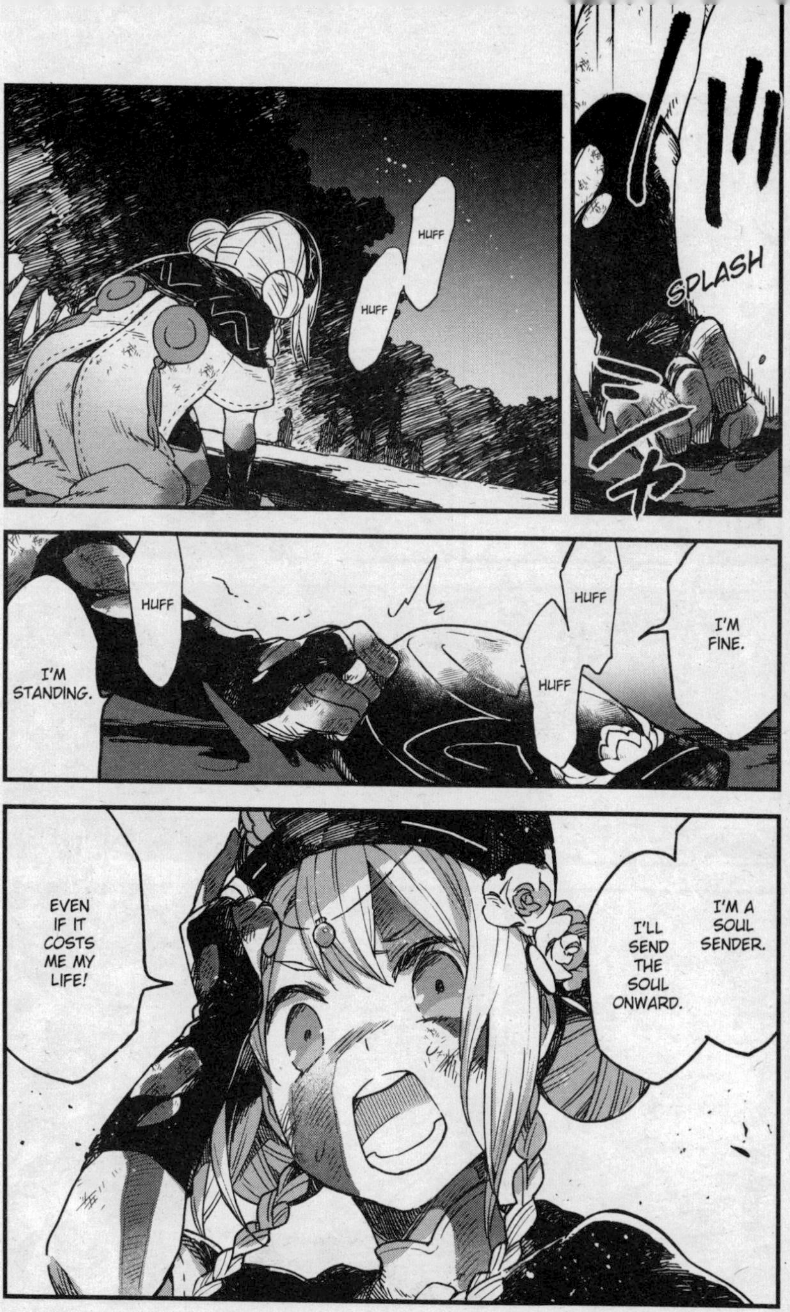
SPLASH
HUFF
HUFF
I'M FINE.
HUFF
HUFF
HUFF
I'M STANDING.
I'M A SOUL SENDER.
I'LL SEND THE SOUL ONWARD.
EVEN IF IT COSTS ME MY LIFE!

CREAK

CREAK

GONG

GONG

GLINT

GONG

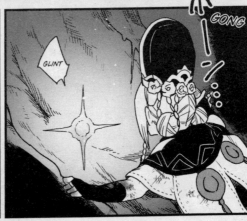

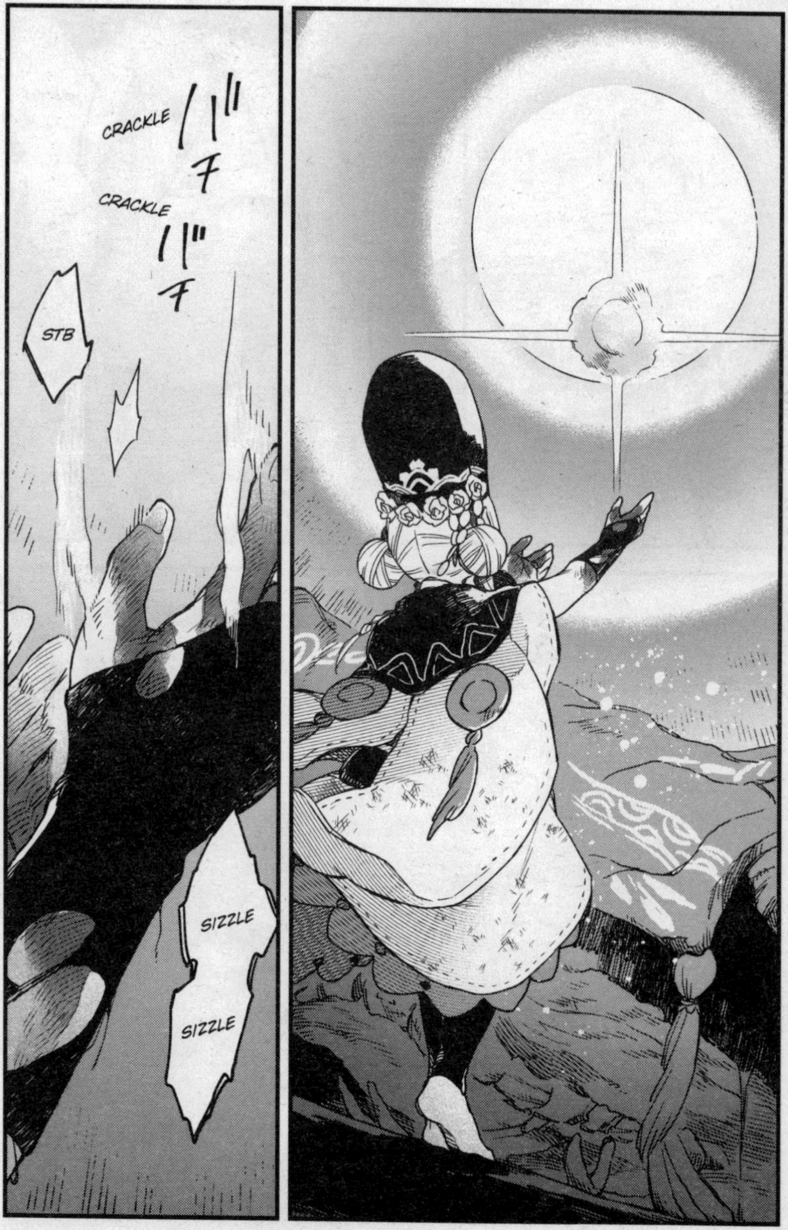
CRACKLE
バチ
CRACKLE
バチ
STB
SIZZLE
SIZZLE

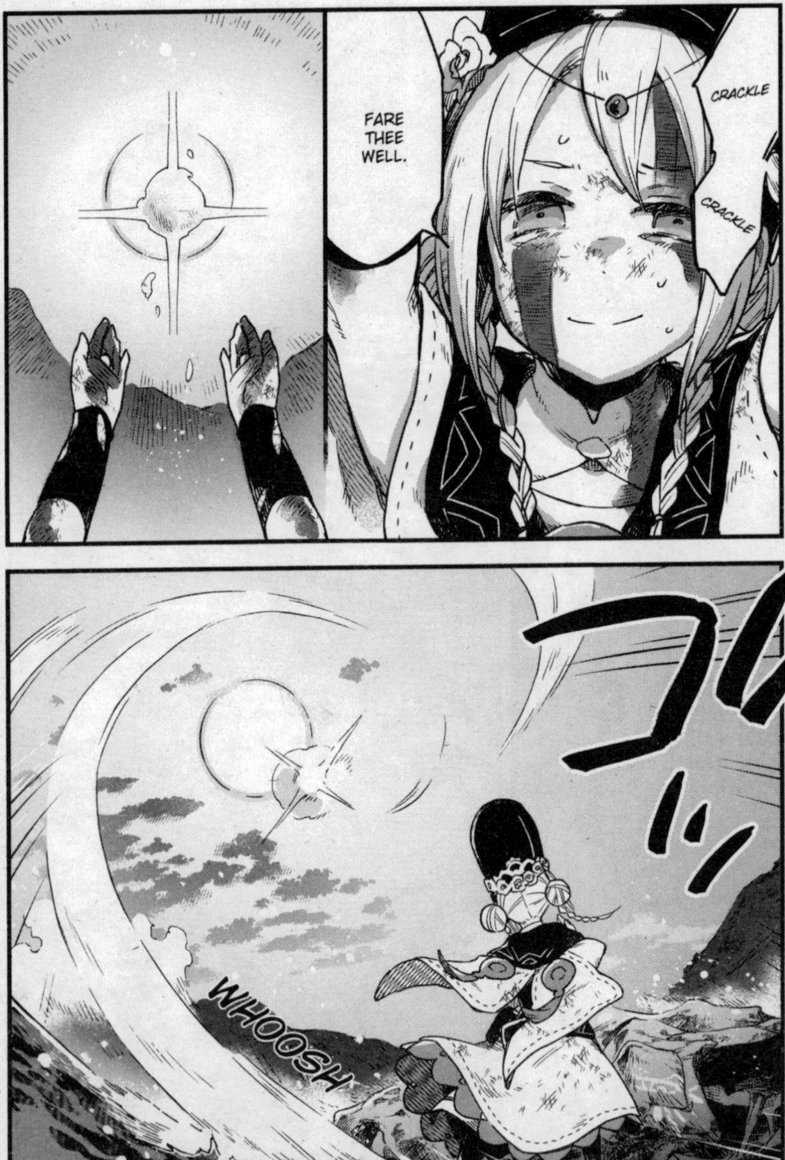
FARE THEE WELL.
CRACKLE
CRACKLE
ゴッ
WHOOSH

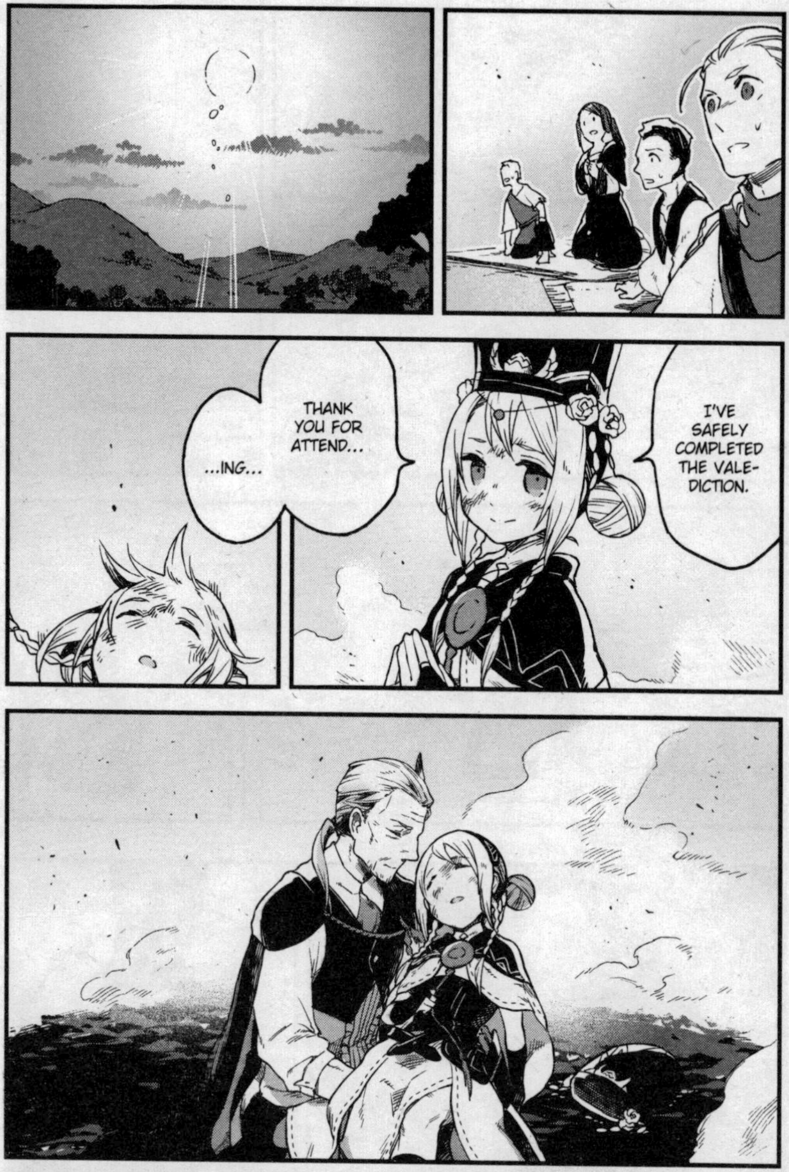
I'VE SAFELY COMPLETED THE VALE-DICTION.
THANK YOU FOR ATTEND...
...ING...

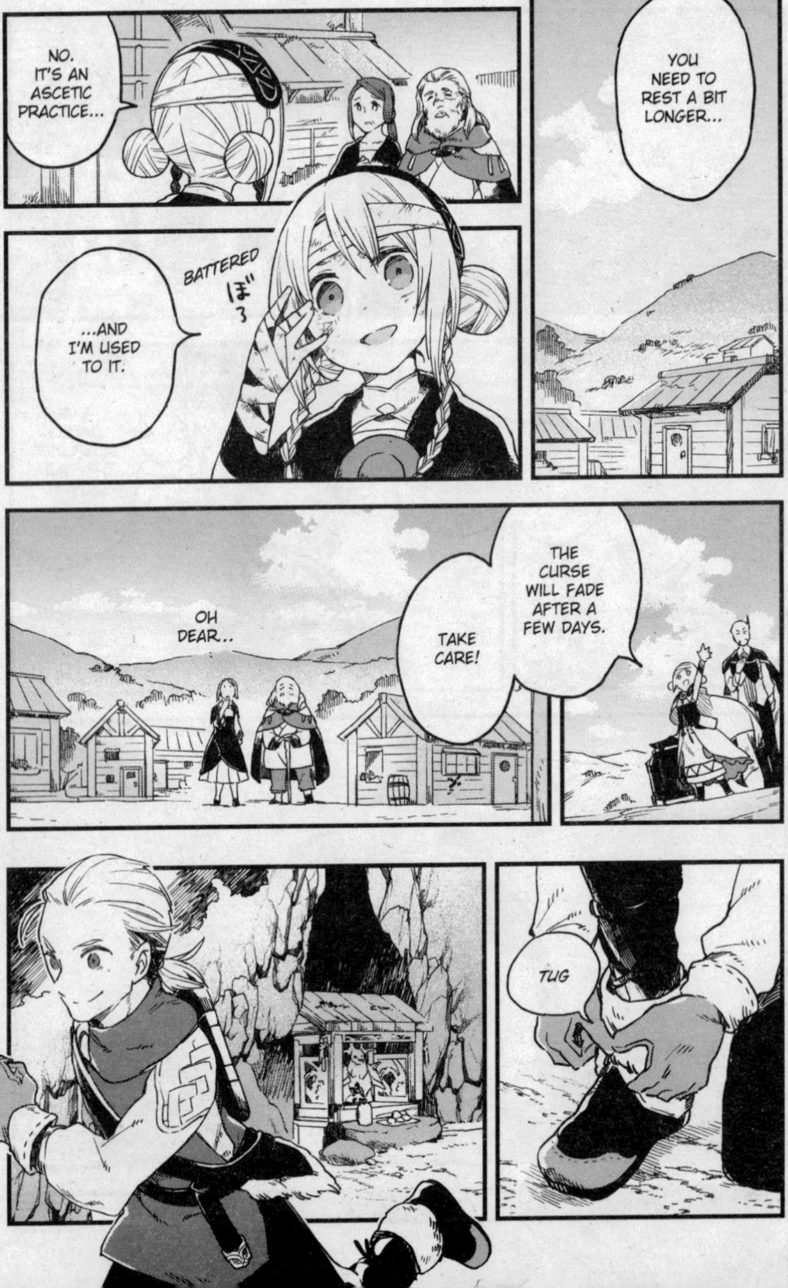
YOU NEED TO REST A BIT LONGER...
NO. IT'S AN ASCETIC PRACTICE...
BATTERED ぼろ
...AND I'M USED TO IT.
THE CURSE WILL FADE AFTER A FEW DAYS.
TAKE CARE!
OH DEAR..
TUG

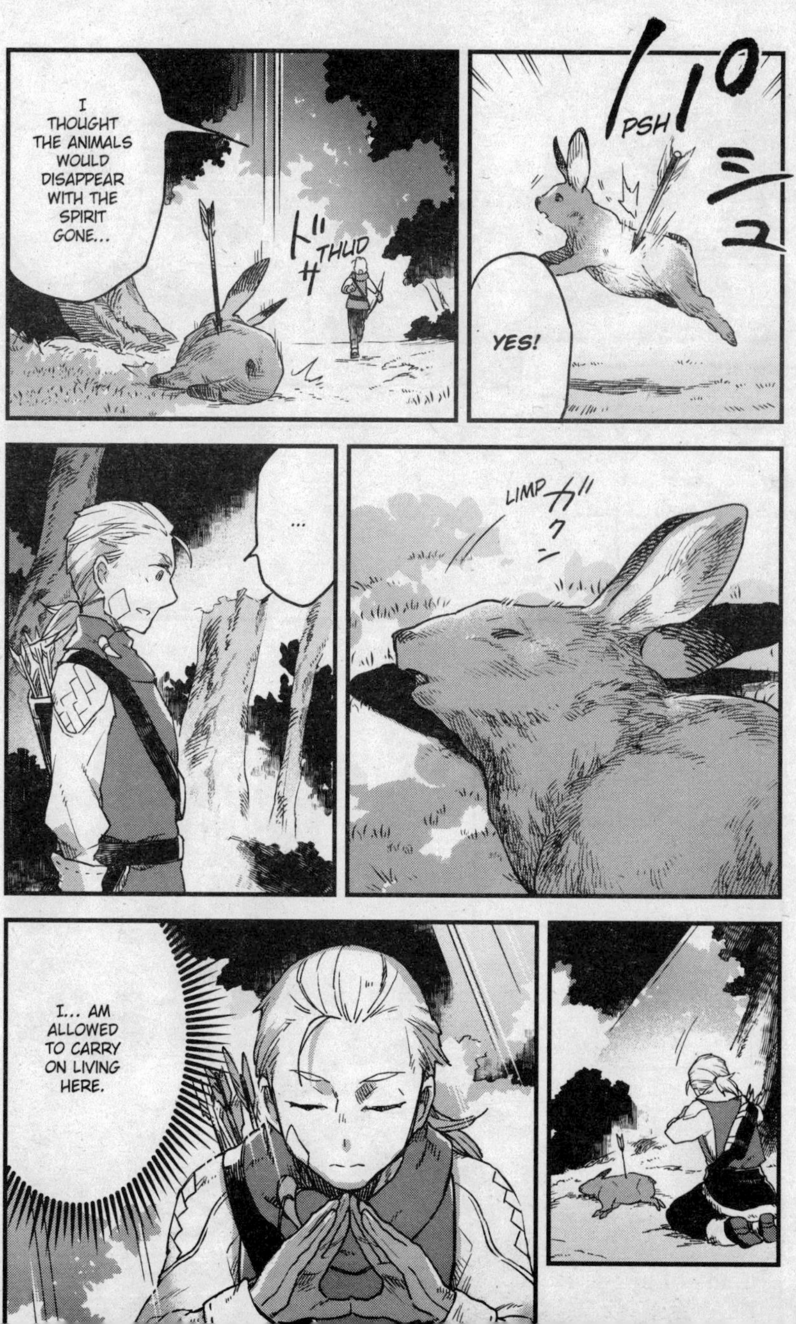
パシュ
PSH
YES!
I THOUGHT THE ANIMALS WOULD DISAPPEAR WITH THE SPIRIT GONE...
ドサ
THUD
LIMP
ガクン
...
I... AM ALLOWED TO CARRY ON LIVING HERE.

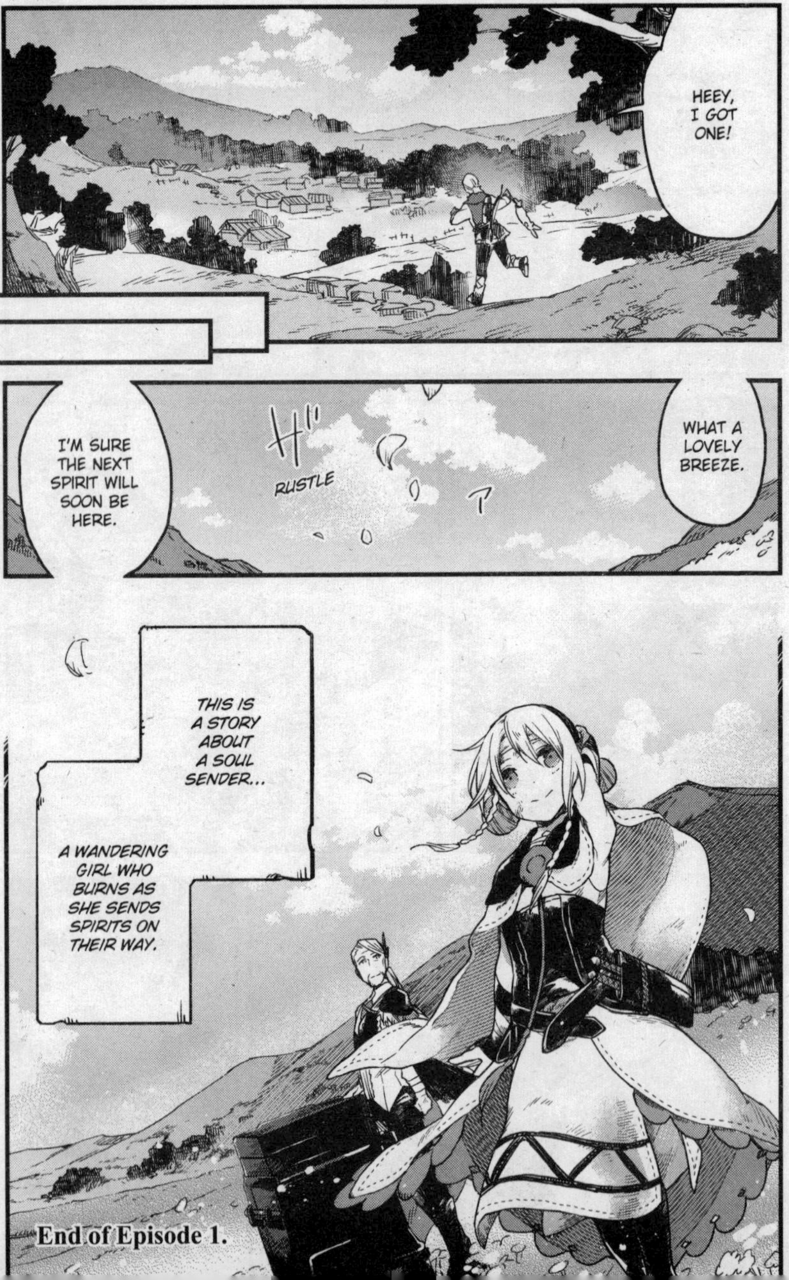
HEEY, I GOT ONE!
WHAT A LOVELY BREEZE.
ザ
RUSTLE
I'M SURE THE NEXT SPIRIT WILL SOON BE HERE.
THIS IS A STORY ABOUT A SOUL SENDER...
A WANDERING GIRL WHO BURNS AS SHE SENDS SPIRITS ON THEIR WAY.
End of Episode 1.

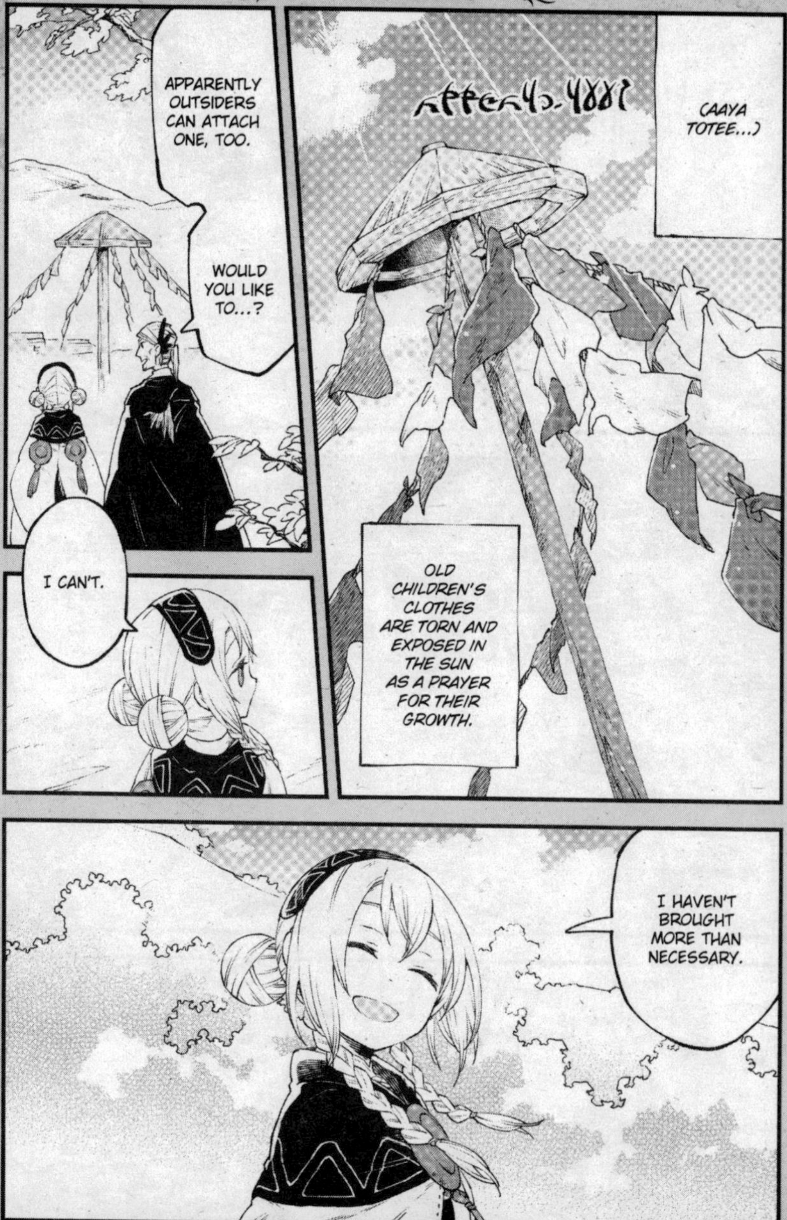
(AAYA TOTEE...)
OLD CHILDREN'S CLOTHES ARE TORN AND EXPOSED IN THE SUN AS A PRAYER FOR THEIR GROWTH.
APPARENTLY OUTSIDERS CAN ATTACH ONE, TOO.
WOULD YOU LIKE TO...?
I CAN'T.
I HAVEN'T BROUGHT MORE THAN NECESSARY.

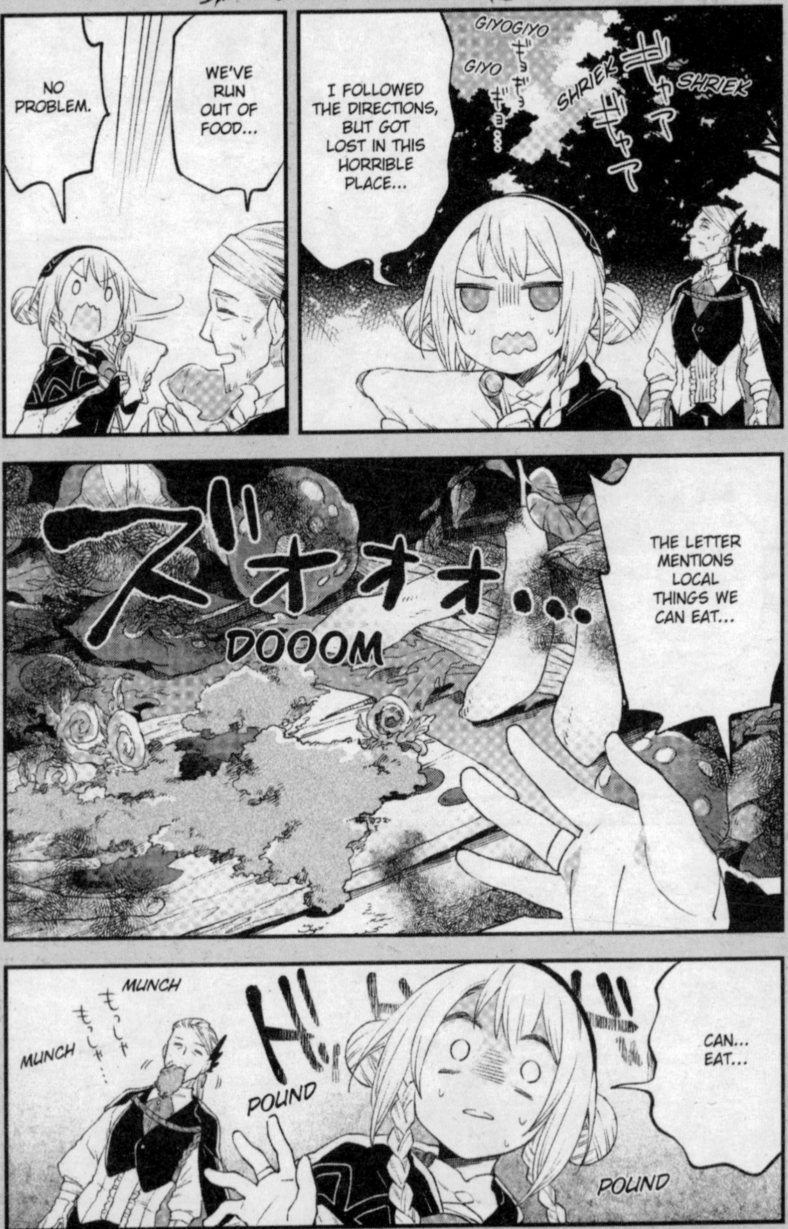
GIYOGIYO
ギョギョ
GIYO
ギョ…
SHRIEK
ギャア
SHRIEK
ギャア
I FOLLOWED THE DIRECTIONS, BUT GOT LOST IN THIS HORRIBLE PLACE…
WE'VE RUN OUT OF FOOD…
NO PROBLEM.
THE LETTER MENTIONS LOCAL THINGS WE CAN EAT…
ズオオオ…
DOOOM
CAN… EAT…
POUND
POUND
MUNCH
もっしゃ
MUNCH
もっしゃ…

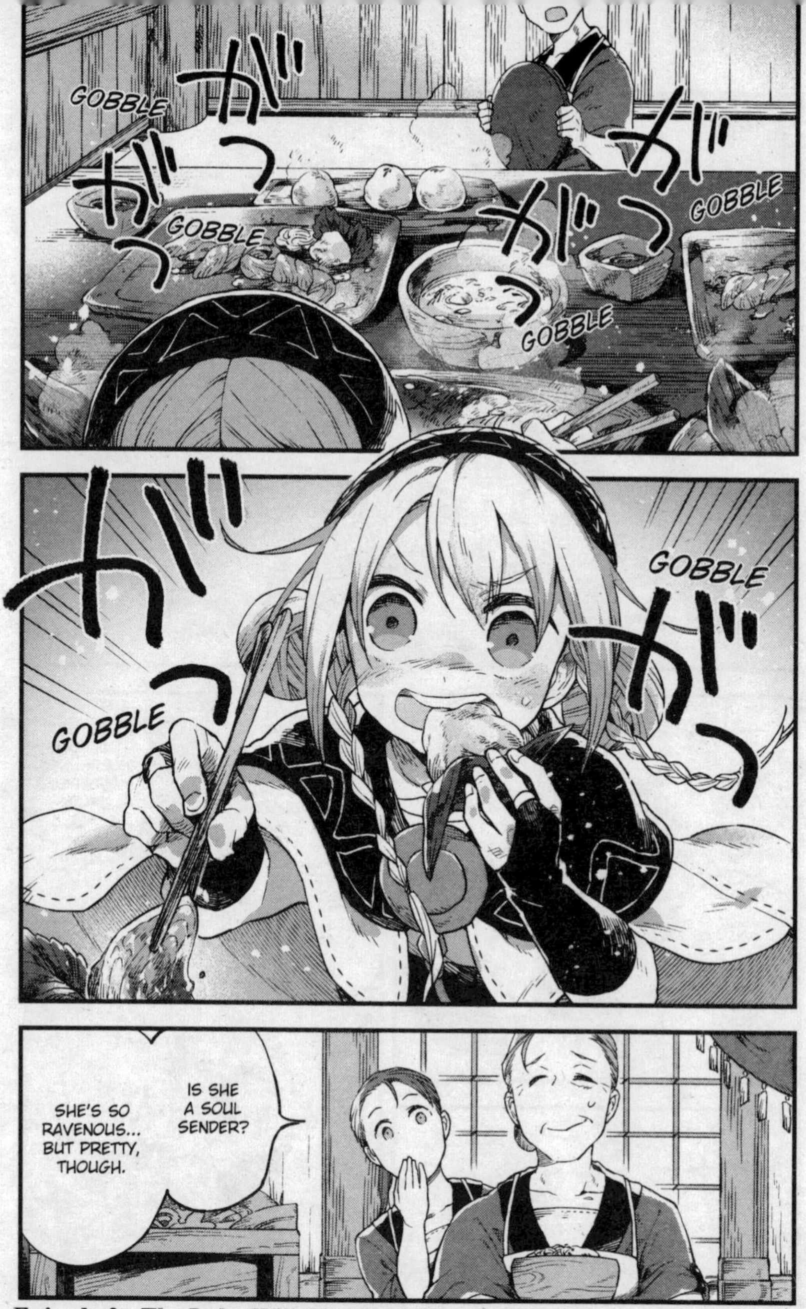
GOBBLE
GOBBLE
GOBBLE
GOBBLE
GOBBLE
GOBBLE
IS SHE A SOUL SENDER?
SHE'S SO RAVENOUS... BUT PRETTY, THOUGH.

Episode 2 - The Lake With The Dark Purple Waters.

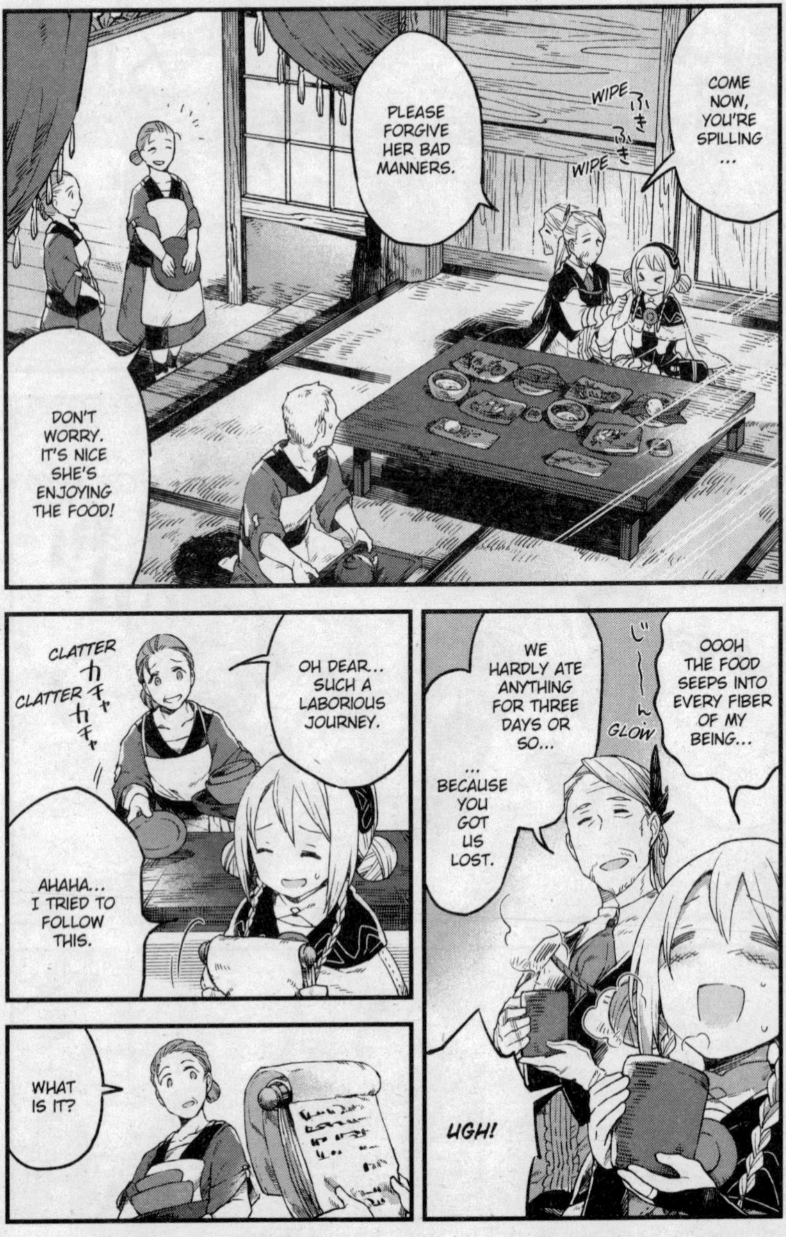
COME NOW, YOU'RE SPILLING ...
WIPE ふき
ふき WIPE
PLEASE FORGIVE HER BAD MANNERS.
DON'T WORRY. IT'S NICE SHE'S ENJOYING THE FOOD!
OOOH THE FOOD SEEPS INTO EVERY FIBER OF MY BEING...
じ〜ん GLOW
WE HARDLY ATE ANYTHING FOR THREE DAYS OR SO...
... BECAUSE YOU GOT US LOST.
UGH!
OH DEAR.. SUCH A LABORIOUS JOURNEY.
CLATTER カチャ
CLATTER カチャ
AHAHA... I TRIED TO FOLLOW THIS.
WHAT IS IT?

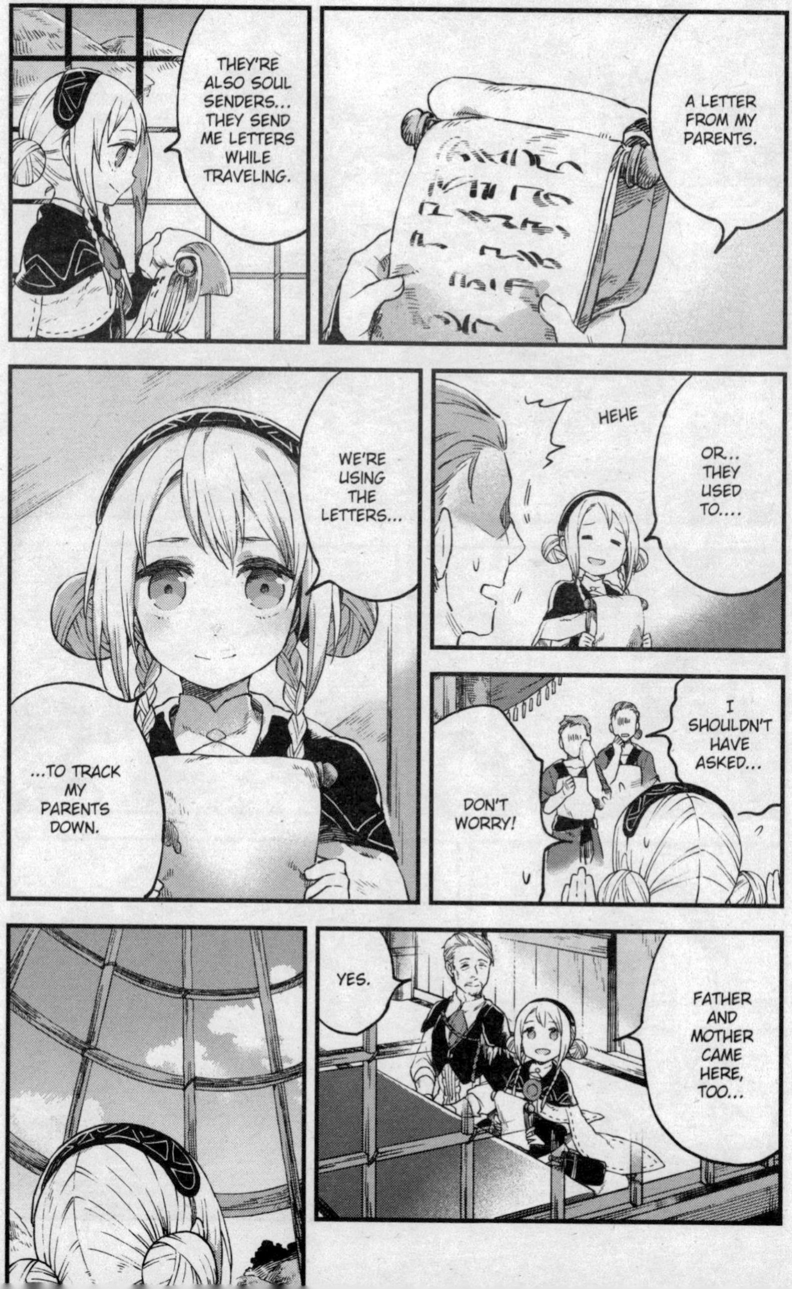
A LETTER FROM MY PARENTS.
THEY'RE ALSO SOUL SENDERS... THEY SEND ME LETTERS WHILE TRAVELING.
OR.. THEY USED TO....
HEHE
I SHOULDN'T HAVE ASKED...
DON'T WORRY!
WE'RE USING THE LETTERS...
...TO TRACK MY PARENTS DOWN.
FATHER AND MOTHER CAME HERE, TOO...
YES.

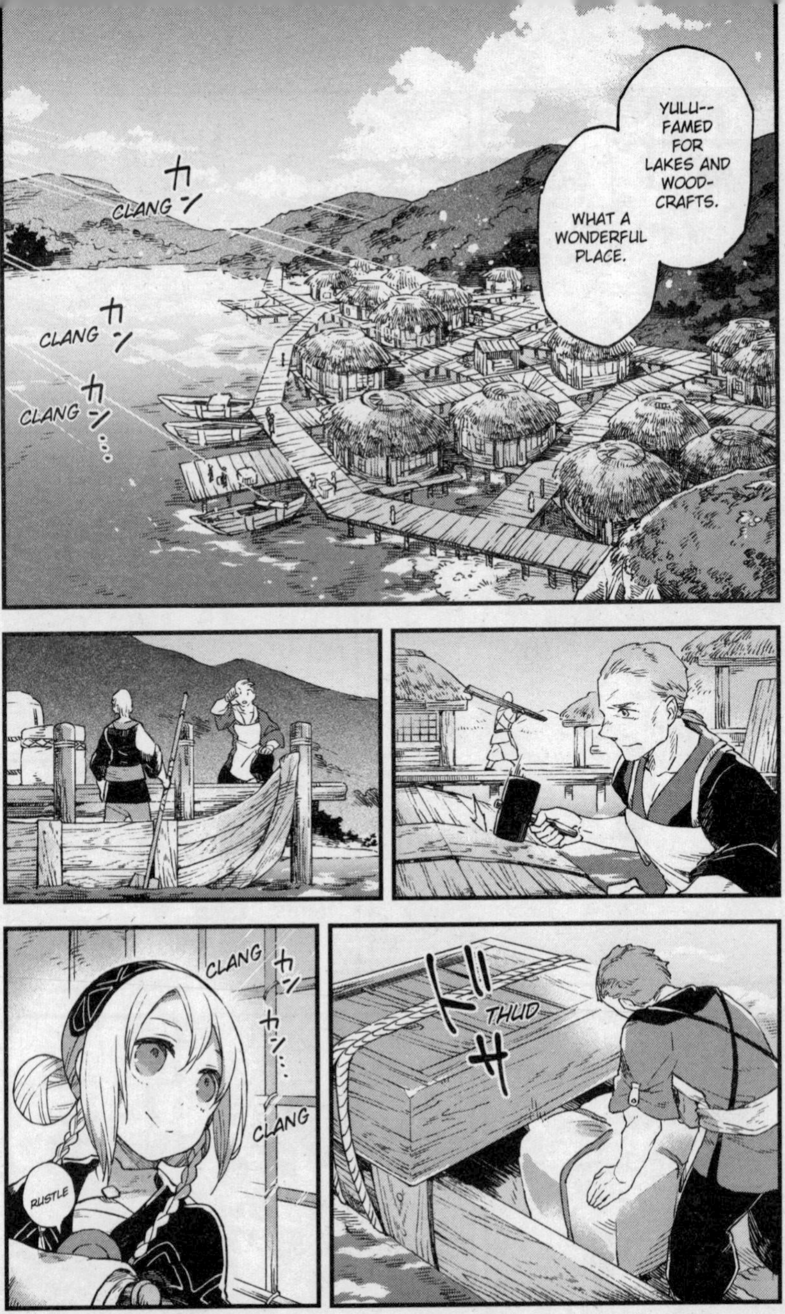
YULU--FAMED FOR LAKES AND WOOD-CRAFTS.
WHAT A WONDERFUL PLACE.
CLANG
CLANG
CLANG
THUD
CLANG
CLANG
RUSTLE

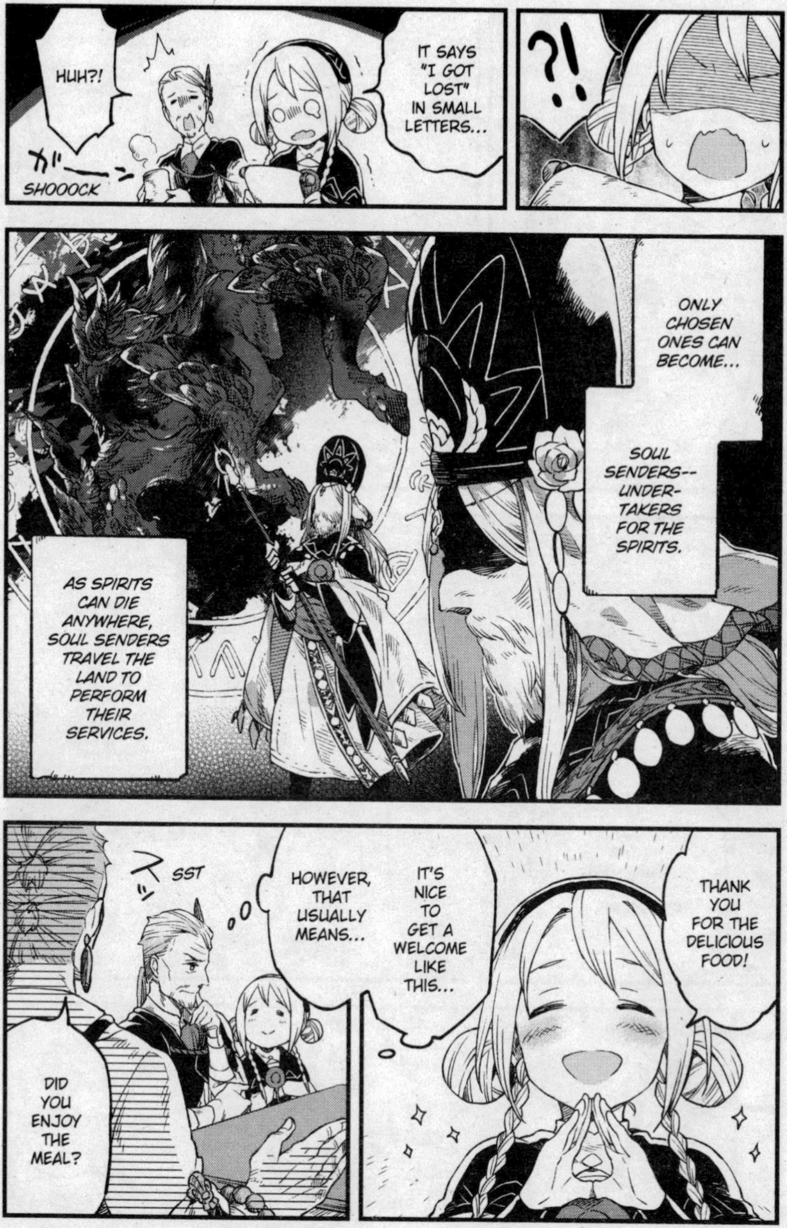
?!
IT SAYS "I GOT LOST" IN SMALL LETTERS...
HUH?!
ガー
SHOOOCK
ONLY CHOSEN ONES CAN BECOME...
SOUL SENDERS-- UNDER-TAKERS FOR THE SPIRITS.
AS SPIRITS CAN DIE ANYWHERE, SOUL SENDERS TRAVEL THE LAND TO PERFORM THEIR SERVICES.
THANK YOU FOR THE DELICIOUS FOOD!
IT'S NICE TO GET A WELCOME LIKE THIS...
HOWEVER, THAT USUALLY MEANS...
スッ
SST
DID YOU ENJOY THE MEAL?

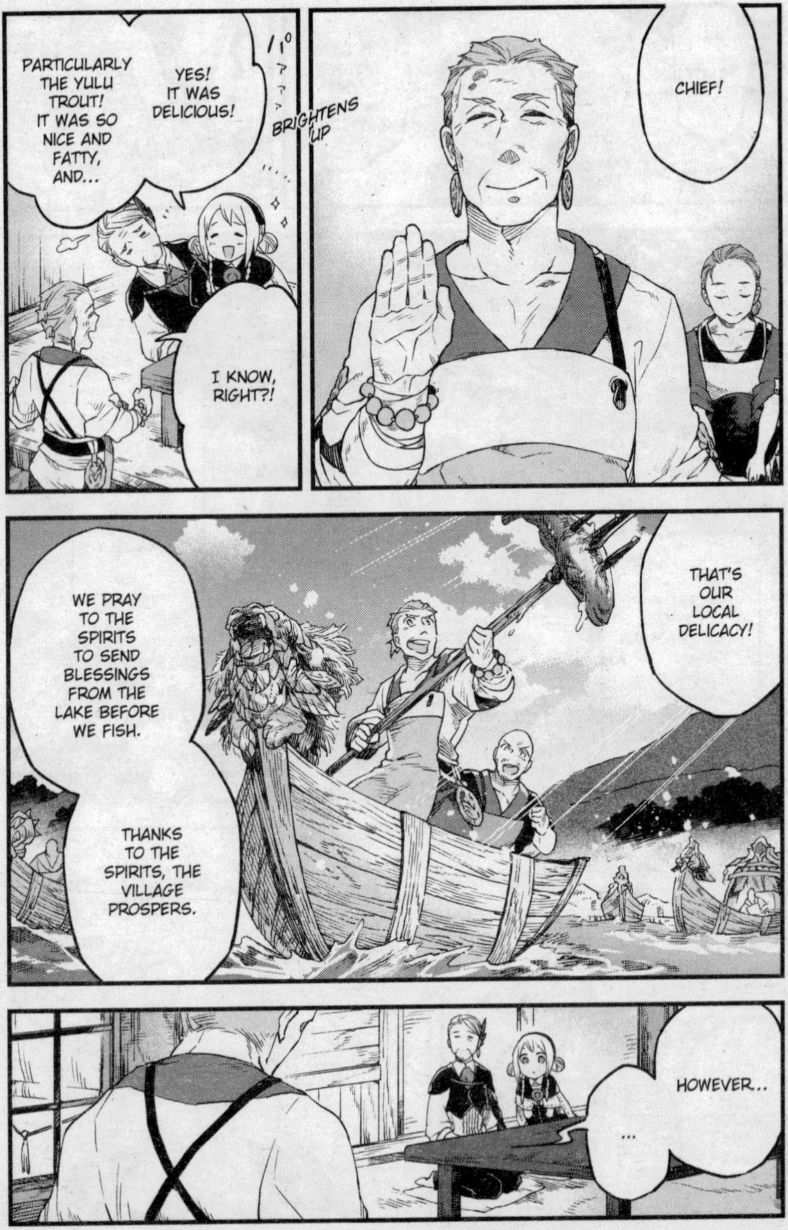
CHIEF!
YES! IT WAS DELICIOUS!
BRIGHTENS UP
PARTICULARLY THE YULU TROUT! IT WAS SO NICE AND FATTY, AND...
I KNOW, RIGHT?!
THAT'S OUR LOCAL DELICACY!
WE PRAY TO THE SPIRITS TO SEND BLESSINGS FROM THE LAKE BEFORE WE FISH.
THANKS TO THE SPIRITS, THE VILLAGE PROSPERS.
HOWEVER..
...

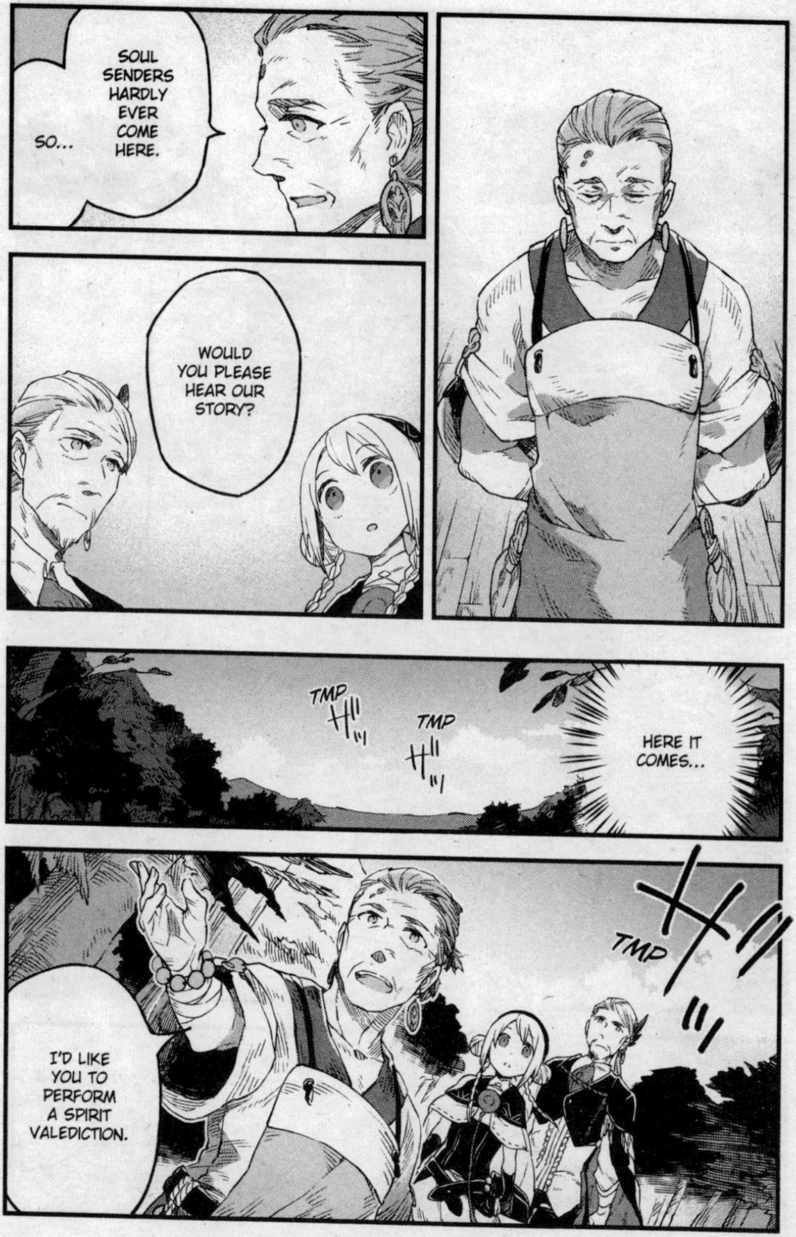

SOUL SENDERS HARDLY EVER COME HERE.
SO...
WOULD YOU PLEASE HEAR OUR STORY?
HERE IT COMES...
TMP
TMP
TMP
I'D LIKE YOU TO PERFORM A SPIRIT VALEDICTION.

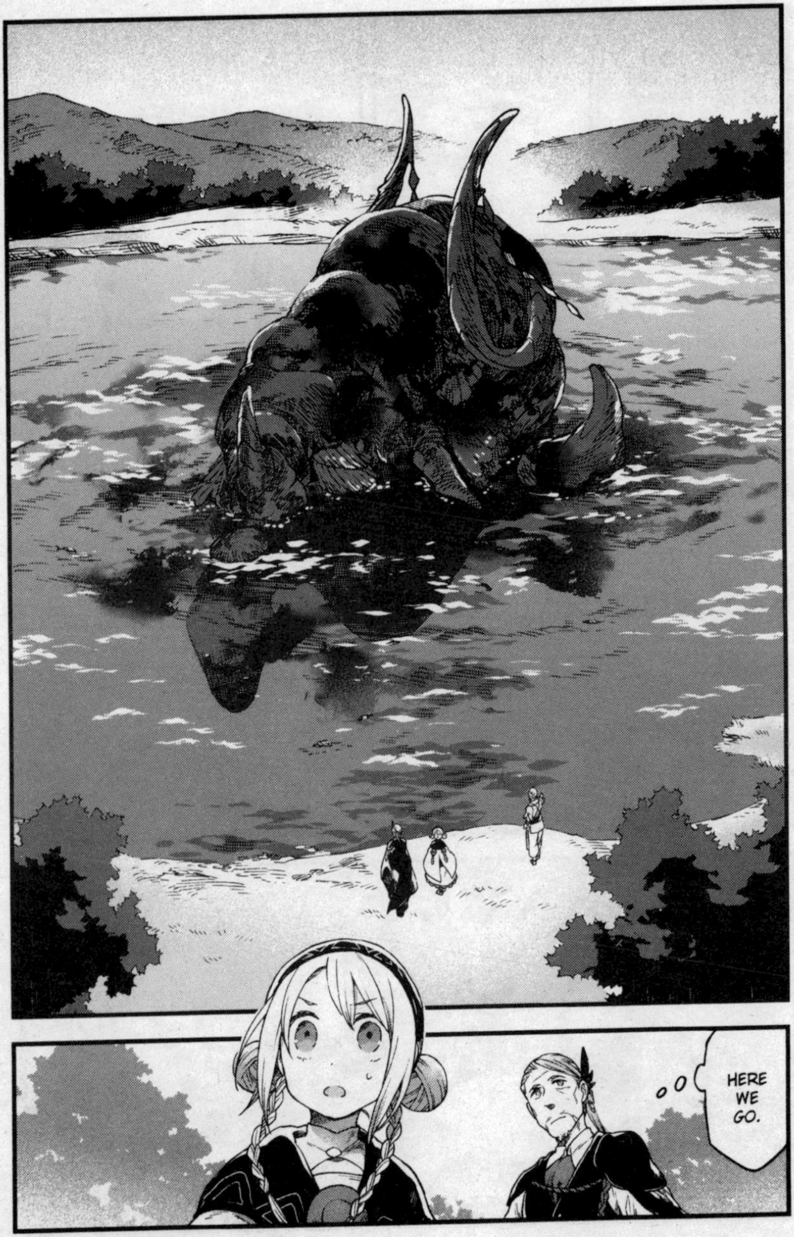
HERE WE GO.

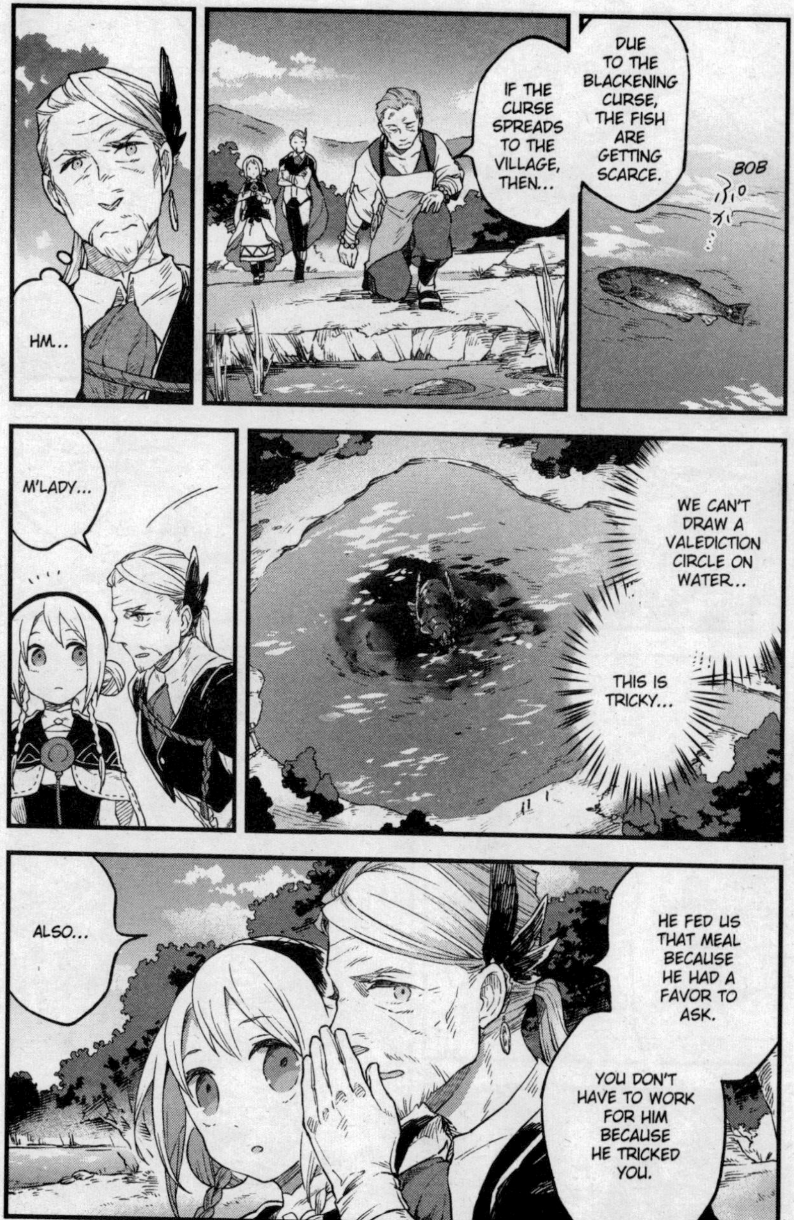

DUE TO THE BLACKENING CURSE, THE FISH ARE GETTING SCARCE.
BOB
IF THE CURSE SPREADS TO THE VILLAGE, THEN...
HM...
WE CAN'T DRAW A VALEDICTION CIRCLE ON WATER...
THIS IS TRICKY...
M'LADY...
HE FED US THAT MEAL BECAUSE HE HAD A FAVOR TO ASK.
ALSO...
YOU DON'T HAVE TO WORK FOR HIM BECAUSE HE TRICKED YOU.

THIS SCALE OF CURSE WON'T SPREAD BEYOND THE LAKE.

I FEEL SORRY FOR THEM, BUT YOU MAY AS WELL JUST LEAVE IT.

...

YOU'RE RIGHT, BUT...

...I THINK THE VILLAGERS WOULD LIKE A VALEDICTION.

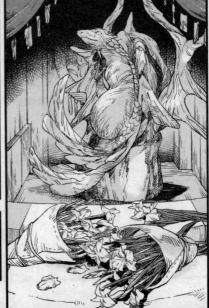

CLENCH

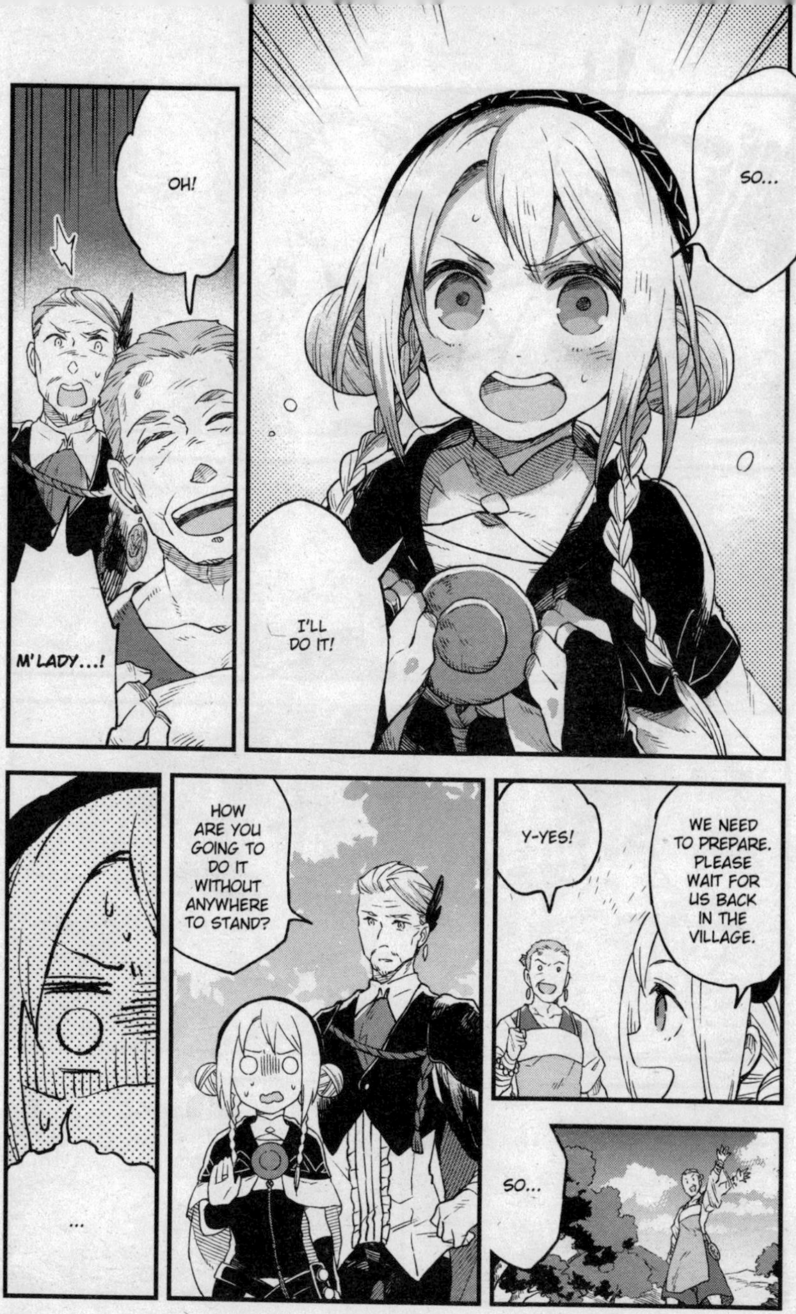
SO...
I'LL DO IT!
OH!
M'LADY...!
WE NEED TO PREPARE. PLEASE WAIT FOR US BACK IN THE VILLAGE.
Y-YES!
SO...
HOW ARE YOU GOING TO DO IT WITHOUT ANYWHERE TO STAND?
...

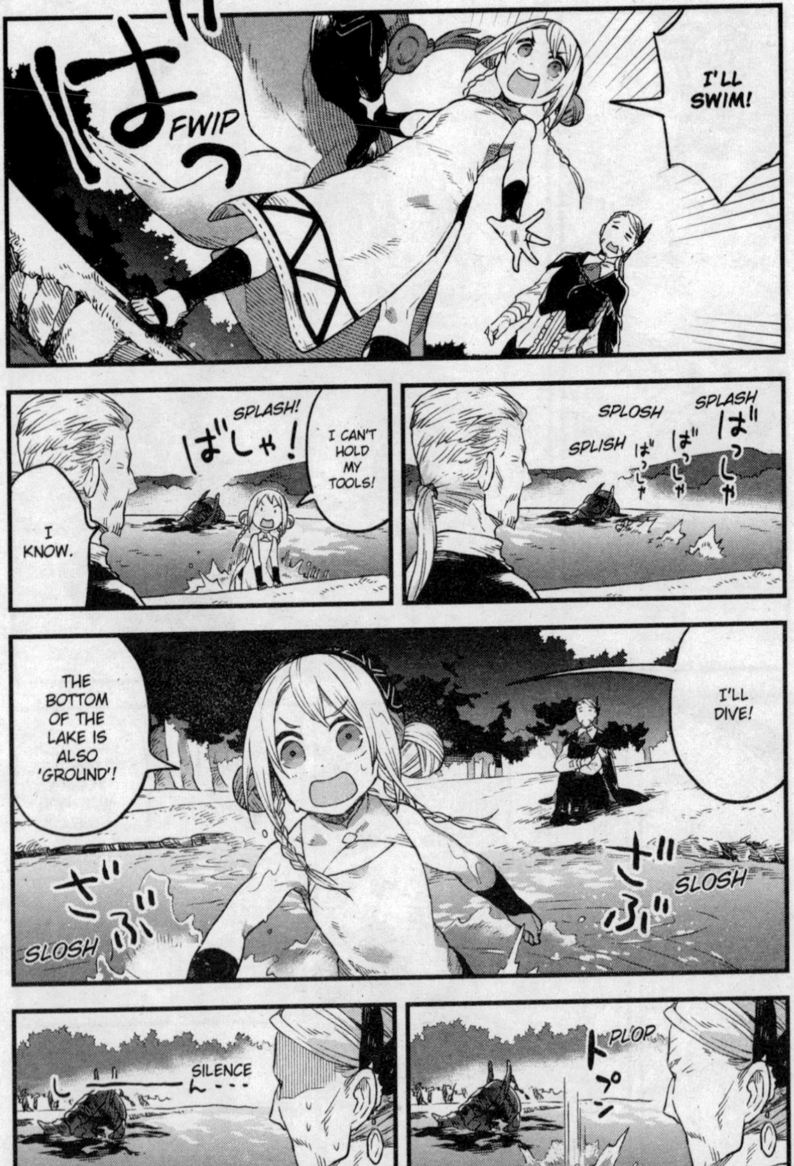
I'LL SWIM!
ばっ
FWIP
SPLASH
ばっしゃ
SPLOSH
ばっしゃ
SPLISH
ばっしゃ
I CAN'T HOLD MY TOOLS!
SPLASH!
ばしゃ!
I KNOW.
I'LL DIVE!
ざぶ
SLOSH
THE BOTTOM OF THE LAKE IS ALSO 'GROUND'!
ざぶ
SLOSH
PLOP
トプン
SILENCE
しーん・・・

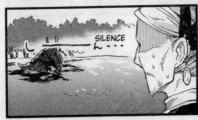

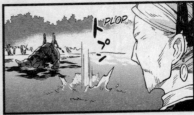

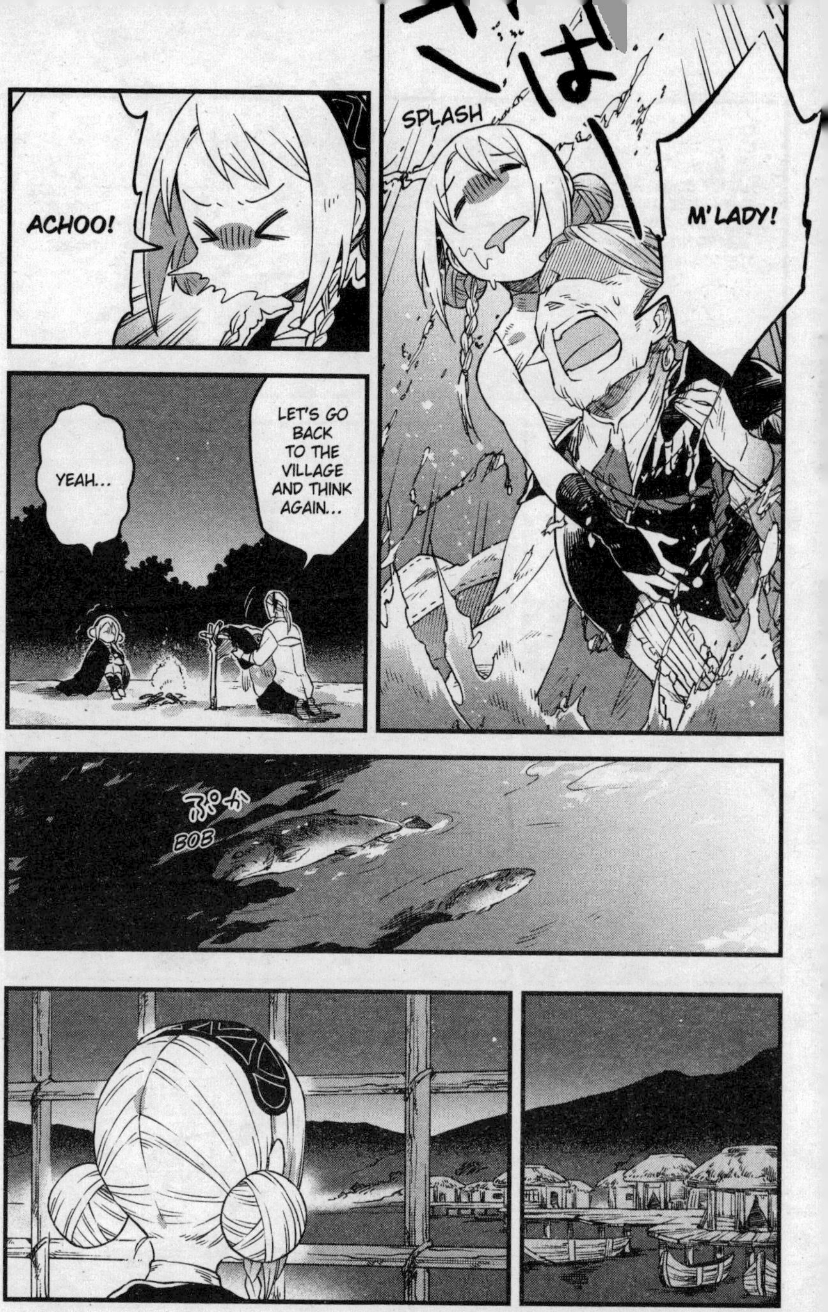
ざば
SPLASH
M'LADY!
ACHOO!
LET'S GO BACK TO THE VILLAGE AND THINK AGAIN...
YEAH...
ぷか
BOB

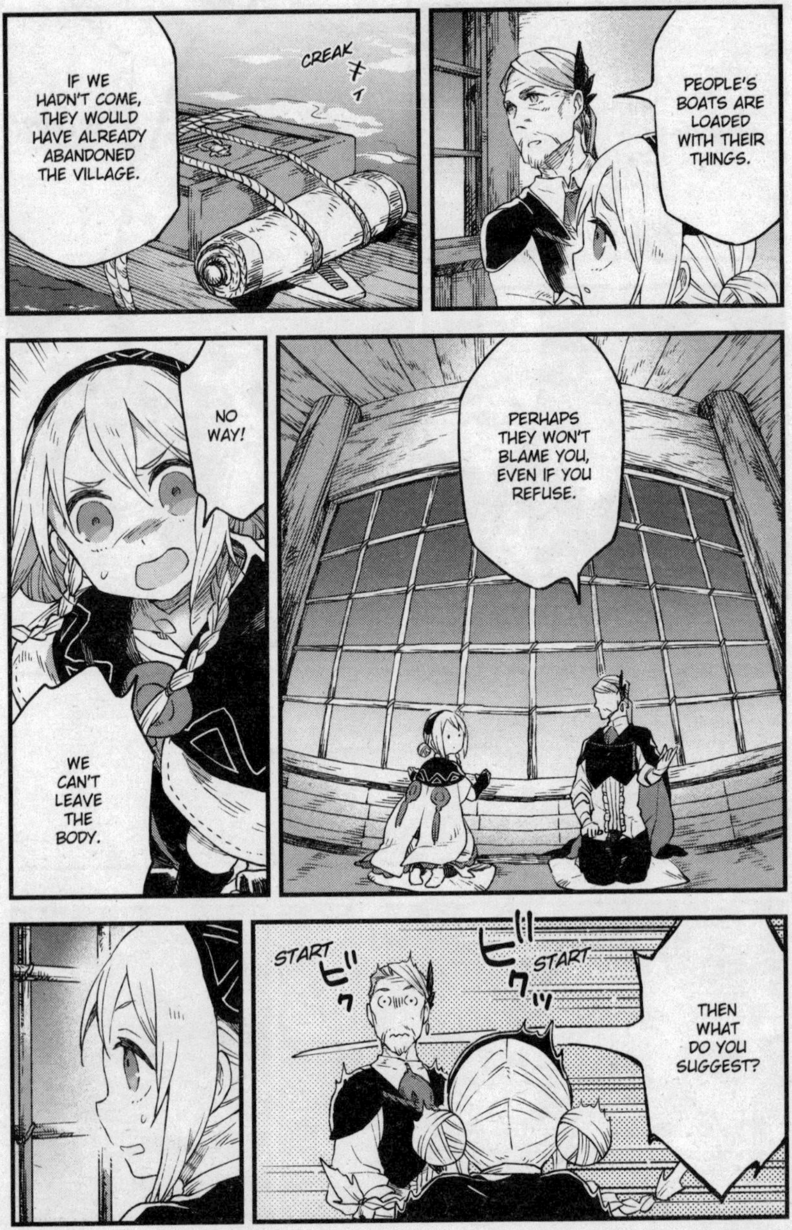
PEOPLE'S BOATS ARE LOADED WITH THEIR THINGS.
CREAK
IF WE HADN'T COME, THEY WOULD HAVE ALREADY ABANDONED THE VILLAGE.
PERHAPS THEY WON'T BLAME YOU, EVEN IF YOU REFUSE.
NO WAY!
WE CAN'T LEAVE THE BODY.
START
START
THEN WHAT DO YOU SUGGEST?

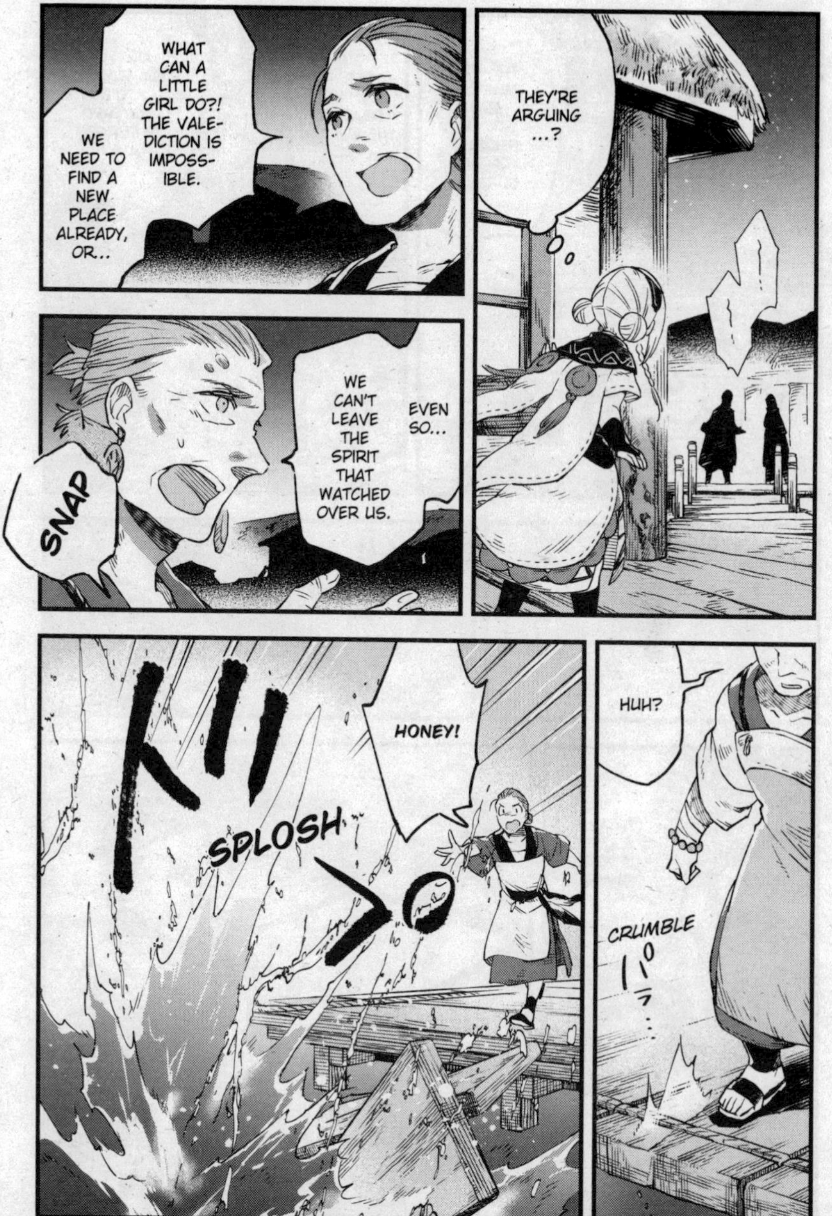
THEY'RE ARGUING ...?
WHAT CAN A LITTLE GIRL DO?! THE VALE-DICTION IS IMPOSS-IBLE.
WE NEED TO FIND A NEW PLACE ALREADY, OR...
EVEN SO...
WE CAN'T LEAVE THE SPIRIT THAT WATCHED OVER US.
SNAP
HUH?
CRUMBLE
HONEY!
SPLOSH

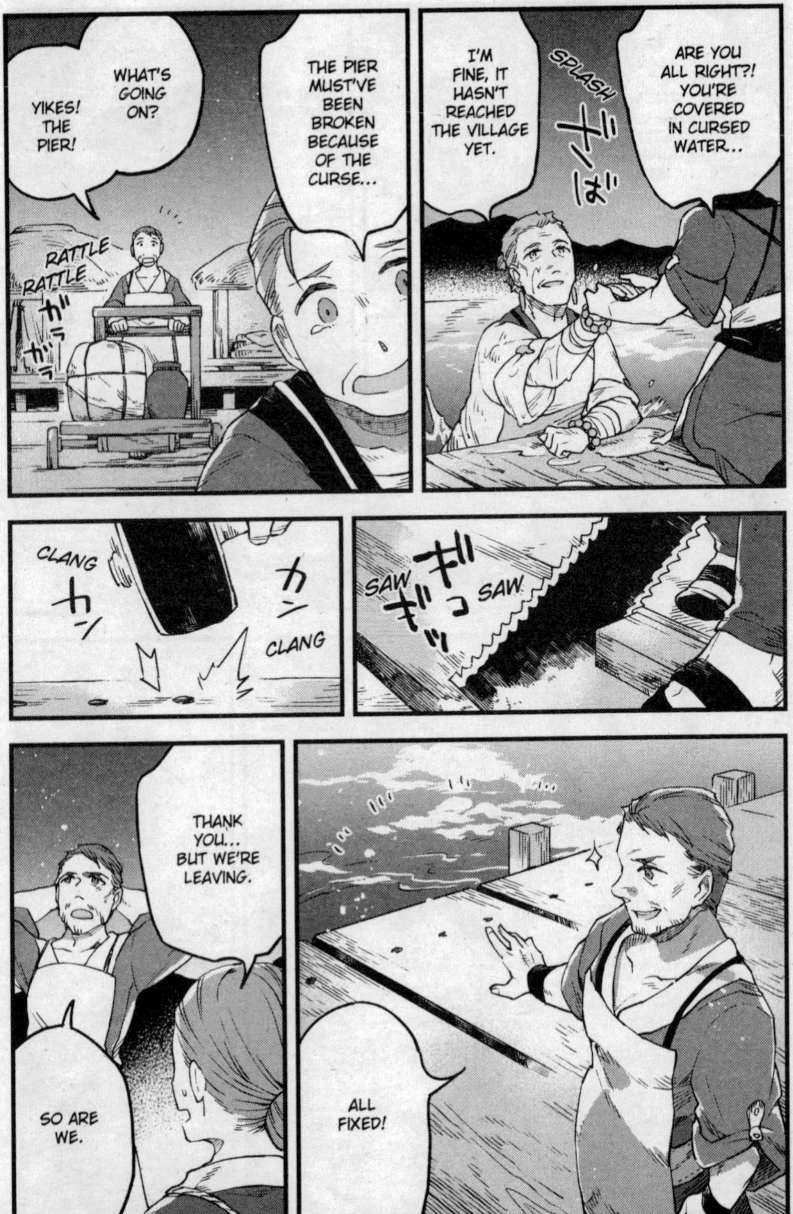

ARE YOU ALL RIGHT?! YOU'RE COVERED IN CURSED WATER...
SPLASH
I'M FINE, IT HASN'T REACHED THE VILLAGE YET.
THE PIER MUST'VE BEEN BROKEN BECAUSE OF THE CURSE...
WHAT'S GOING ON?
YIKES! THE PIER!
RATTLE RATTLE
SAW SAW
CLANG
CLANG
ALL FIXED!
THANK YOU... BUT WE'RE LEAVING.
SO ARE WE.

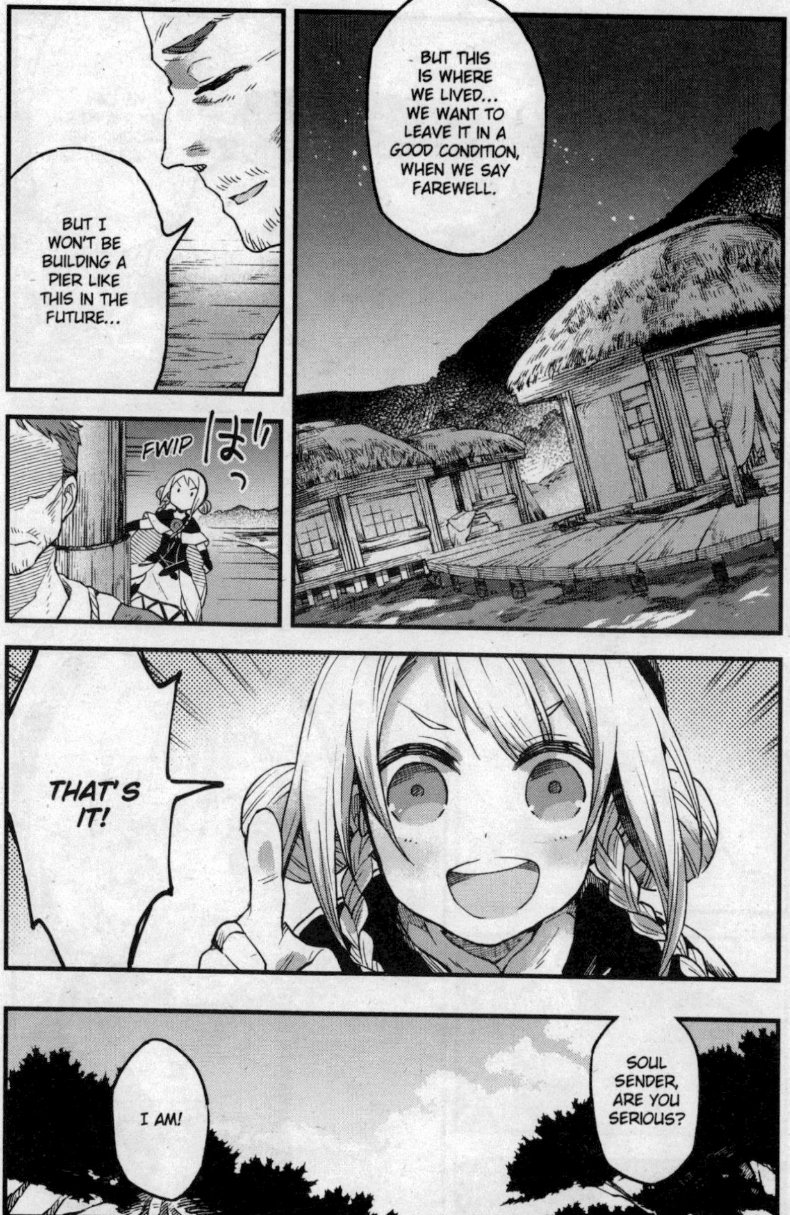
BUT THIS IS WHERE WE LIVED... WE WANT TO LEAVE IT IN A GOOD CONDITION, WHEN WE SAY FAREWELL.
BUT I WON'T BE BUILDING A PIER LIKE THIS IN THE FUTURE...
はっ
FWIP
THAT'S IT!
SOUL SENDER, ARE YOU SERIOUS?
I AM!

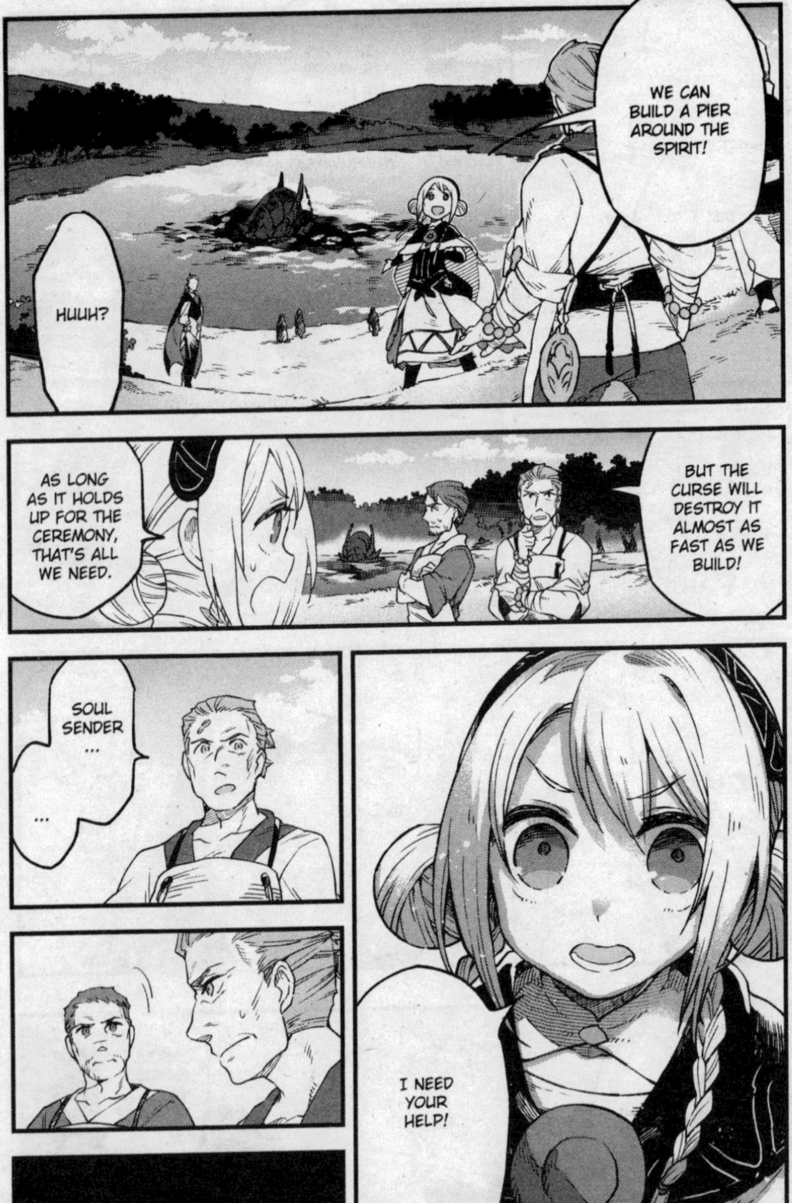
WE CAN BUILD A PIER AROUND THE SPIRIT!
HUUH?
BUT THE CURSE WILL DESTROY IT ALMOST AS FAST AS WE BUILD!
AS LONG AS IT HOLDS UP FOR THE CEREMONY, THAT'S ALL WE NEED.
I NEED YOUR HELP!
SOUL SENDER ...
...

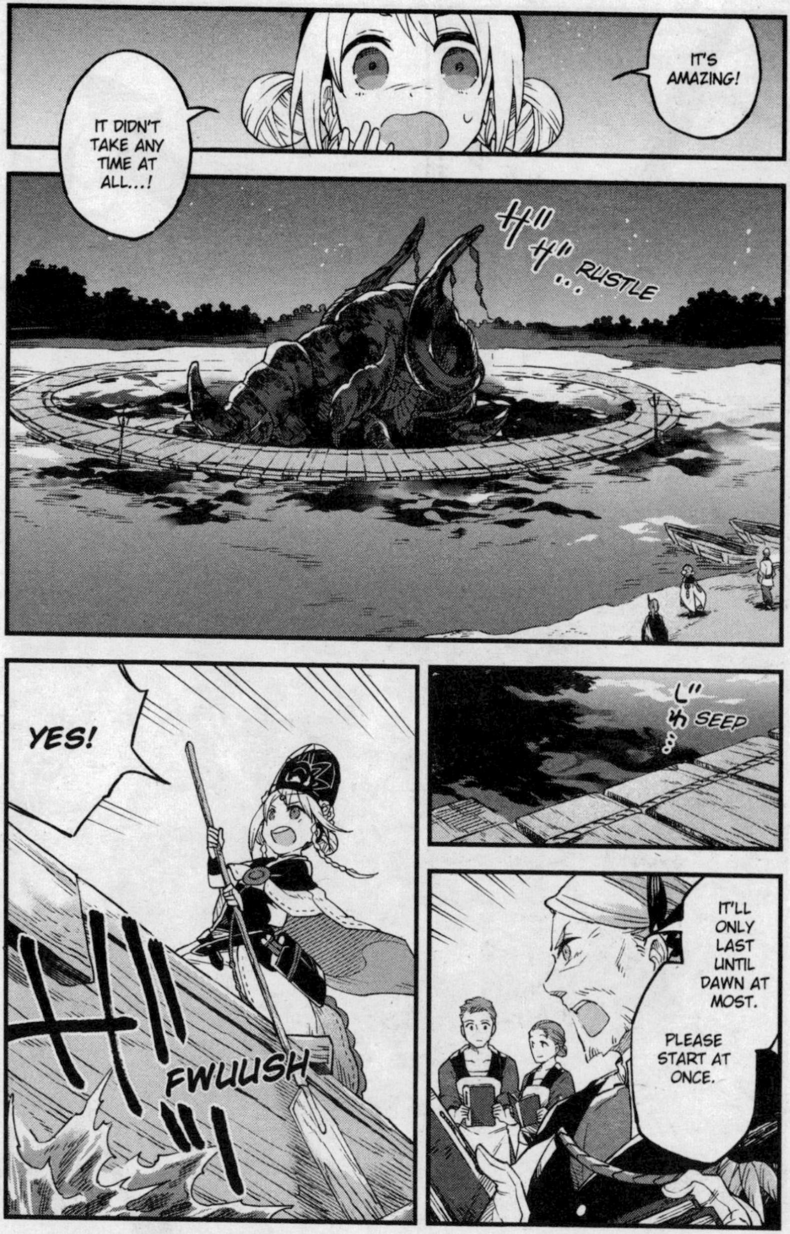
IT'S AMAZING!
IT DIDN'T TAKE ANY TIME AT ALL...!
RUSTLE
SEEP
IT'LL ONLY LAST UNTIL DAWN AT MOST.
PLEASE START AT ONCE.
YES!
FWUUSH

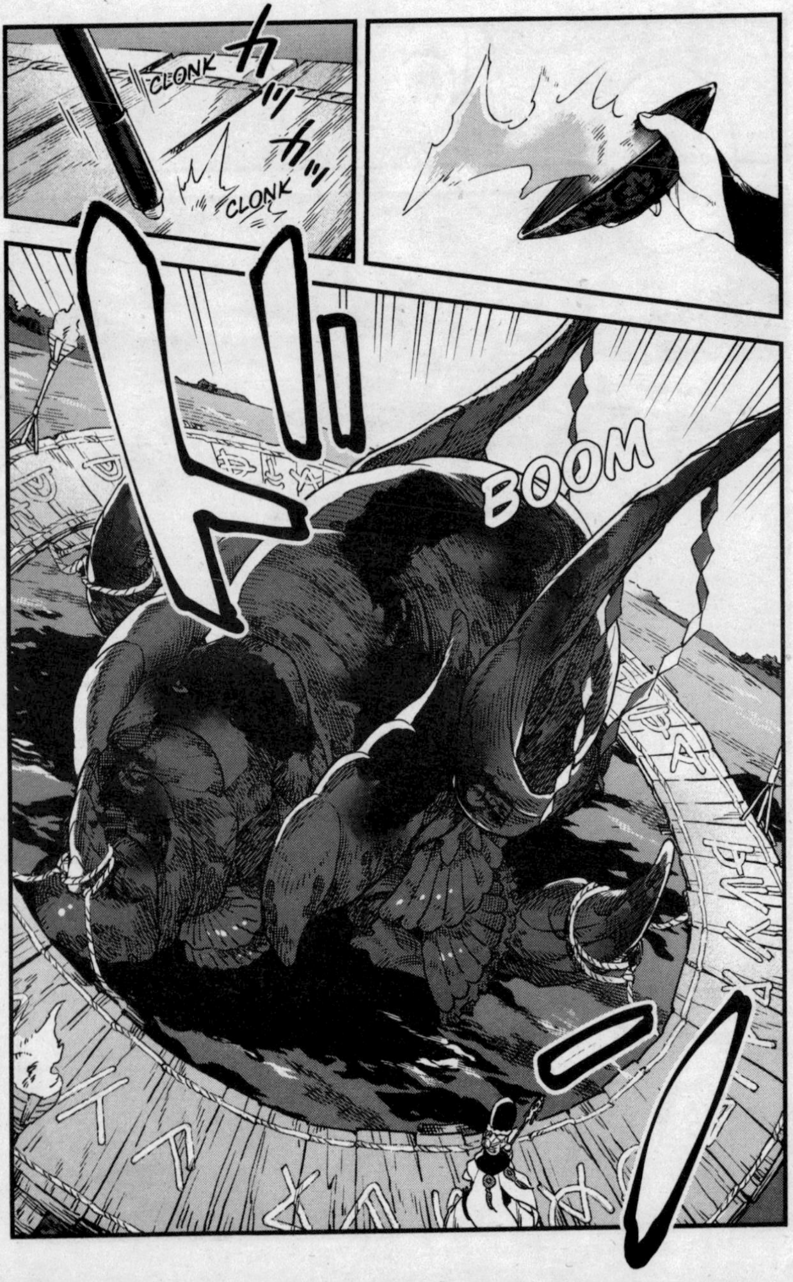
CLONK
カッ
カッ
CLONK
BOOM

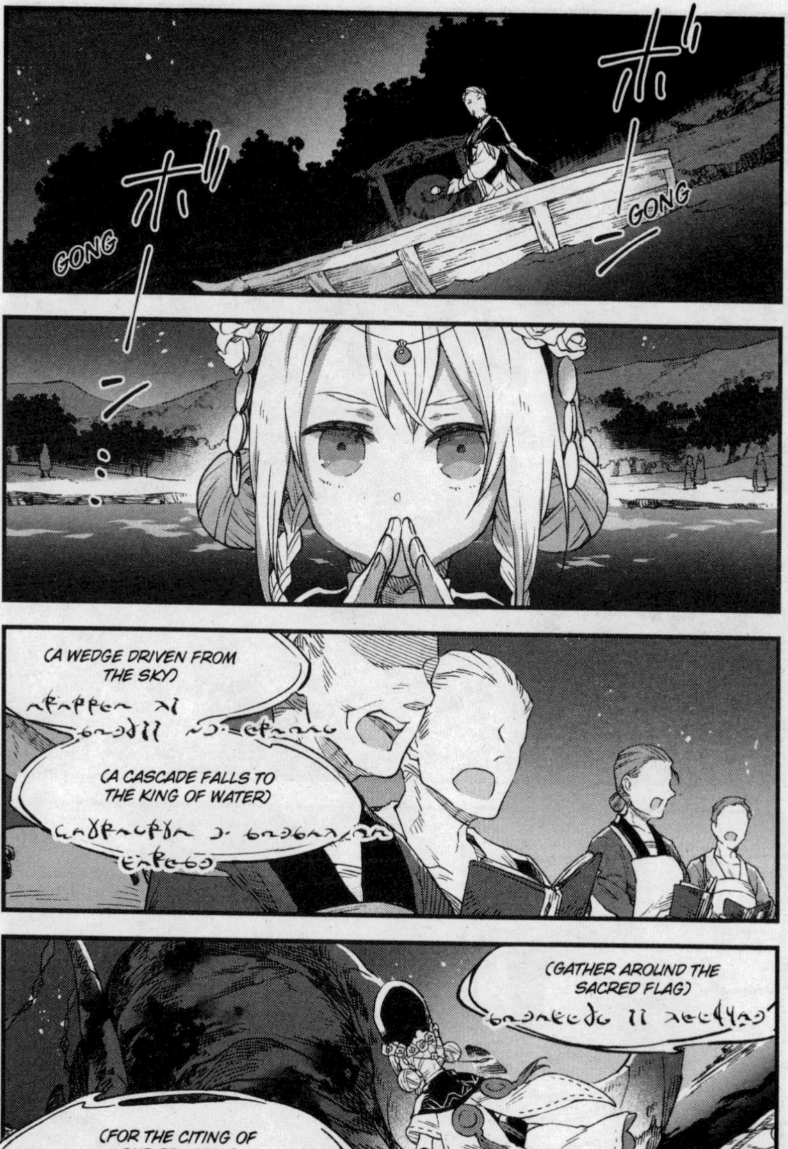

ボーン
GONG
ボーン
GONG
(A WEDGE DRIVEN FROM THE SKY)
(A CASCADE FALLS TO THE KING OF WATER)
(GATHER AROUND THE SACRED FLAG)
(FOR THE CITING OF OUR PRAYERS)

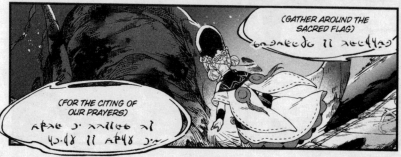

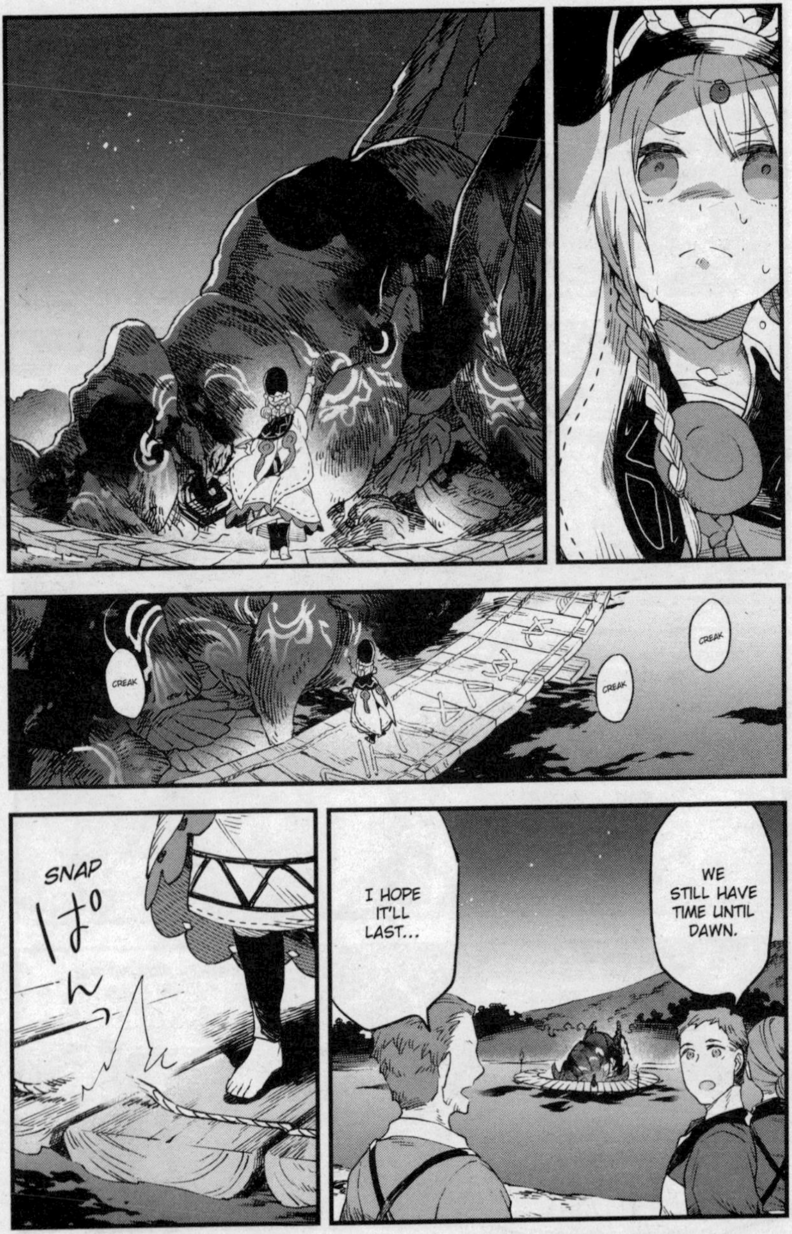
CREAK
CREAK
CREAK
WE STILL HAVE TIME UNTIL DAWN.
I HOPE IT'LL LAST...
SNAP
ぱんっ

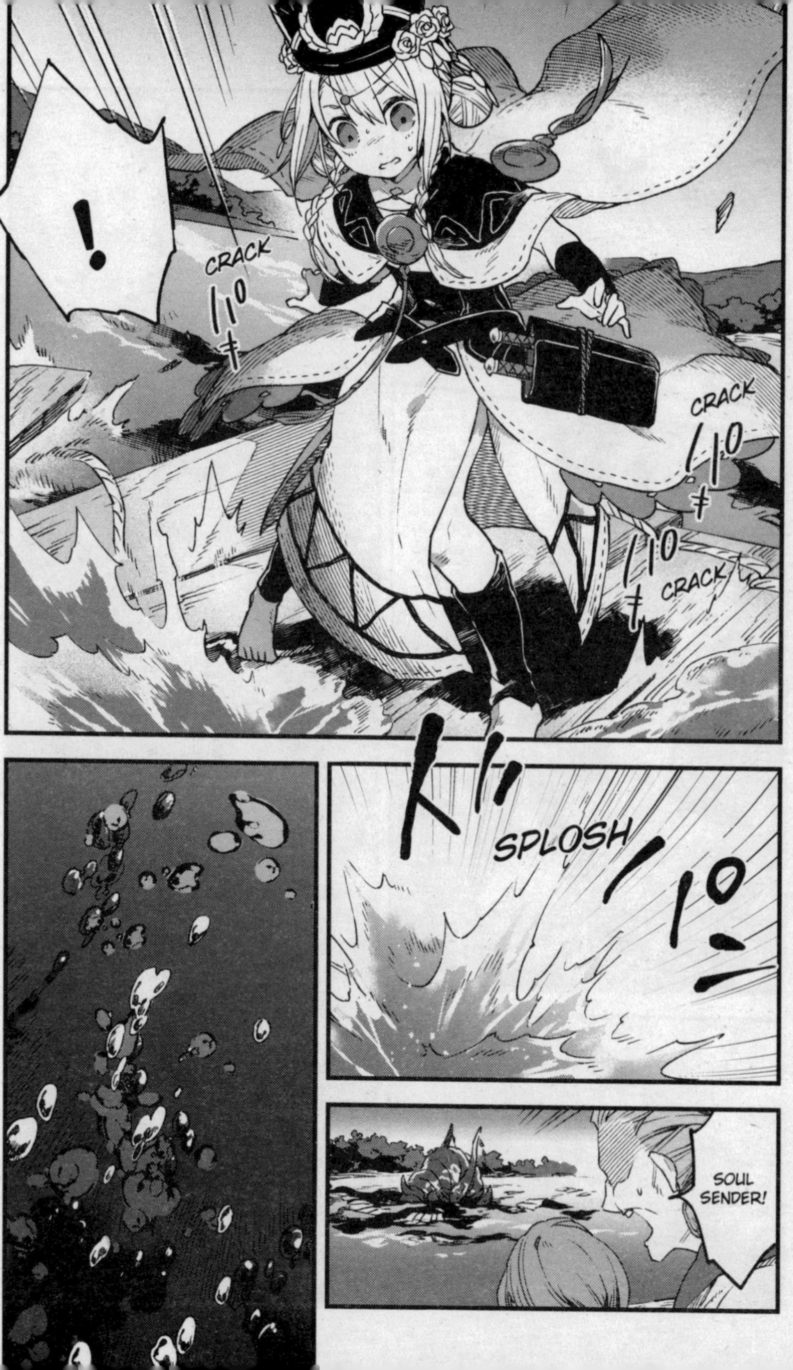
!
CRACK
CRACK
CRACK
SPLOSH
SOUL SENDER!

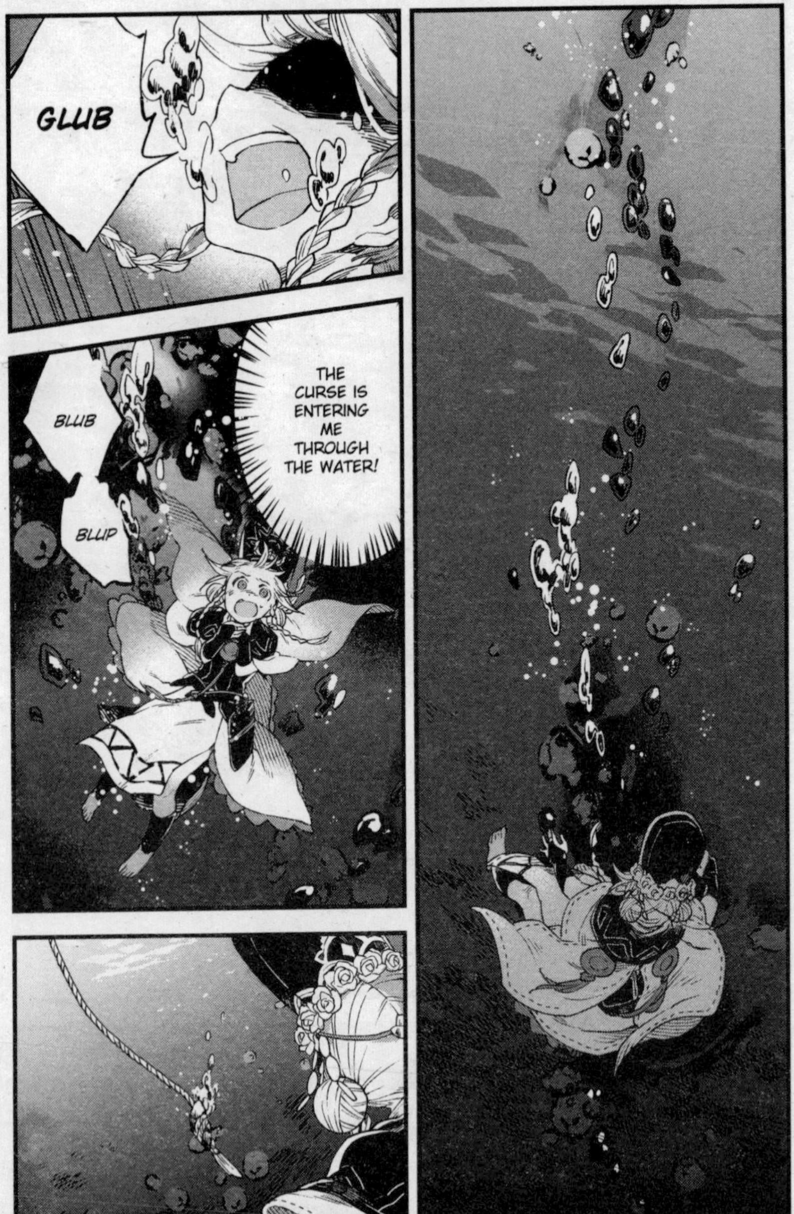
GLUB
THE CURSE IS ENTERING ME THROUGH THE WATER!
BLUB
BLUP

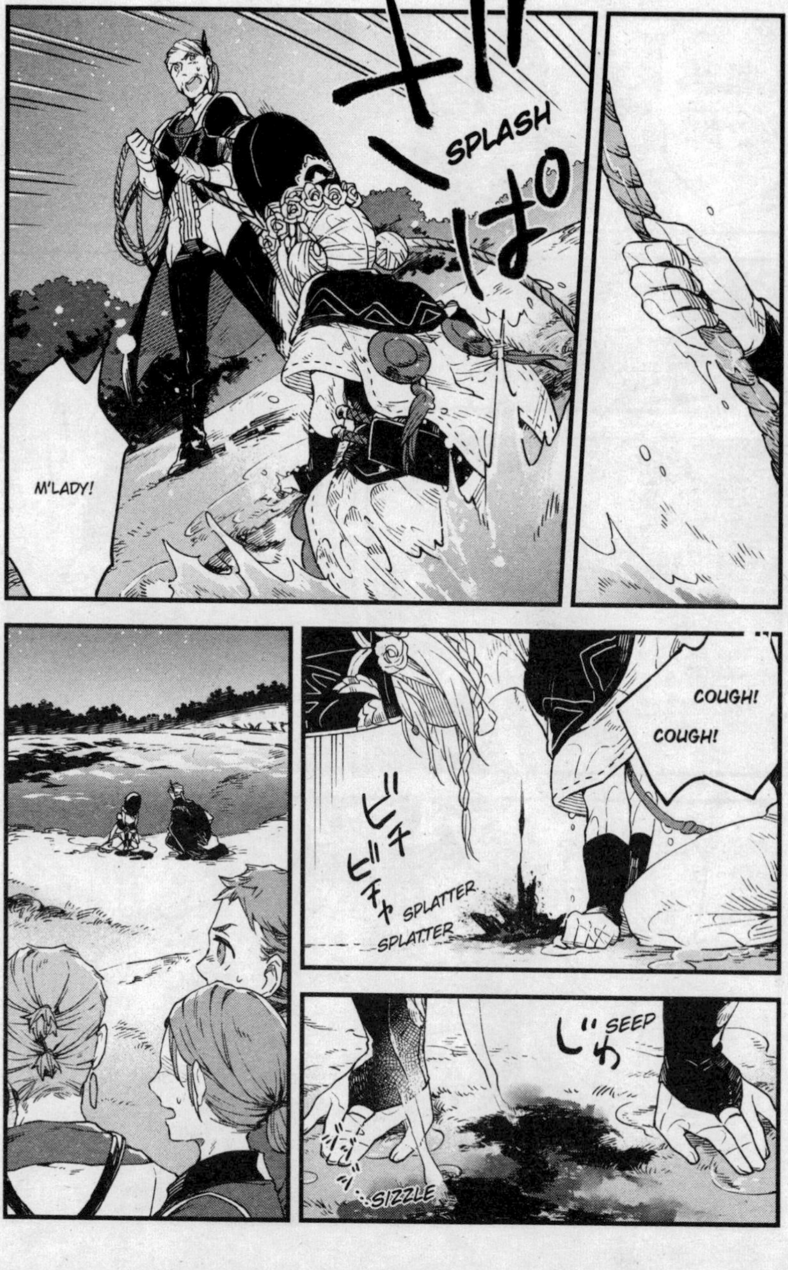
ざぱ
SPLASH
M'LADY!
COUGH!
COUGH!
ビチビチャ
SPLATTER
SPLATTER
じわ
SEEP
...SIZZLE

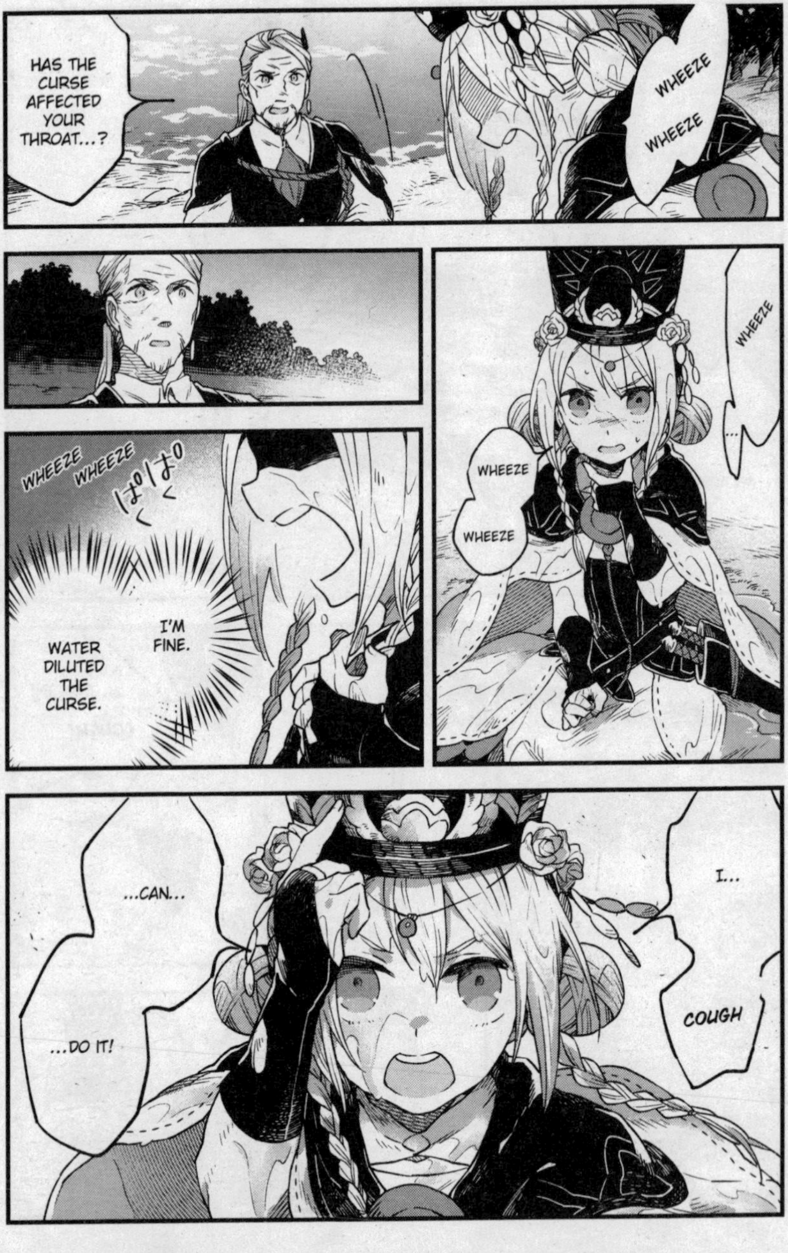
WHEEZE
WHEEZE
HAS THE CURSE AFFECTED YOUR THROAT...?
WHEEZE
...
WHEEZE
WHEEZE
WHEEZE
WHEEZE
ぱくぱく
I'M FINE.
WATER DILUTED THE CURSE.
I...
COUGH
...CAN...
...DO IT!

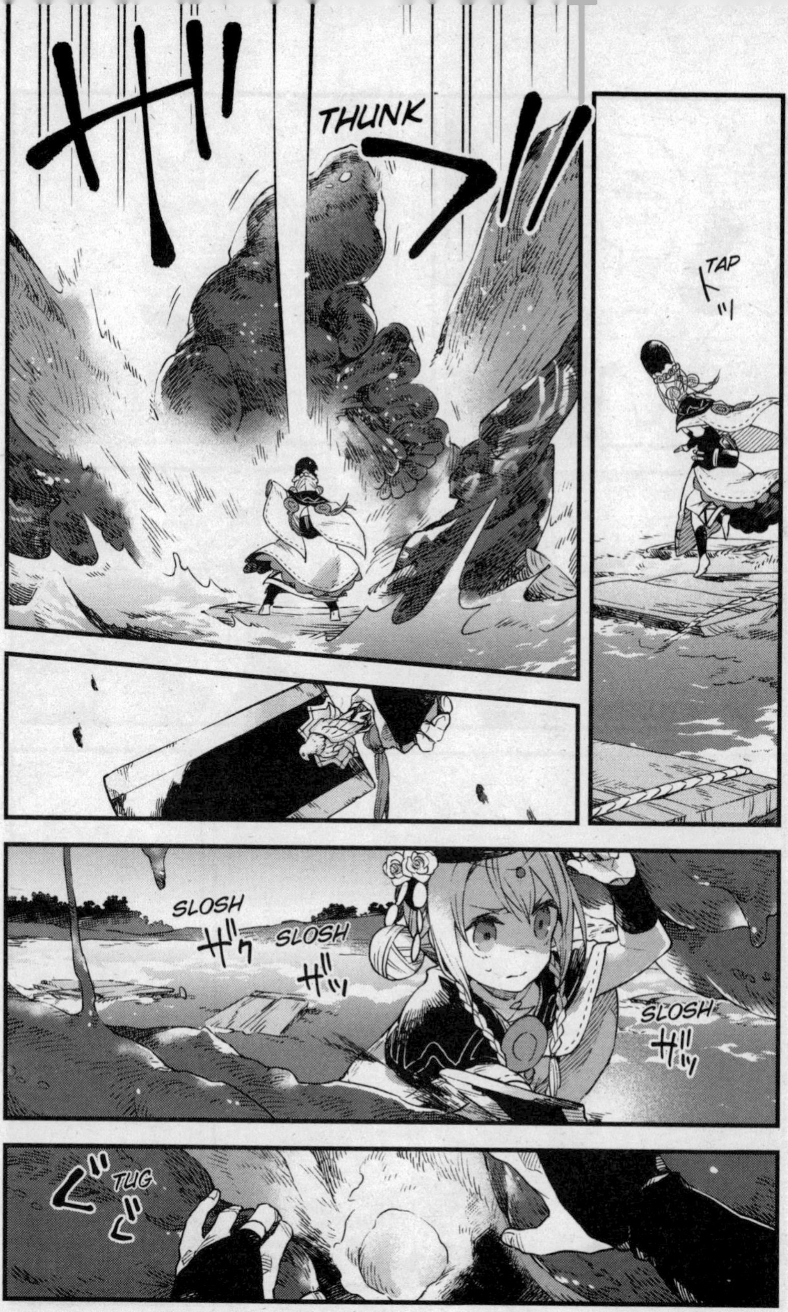
TAP
トッ
THUNK
SLOSH
ザク
SLOSH
ザッ
SLOSH
ザッ
TUG

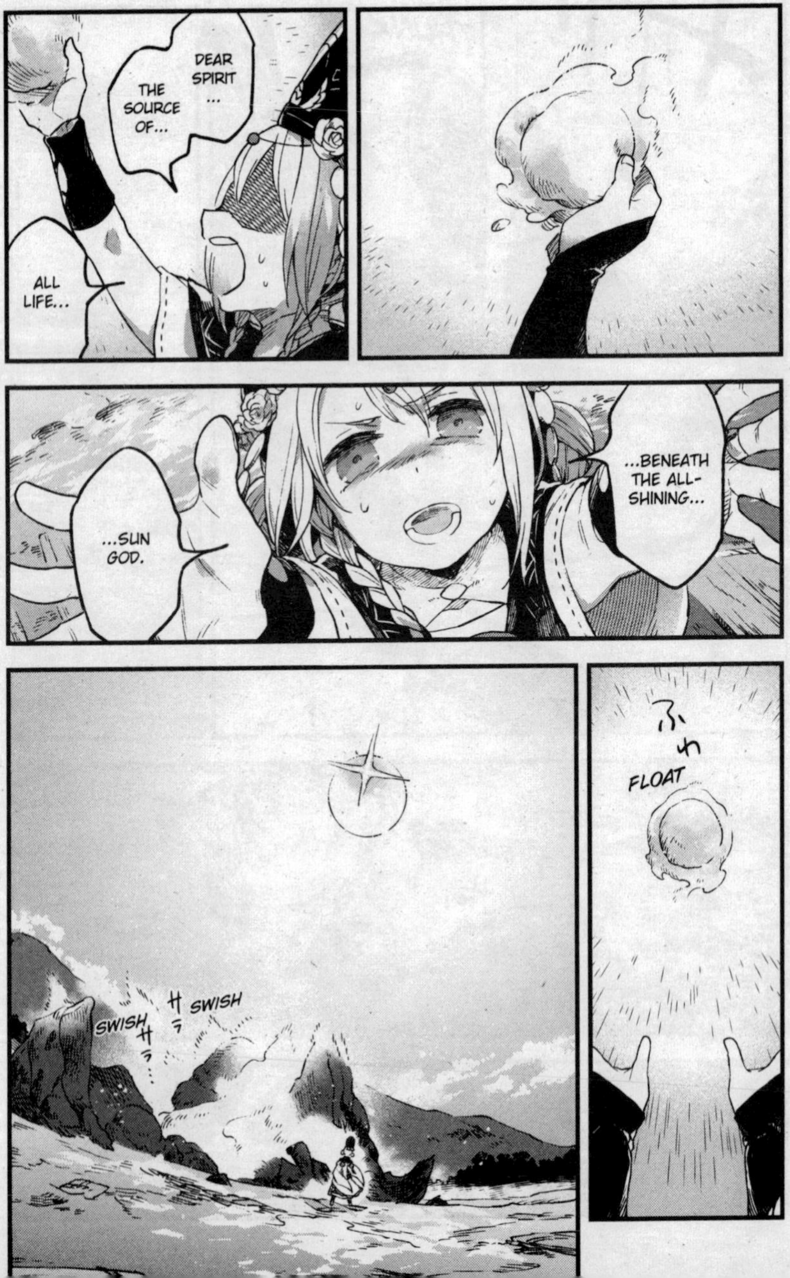
DEAR SPIRIT...
THE SOURCE OF...
ALL LIFE...
...BENEATH THE ALL-SHINING...
...SUN GOD.
ふわ
FLOAT
サラ
SWISH
サラ...
SWISH

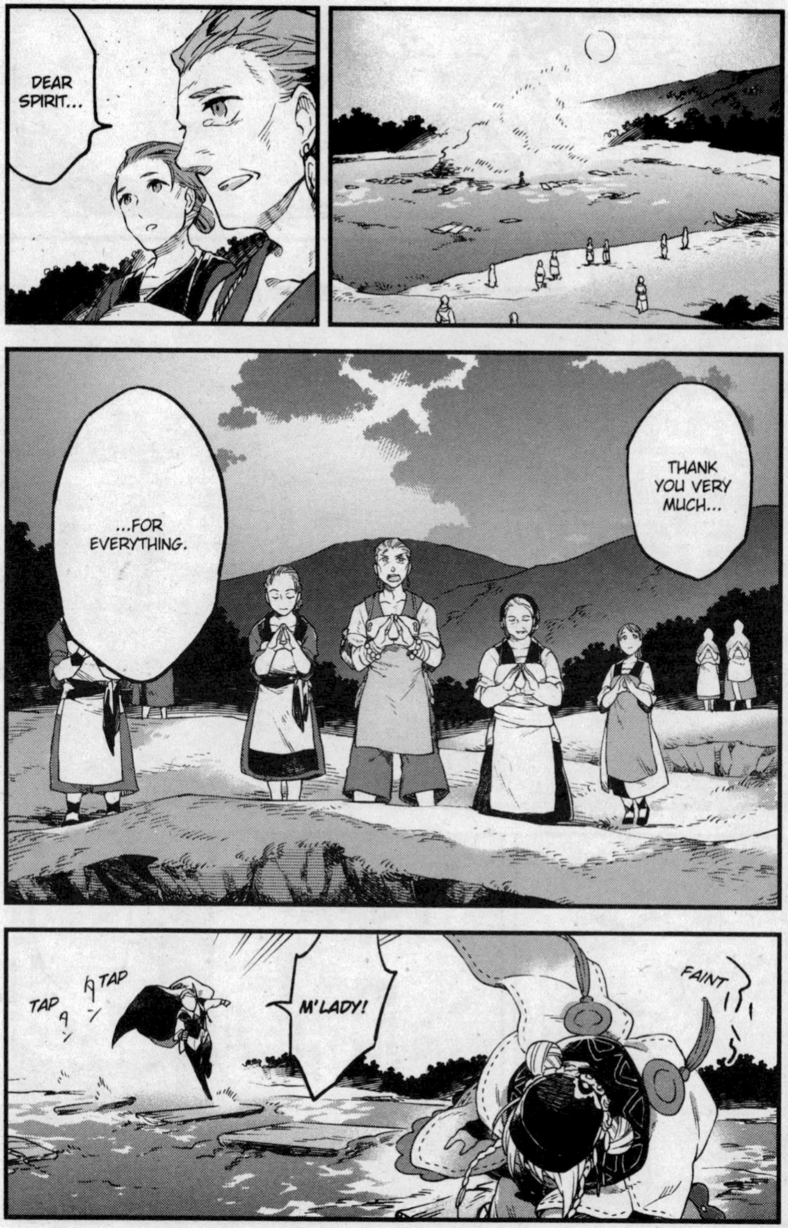
DEAR SPIRIT...
THANK YOU VERY MUCH...
...FOR EVERYTHING.
FAINT
M'LADY!
TAP
TAP

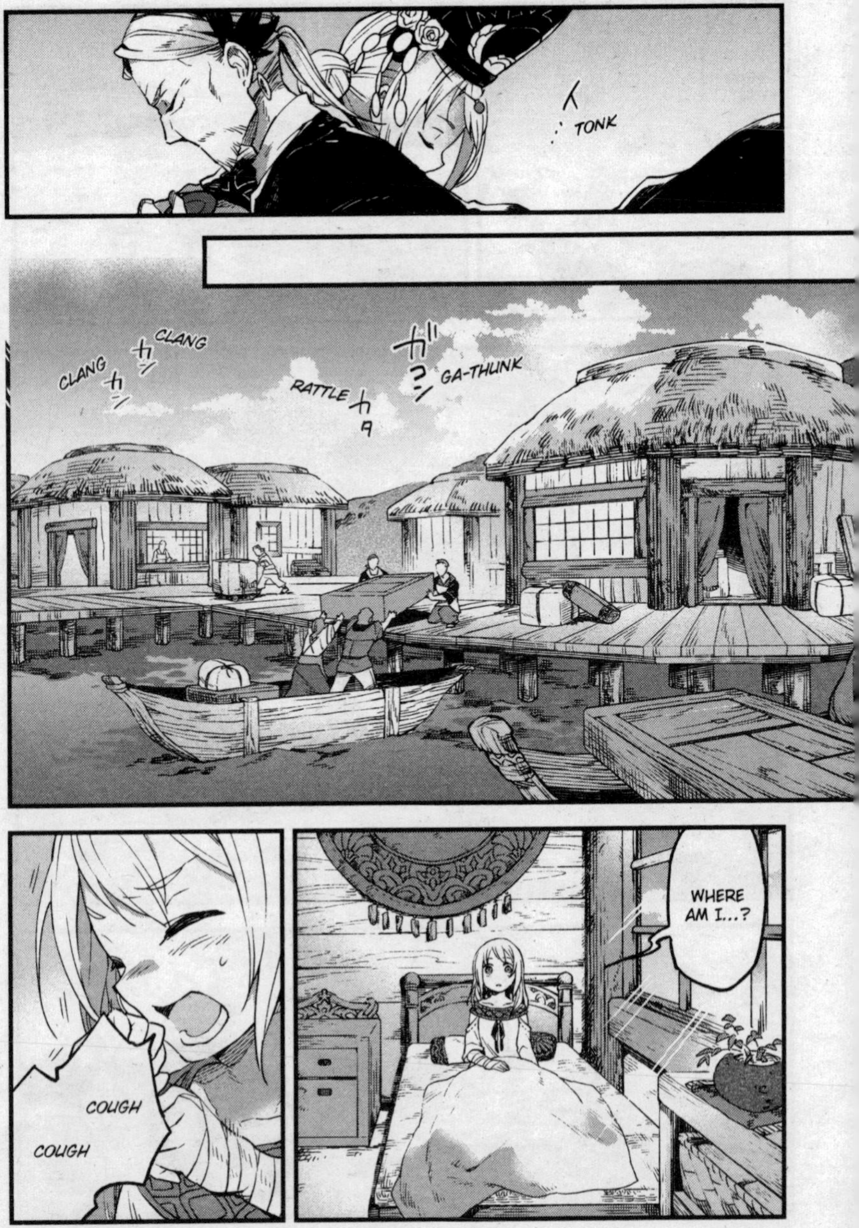
TONK
GA-THUNK
RATTLE
CLANG
CLANG
WHERE AM I...?
COUGH
COUGH

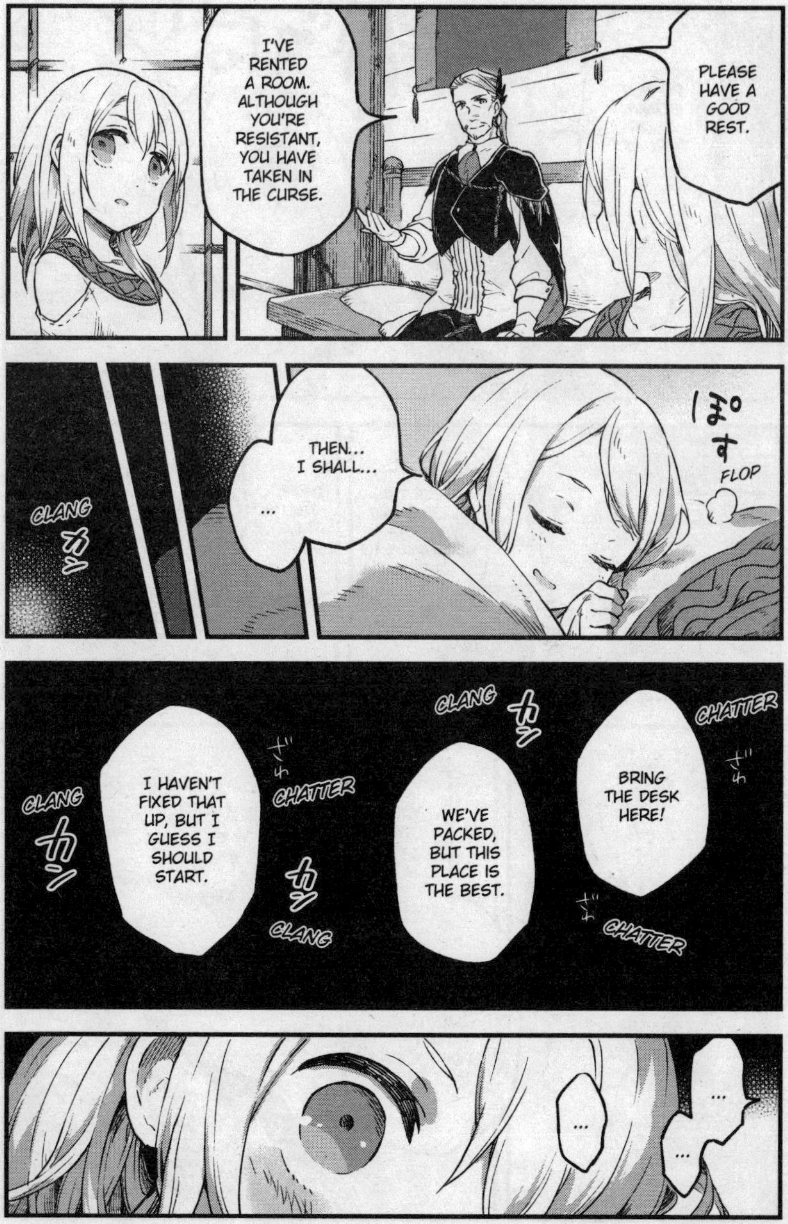
PLEASE HAVE A GOOD REST.
I'VE RENTED A ROOM. ALTHOUGH YOU'RE RESISTANT, YOU HAVE TAKEN IN THE CURSE.
ぽす
FLOP
THEN... I SHALL...
...
CLANG
カン
CHATTER
ざわ
BRING THE DESK HERE!
ざわ
CHATTER
CLANG
カン
WE'VE PACKED, BUT THIS PLACE IS THE BEST.
カン
CLANG
ざわ
CHATTER
I HAVEN'T FIXED THAT UP, BUT I GUESS I SHOULD START.
CLANG
カン
...
...
...

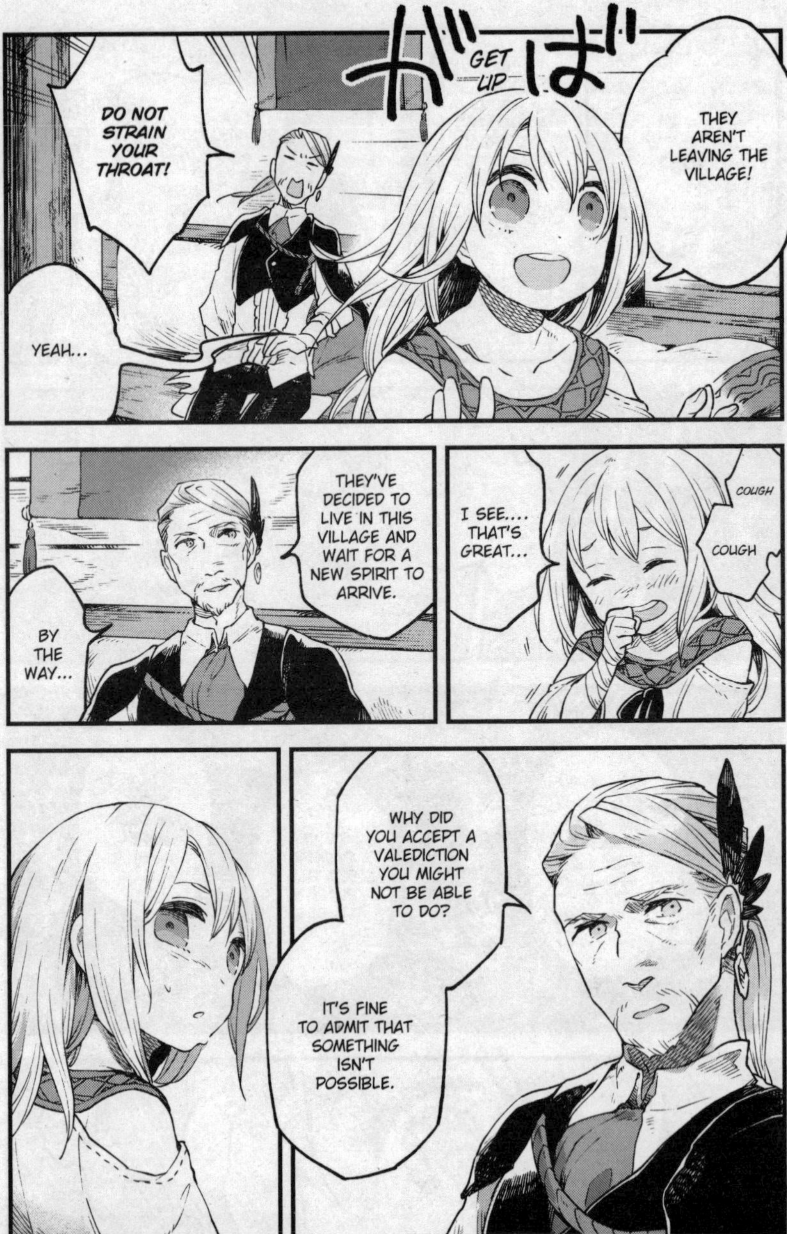
がば
GET UP
THEY AREN'T LEAVING THE VILLAGE!
DO NOT STRAIN YOUR THROAT!
YEAH...
COUGH
COUGH
I SEE.... THAT'S GREAT...
THEY'VE DECIDED TO LIVE IN THIS VILLAGE AND WAIT FOR A NEW SPIRIT TO ARRIVE.
BY THE WAY...
WHY DID YOU ACCEPT A VALEDICTION YOU MIGHT NOT BE ABLE TO DO?
IT'S FINE TO ADMIT THAT SOMETHING ISN'T POSSIBLE.

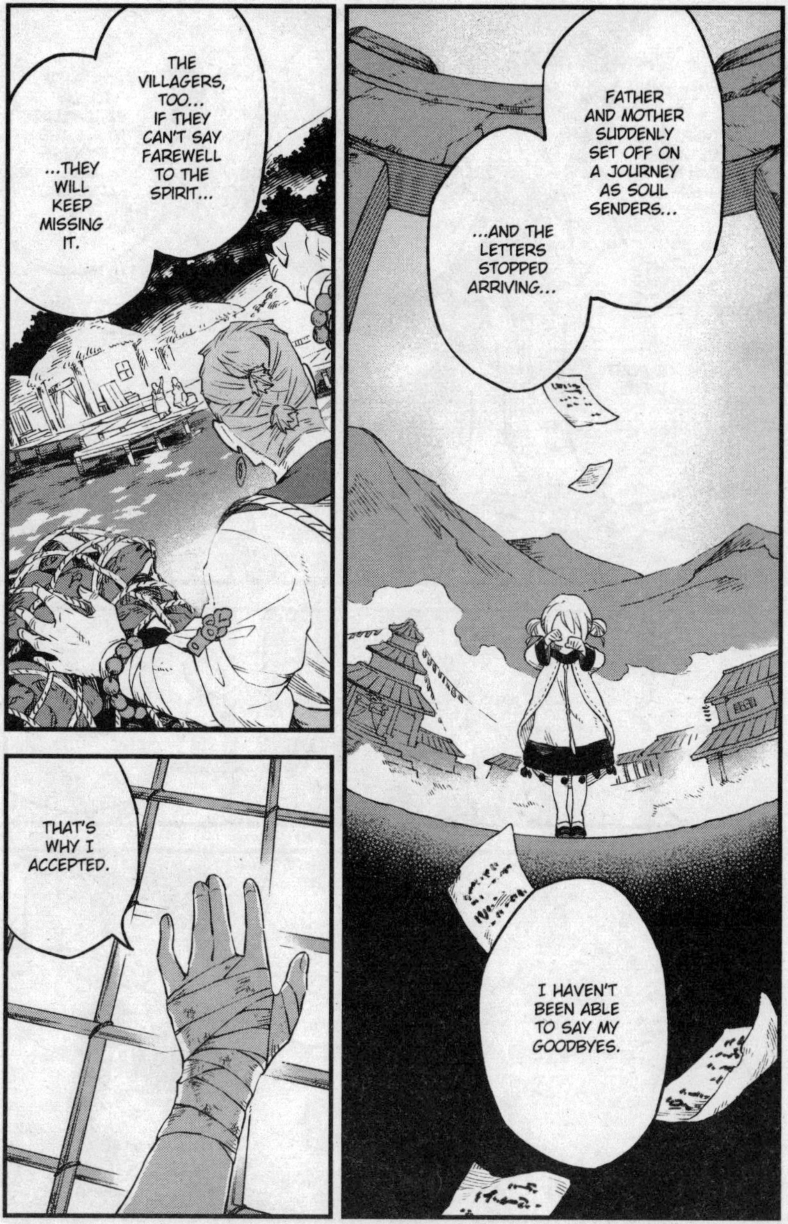
FATHER AND MOTHER SUDDENLY SET OFF ON A JOURNEY AS SOUL SENDERS...
...AND THE LETTERS STOPPED ARRIVING...
I HAVEN'T BEEN ABLE TO SAY MY GOODBYES.
THE VILLAGERS, TOO... IF THEY CAN'T SAY FAREWELL TO THE SPIRIT...
...THEY WILL KEEP MISSING IT.
THAT'S WHY I ACCEPTED.

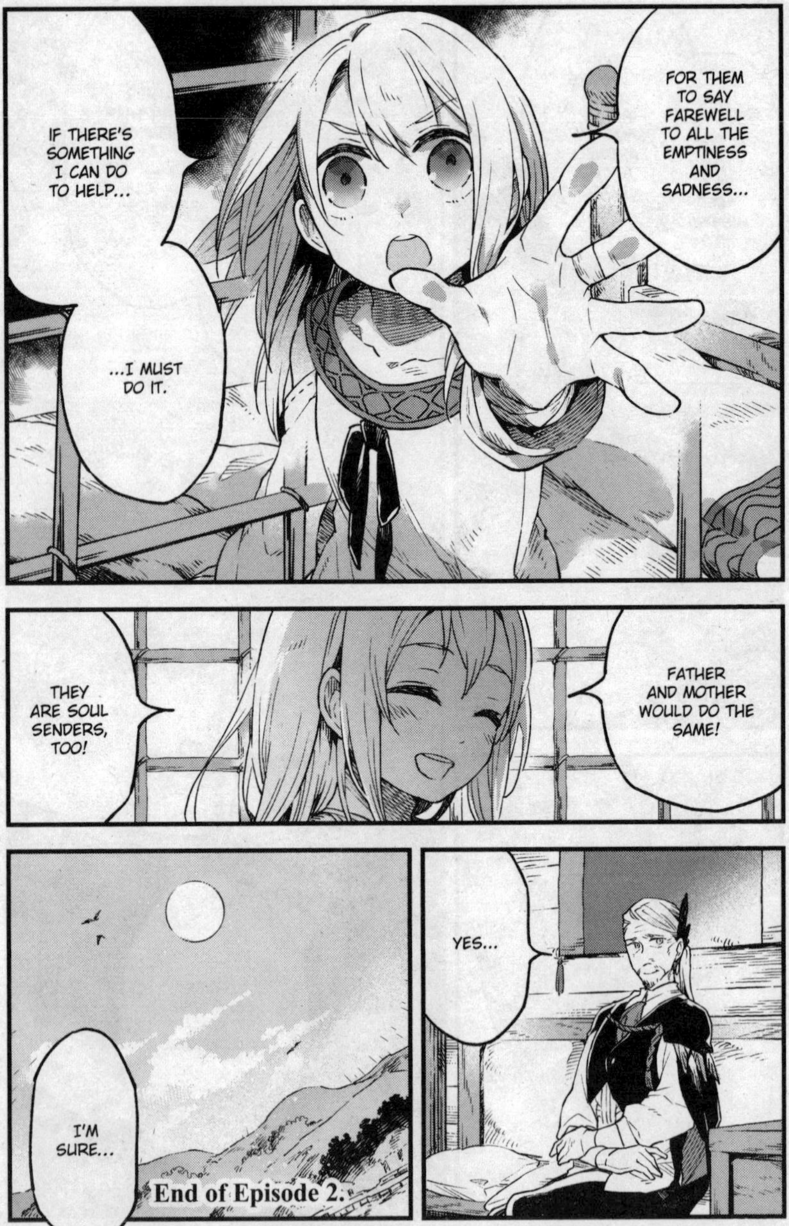
FOR THEM TO SAY FAREWELL TO ALL THE EMPTINESS AND SADNESS...
IF THERE'S SOMETHING I CAN DO TO HELP...
...I MUST DO IT.
FATHER AND MOTHER WOULD DO THE SAME!
THEY ARE SOUL SENDERS, TOO!
YES...
I'M SURE...
End of Episode 2.

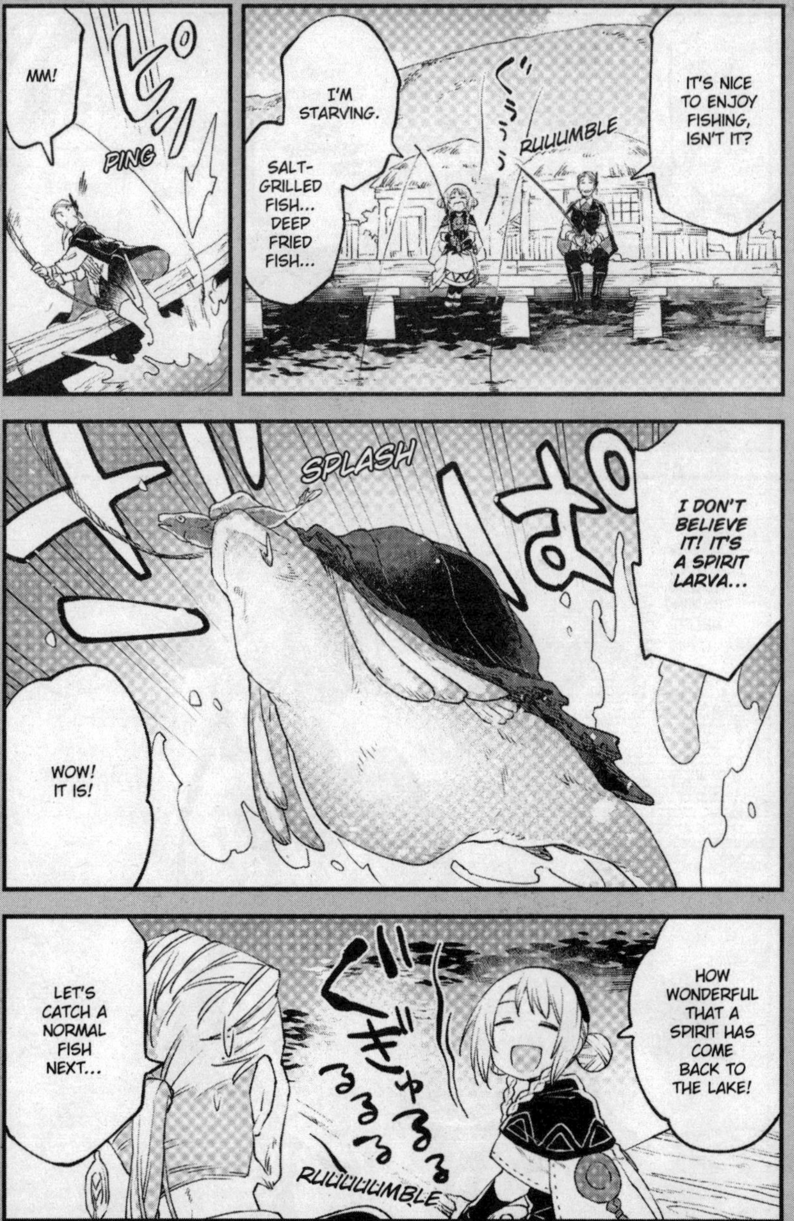
IT'S NICE TO ENJOY FISHING, ISN'T IT?
RUUUMBLE
I'M STARVING.
SALT-GRILLED FISH... DEEP FRIED FISH...
MM!
PING
SPLASH
I DON'T BELIEVE IT! IT'S A SPIRIT LARVA...
WOW! IT IS!
HOW WONDERFUL THAT A SPIRIT HAS COME BACK TO THE LAKE!
RUUUUUUMBLE
LET'S CATCH A NORMAL FISH NEXT...

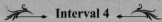

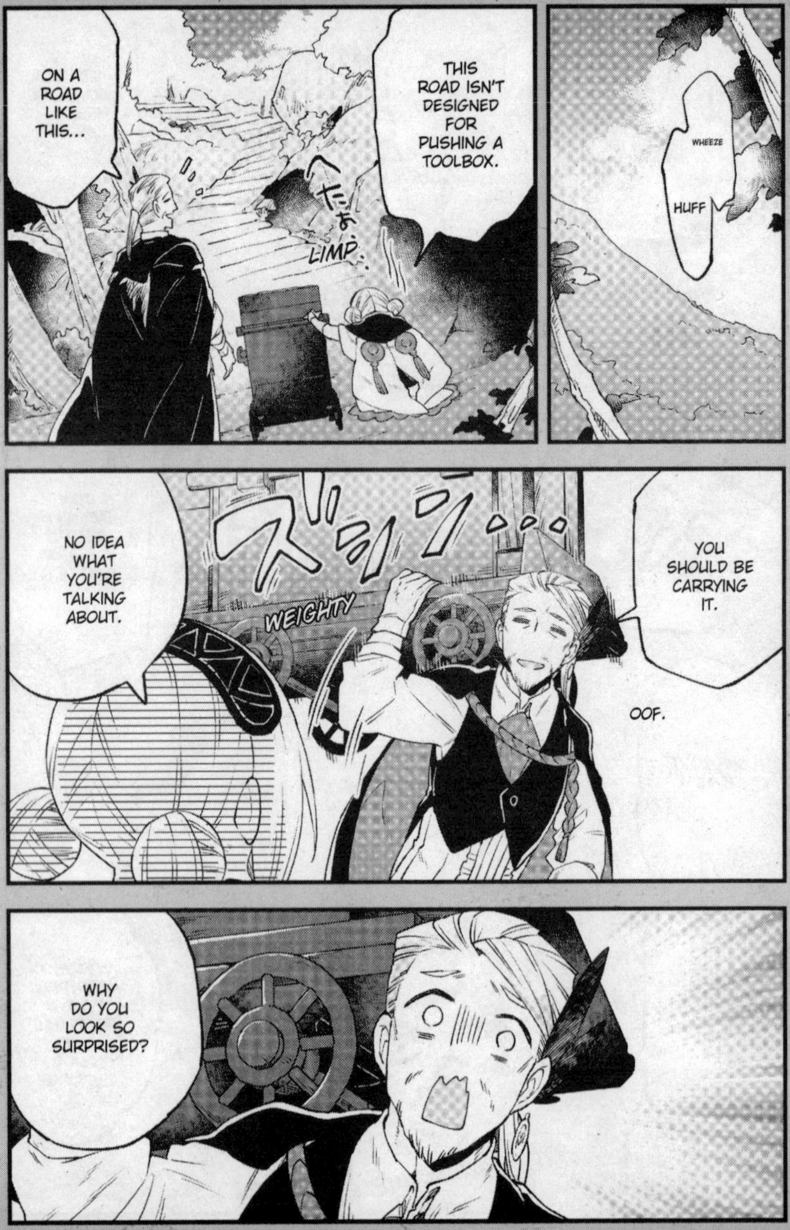
WHEEZE
HUFF
THIS ROAD ISN'T DESIGNED FOR PUSHING A TOOLBOX.
LIMP
ON A ROAD LIKE THIS...
YOU SHOULD BE CARRYING IT.
OOF.
WEIGHTY
NO IDEA WHAT YOU'RE TALKING ABOUT.
WHY DO YOU LOOK SO SURPRISED?

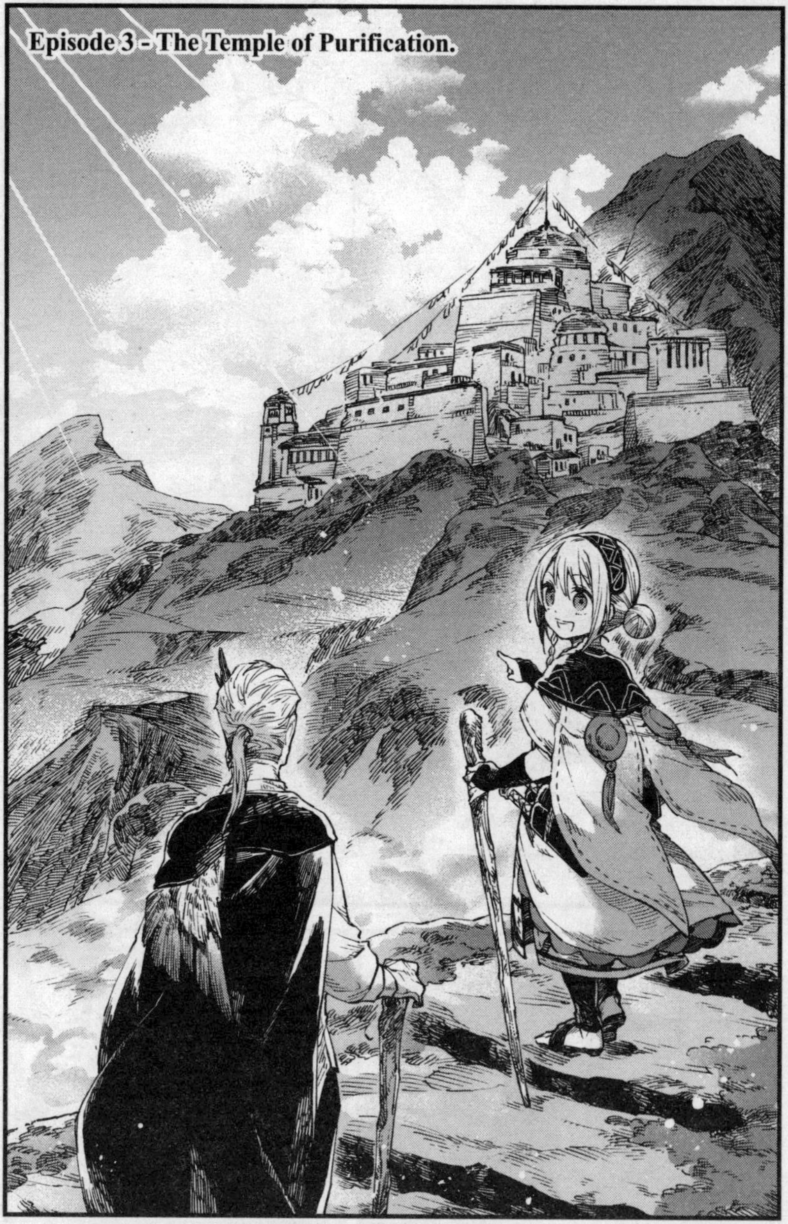
Episode 3 - The Temple of Purification.

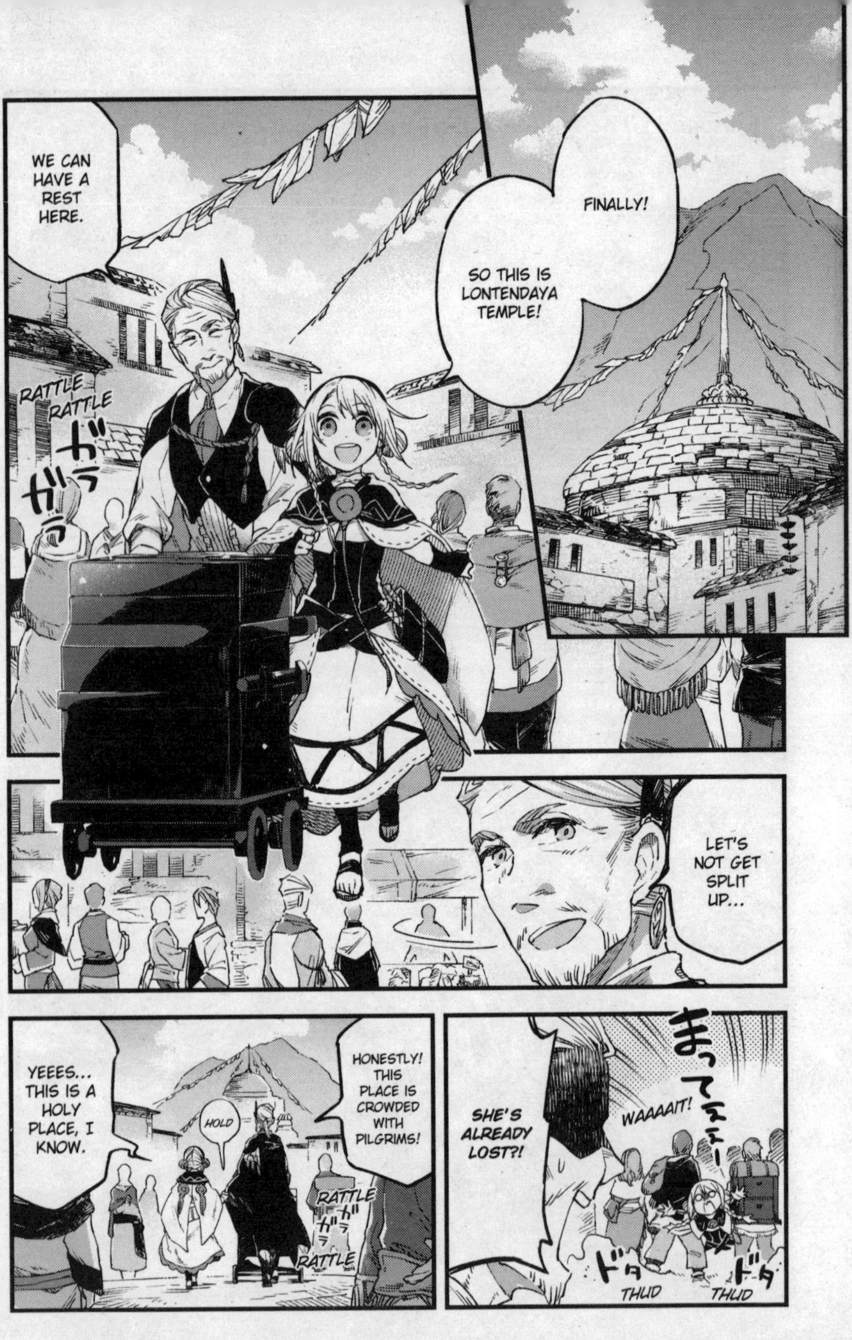
FINALLY!
SO THIS IS LONTENDAYA TEMPLE!
WE CAN HAVE A REST HERE.
RATTLE RATTLE
ガラガラ
LET'S NOT GET SPLIT UP...
まってぇぇー
WAAAAIT!
SHE'S ALREADY LOST?!
ドタ
THUD
ドタ
THUD
HONESTLY! THIS PLACE IS CROWDED WITH PILGRIMS!
HOLD
YEEES... THIS IS A HOLY PLACE, I KNOW.
RATTLE
ガラガラ
RATTLE

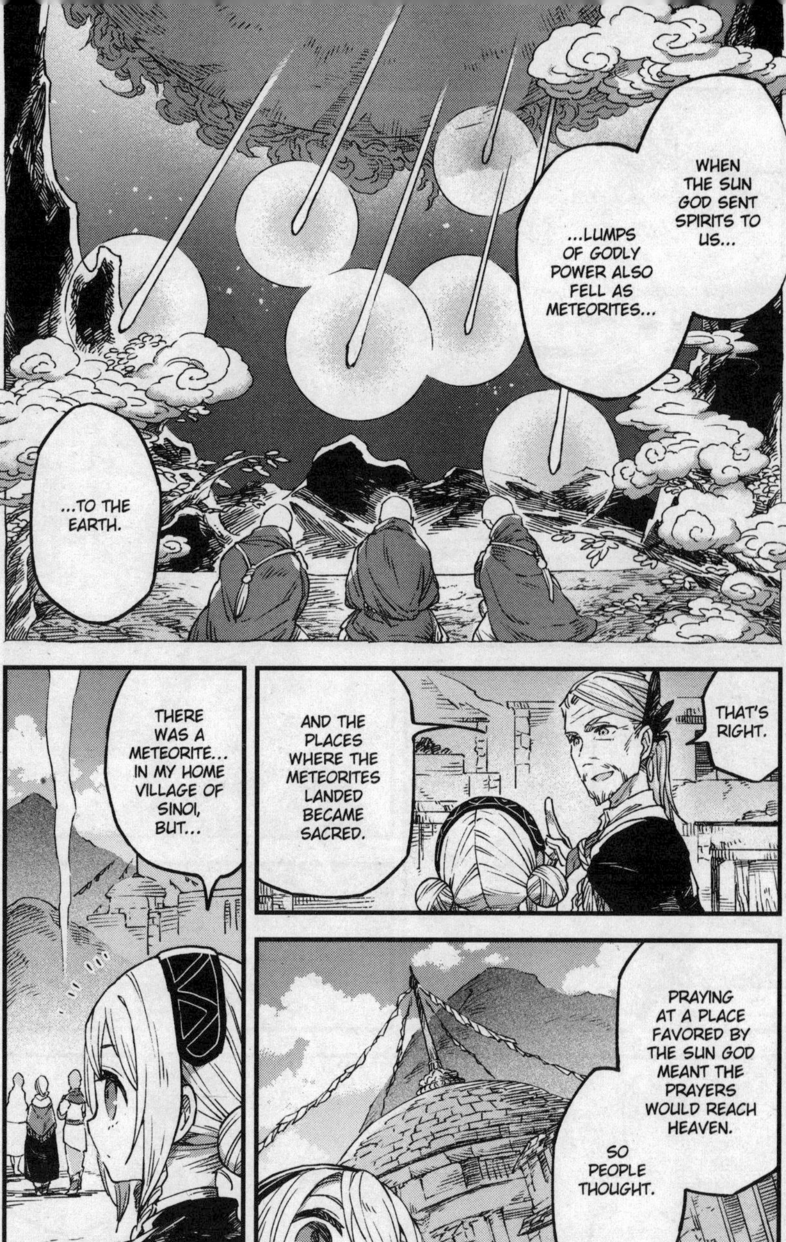
WHEN THE SUN GOD SENT SPIRITS TO US...
...LUMPS OF GODLY POWER ALSO FELL AS METEORITES...
...TO THE EARTH.
THAT'S RIGHT.
AND THE PLACES WHERE THE METEORITES LANDED BECAME SACRED.
PRAYING AT A PLACE FAVORED BY THE SUN GOD MEANT THE PRAYERS WOULD REACH HEAVEN.
SO PEOPLE THOUGHT.
THERE WAS A METEORITE... IN MY HOME VILLAGE OF SINOI, BUT...

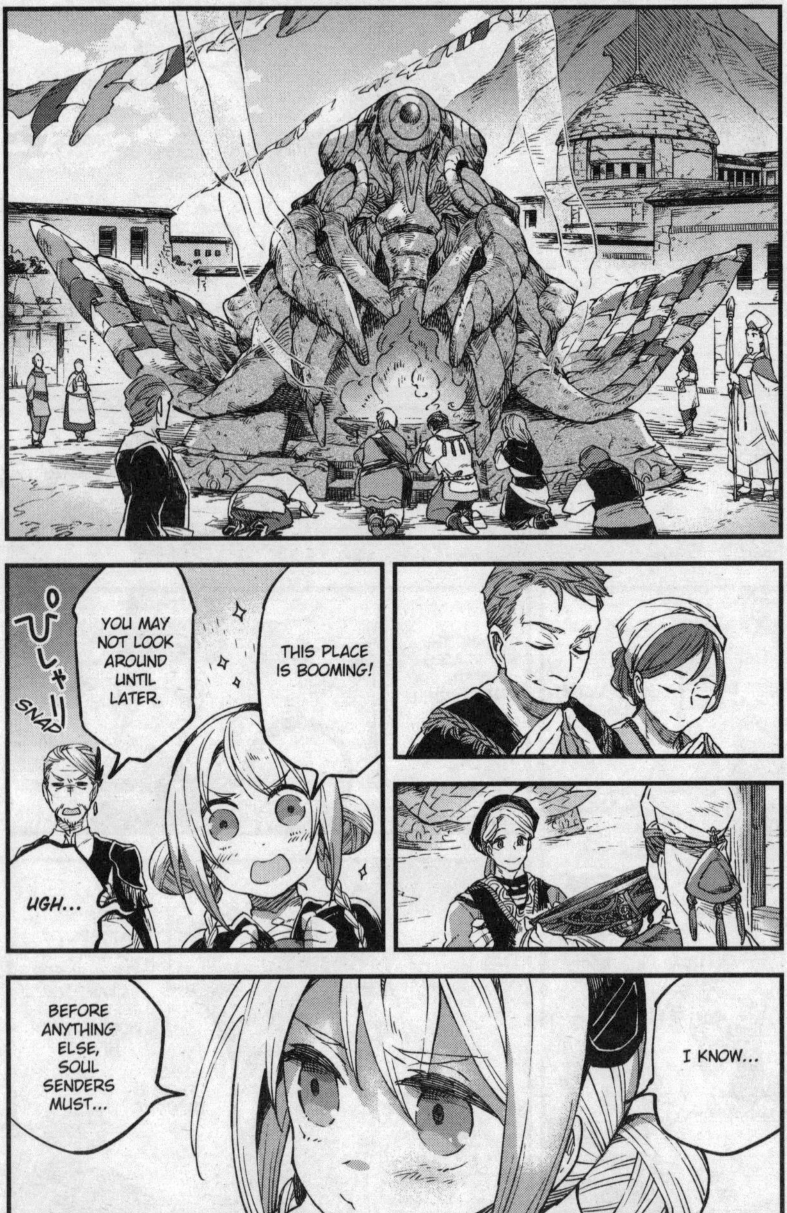
THIS PLACE IS BOOMING!
YOU MAY NOT LOOK AROUND UNTIL LATER.
ぴしゃー
SNAP
UGH...
I KNOW...
BEFORE ANYTHING ELSE, SOUL SENDERS MUST...

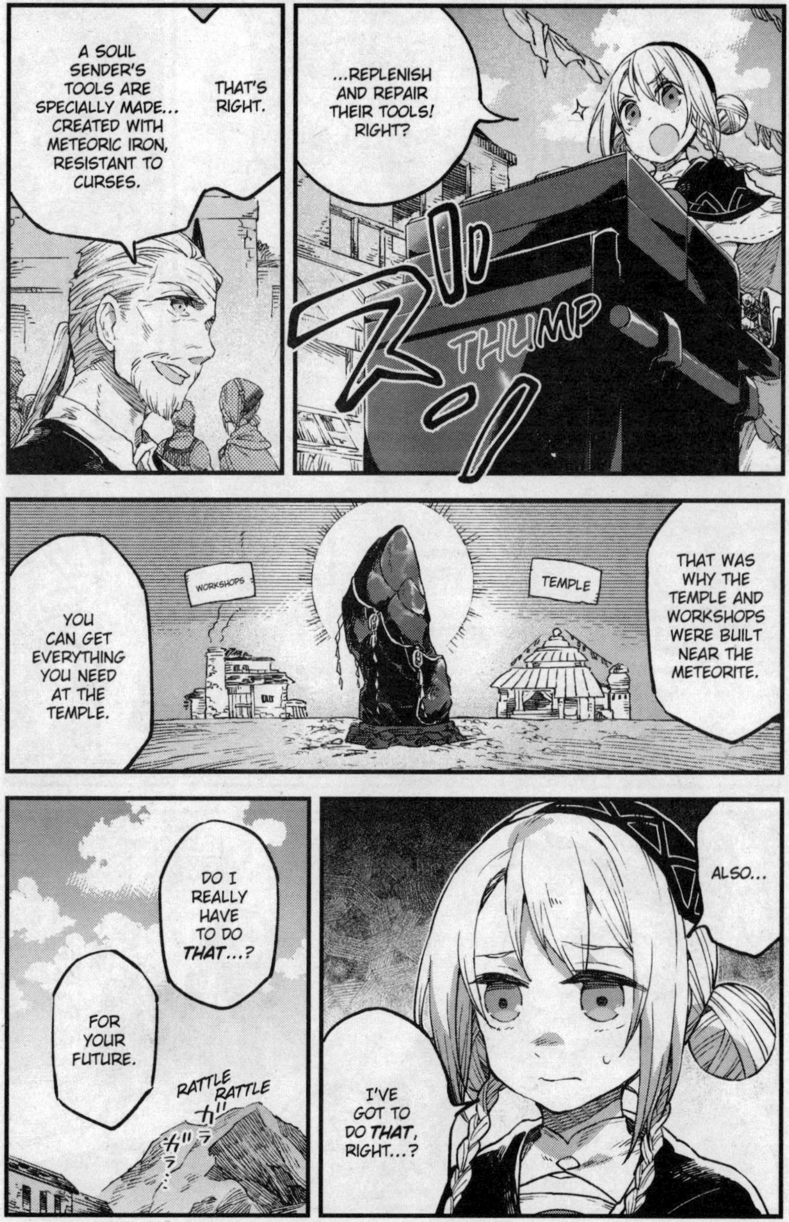

...REPLENISH AND REPAIR THEIR TOOLS! RIGHT?
THUMP
THAT'S RIGHT.
A SOUL SENDER'S TOOLS ARE SPECIALLY MADE... CREATED WITH METEORIC IRON, RESISTANT TO CURSES.
THAT WAS WHY THE TEMPLE AND WORKSHOPS WERE BUILT NEAR THE METEORITE.
TEMPLE
WORKSHOPS
YOU CAN GET EVERYTHING YOU NEED AT THE TEMPLE.
ALSO...
I'VE GOT TO DO *THAT*, RIGHT...?
DO I REALLY HAVE TO DO *THAT*...?
FOR YOUR FUTURE.
RATTLE RATTLE

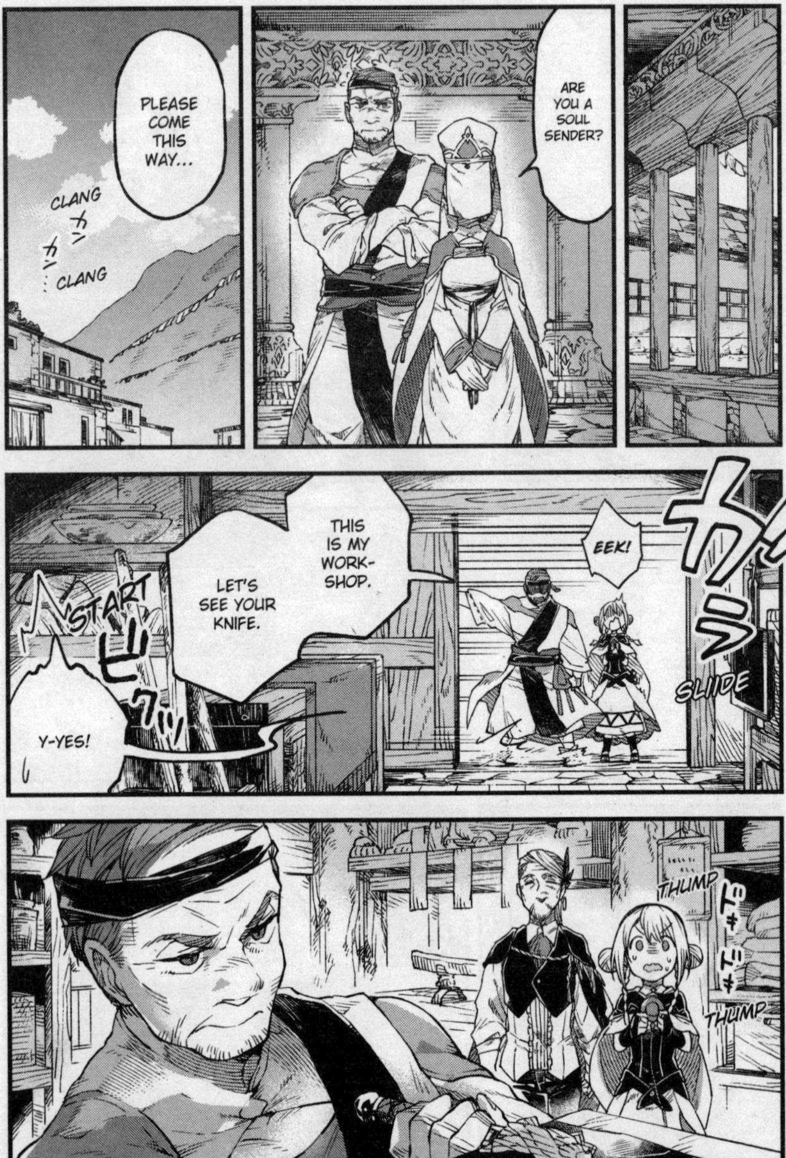
ARE YOU A SOUL SENDER?
PLEASE COME THIS WAY...
CLANG
CLANG
ガラ
SLIIDE
EEK!
THIS IS MY WORK-SHOP.
LET'S SEE YOUR KNIFE.
START
ビクッ
Y-YES!
THUMP
ドキドキ
THUMP

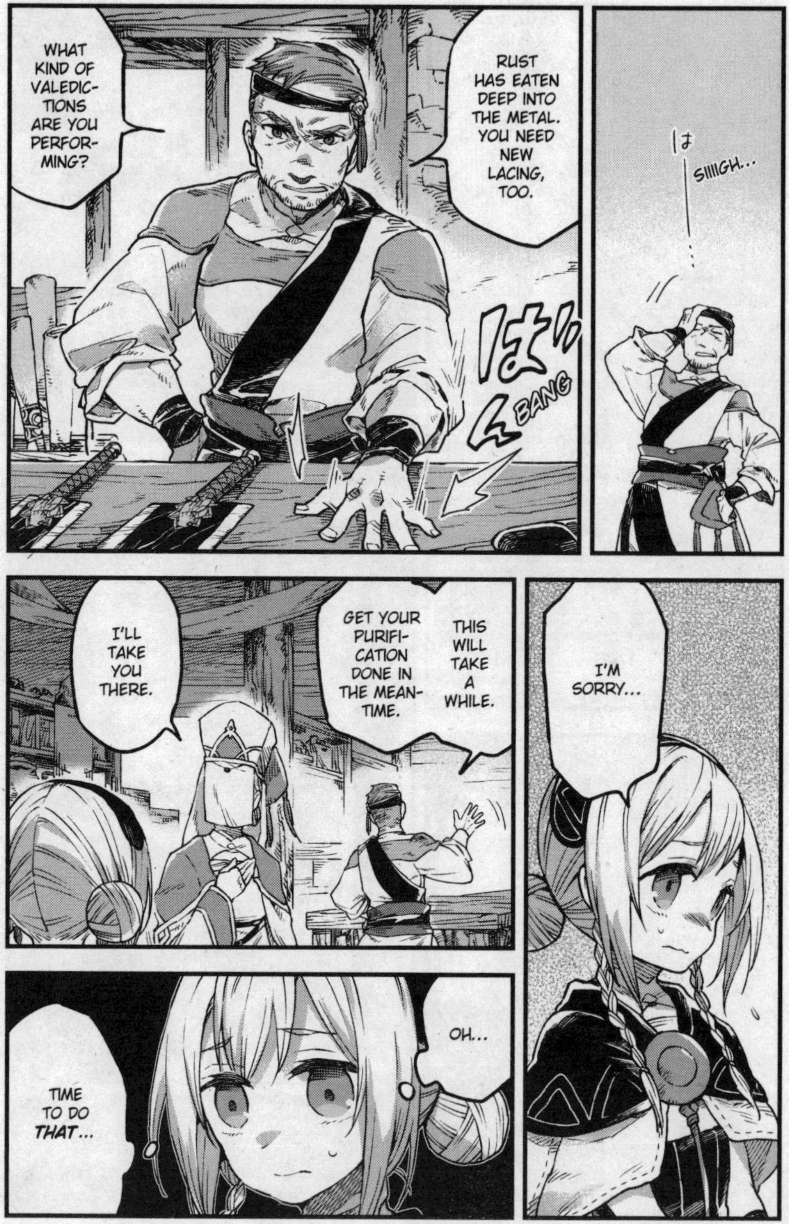
は
SIIIIGH...
RUST HAS EATEN DEEP INTO THE METAL. YOU NEED NEW LACING, TOO.
WHAT KIND OF VALEDIC-TIONS ARE YOU PERFOR-MING?
はん
BANG
I'M SORRY...
THIS WILL TAKE A WHILE.
GET YOUR PURIFI-CATION DONE IN THE MEAN-TIME.
I'LL TAKE YOU THERE.
OH...
TIME TO DO *THAT*...

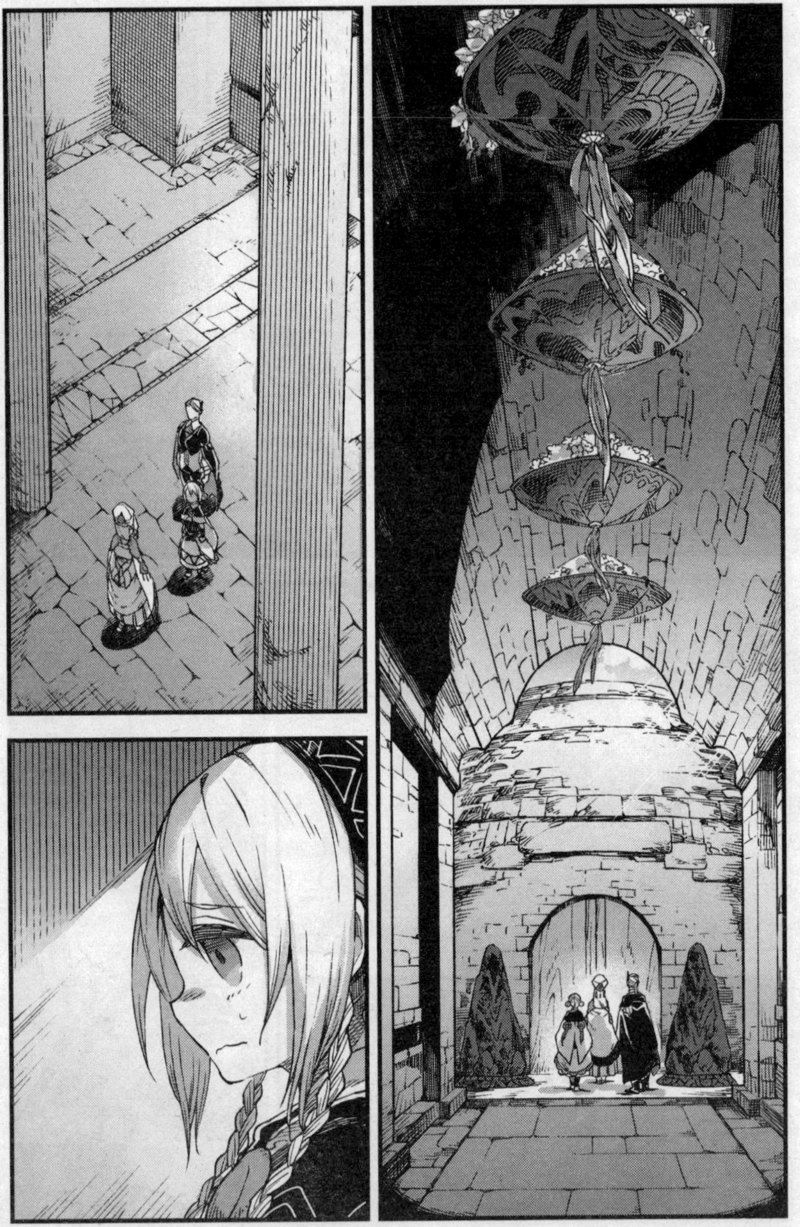

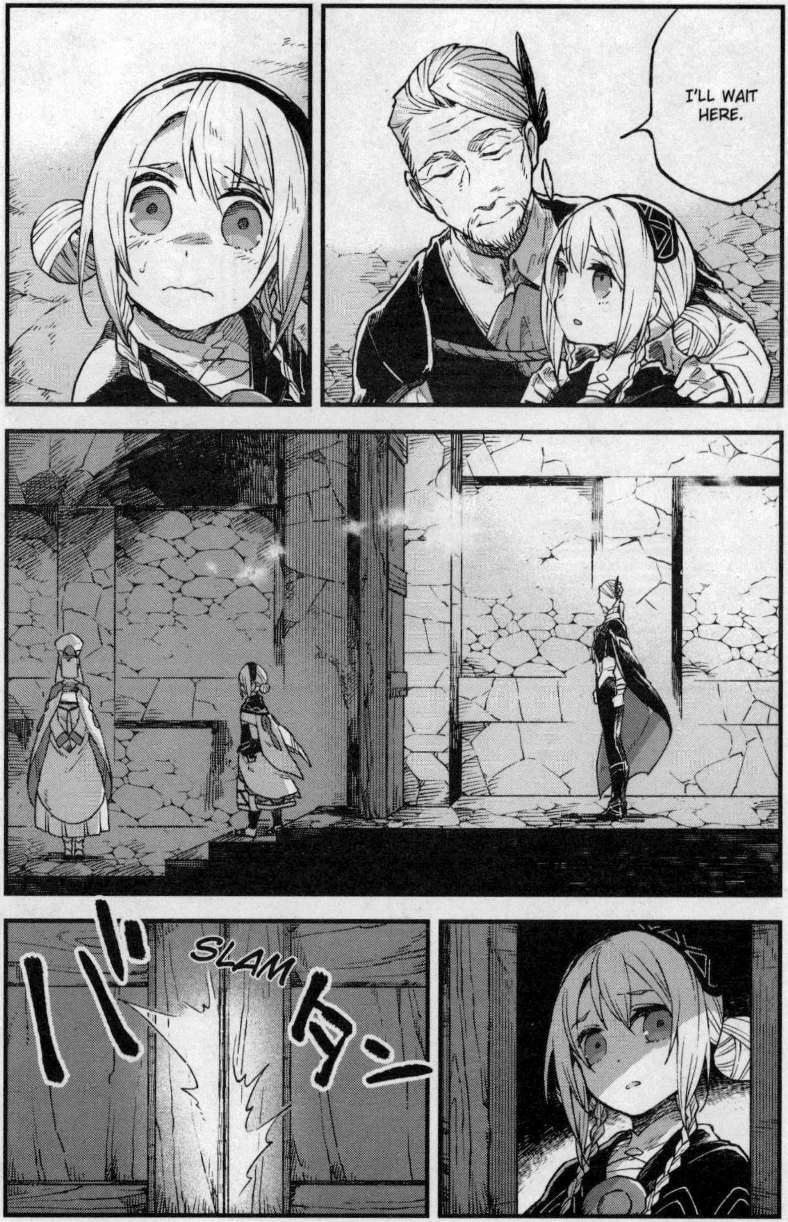
I'LL WAIT HERE.
SLAM
バタン

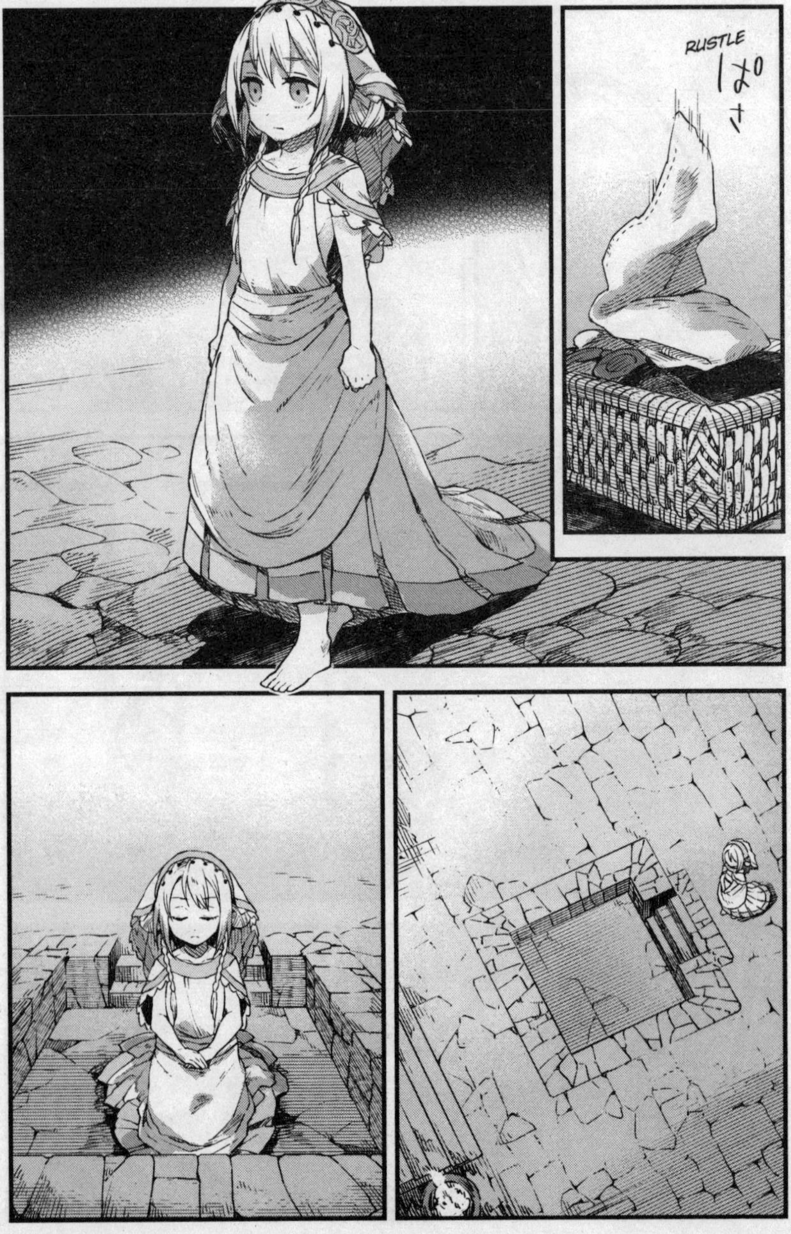
RUSTLE
ぱさ

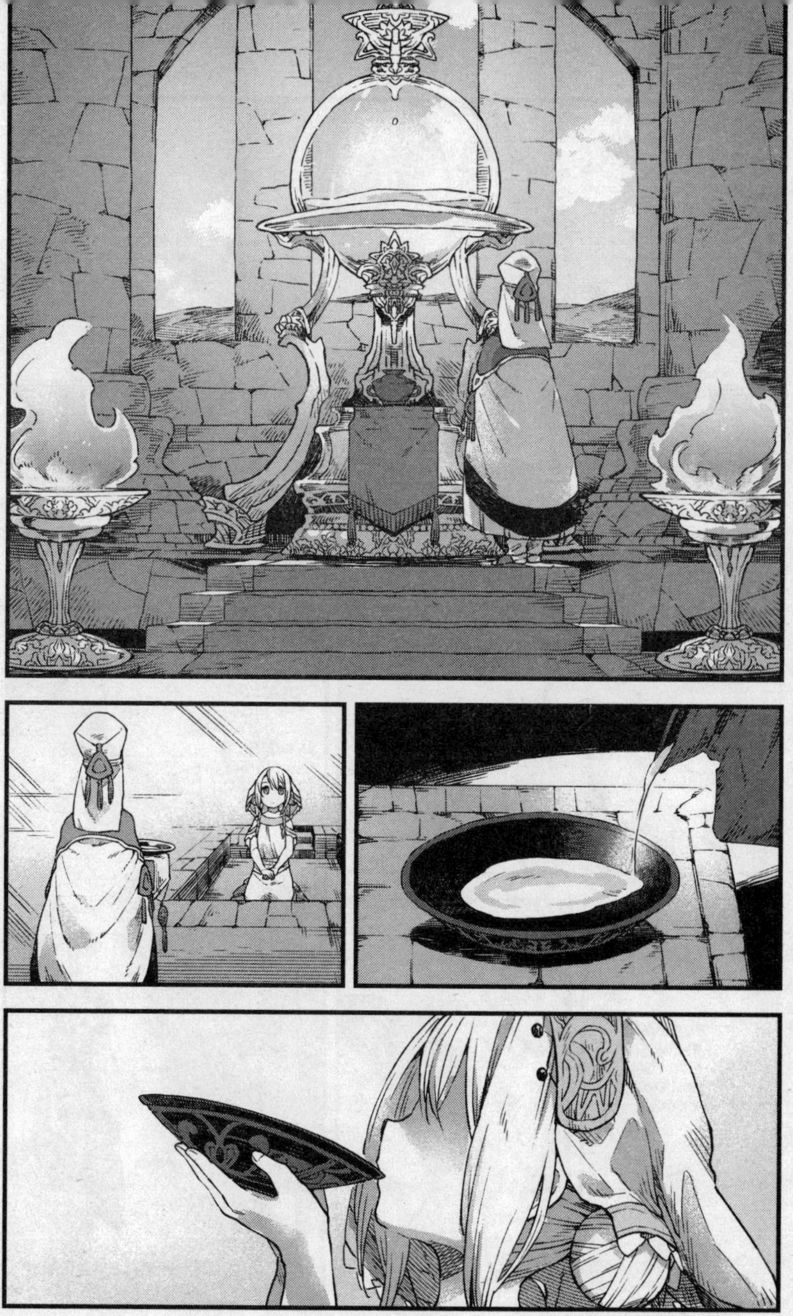

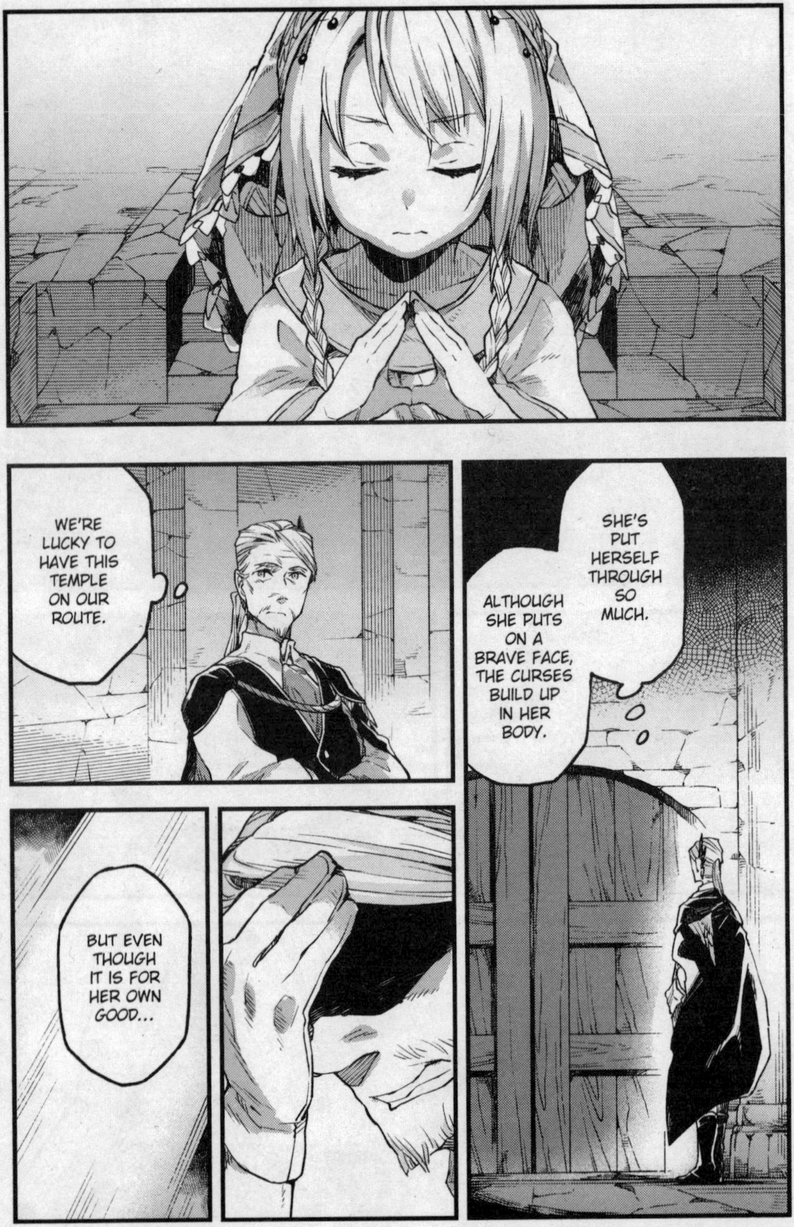
SHE'S PUT HERSELF THROUGH SO MUCH.
ALTHOUGH SHE PUTS ON A BRAVE FACE, THE CURSES BUILD UP IN HER BODY.
WE'RE LUCKY TO HAVE THIS TEMPLE ON OUR ROUTE.
BUT EVEN THOUGH IT IS FOR HER OWN GOOD...

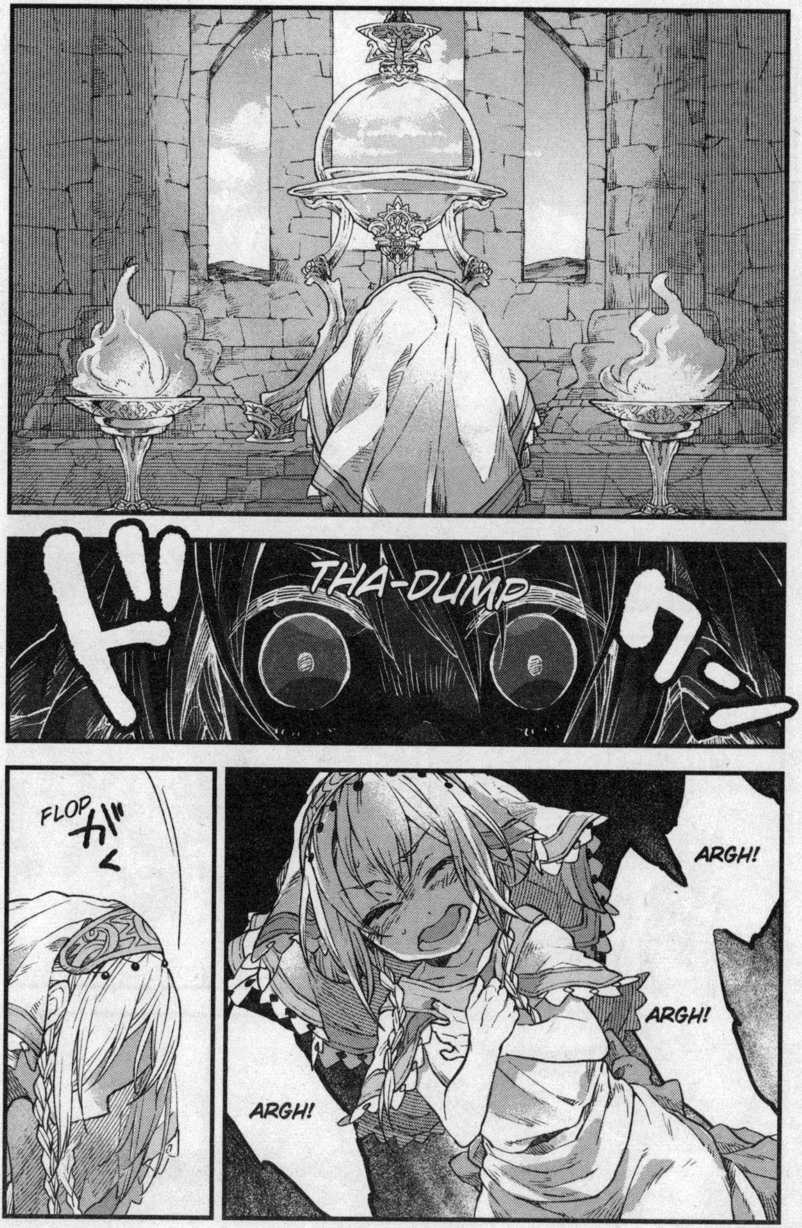
THA-DUMP
ドクン
ARGH!
ARGH!
ARGH!
FLOP
がく

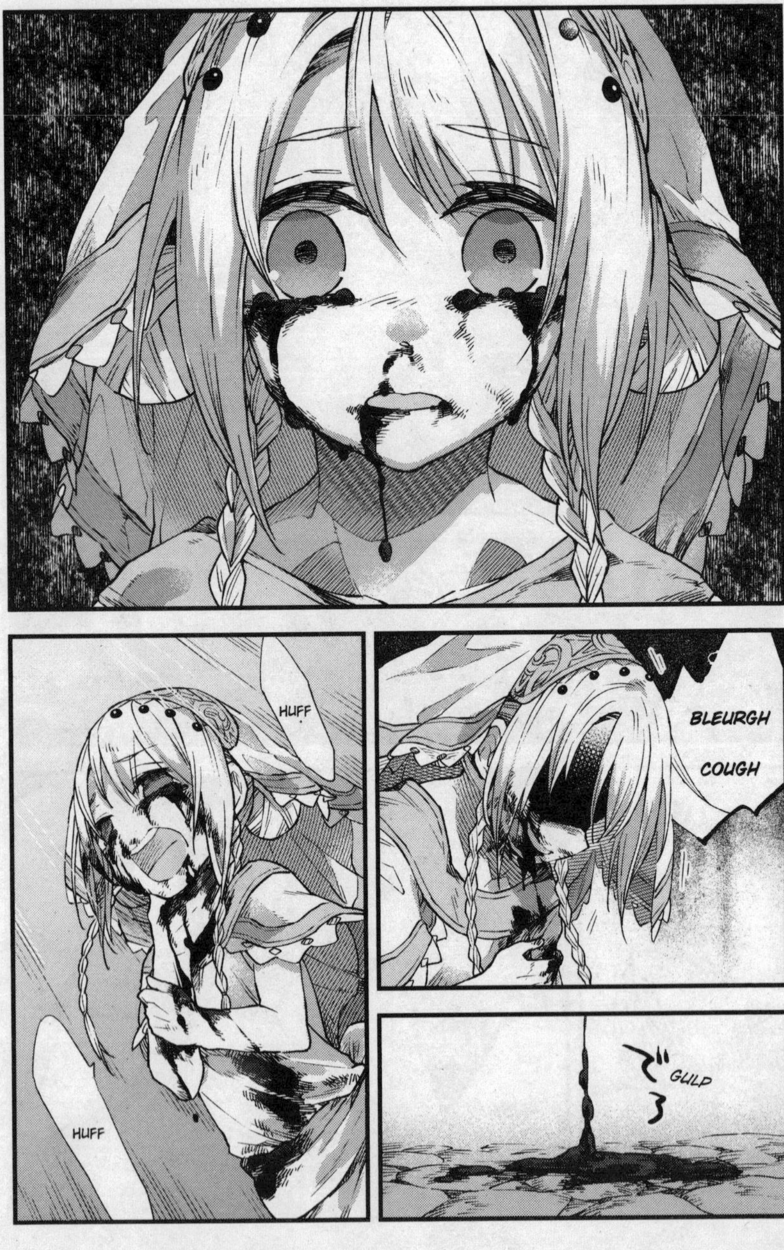
BLEURGH
COUGH
GULP
HUFF
HUFF

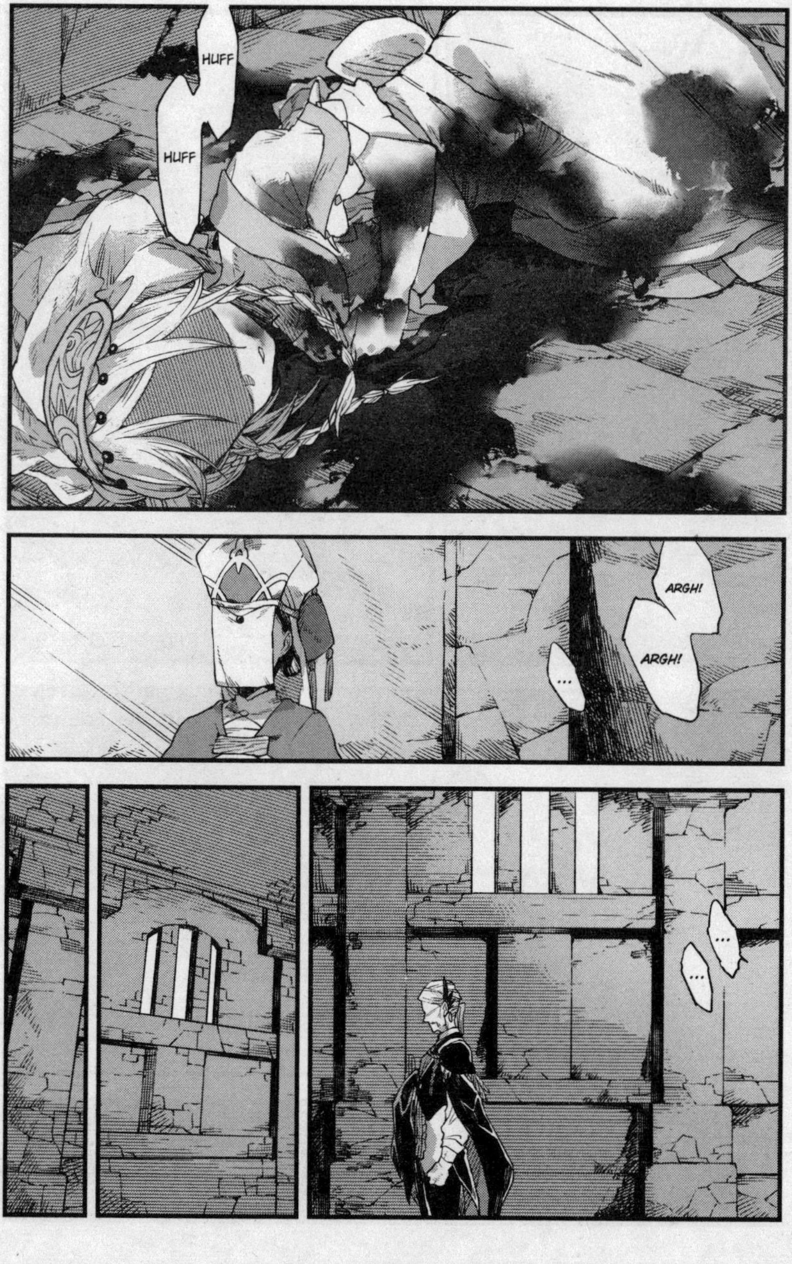
HUFF
HUFF
ARGH!
ARGH!
...
...
...

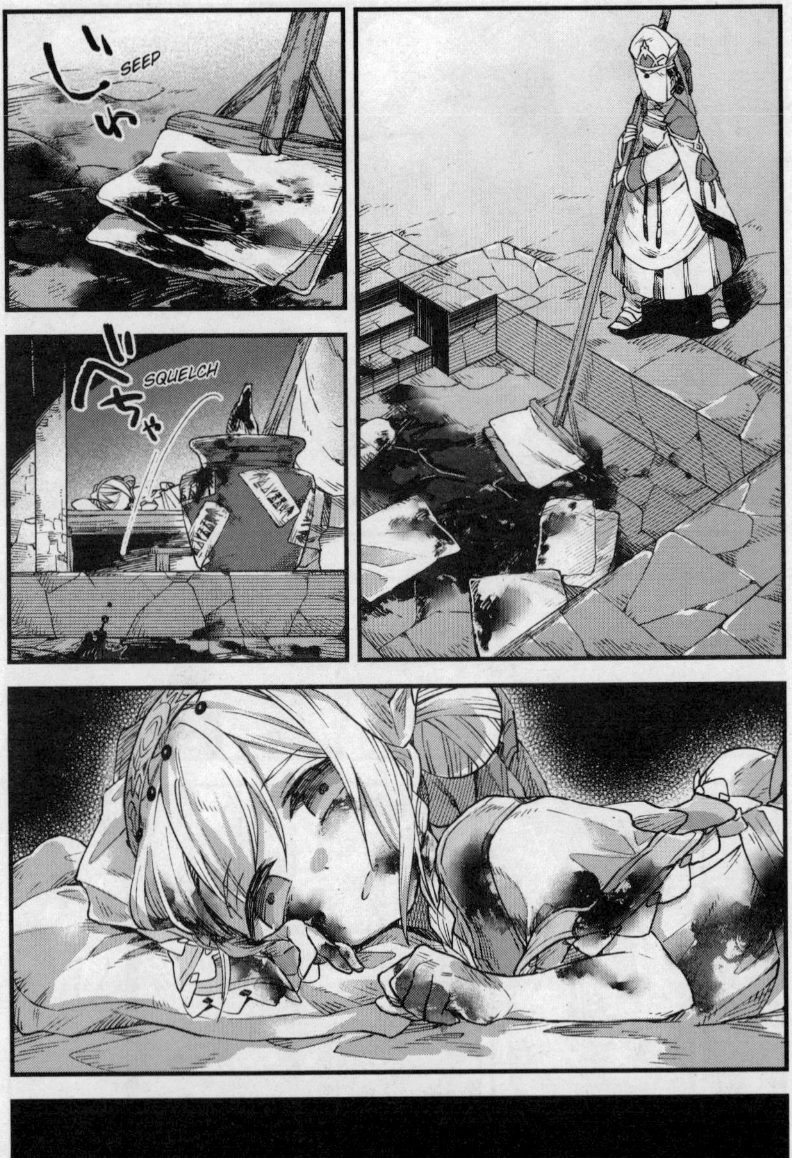
じゅ
SEEP
べちゃ
SQUELCH

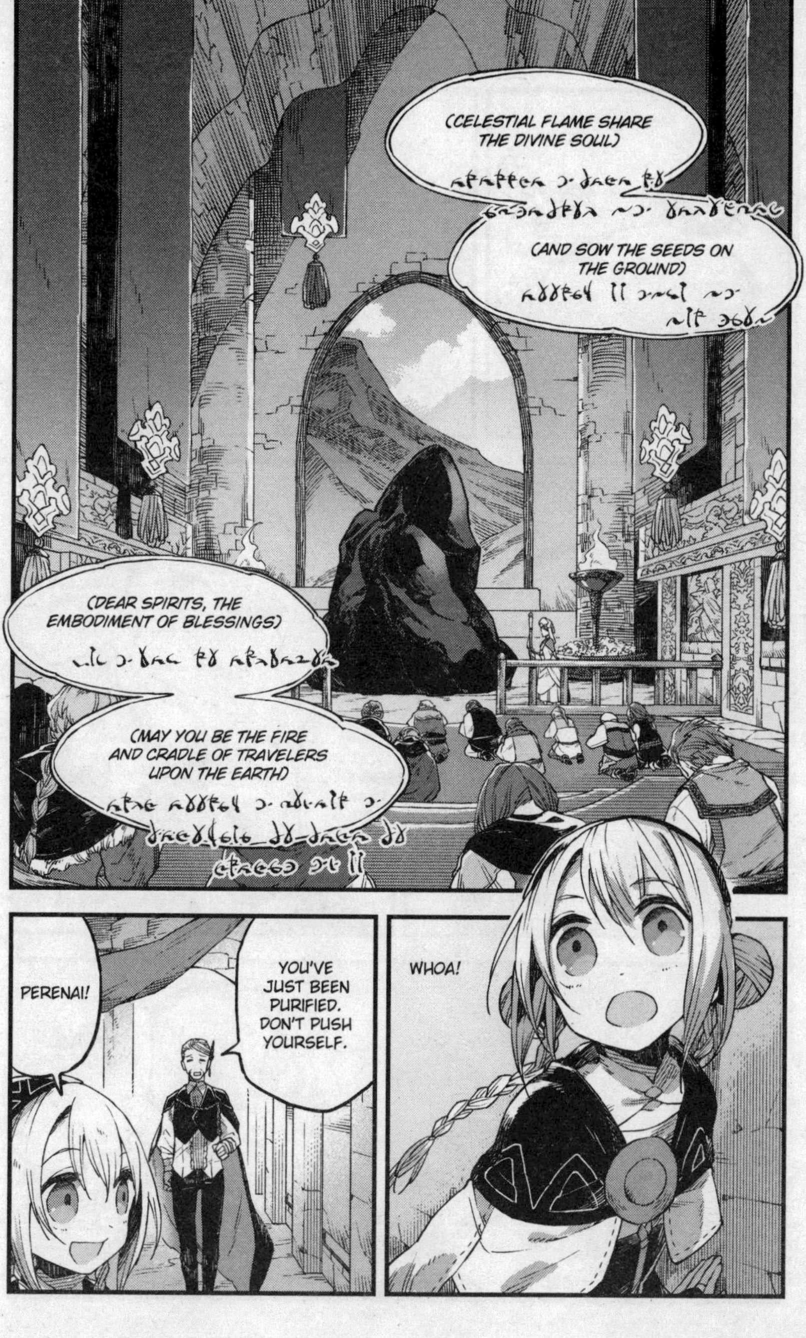
(CELESTIAL FLAME SHARE THE DIVINE SOUL)
(AND SOW THE SEEDS ON THE GROUND)
(DEAR SPIRITS, THE EMBODIMENT OF BLESSINGS)
(MAY YOU BE THE FIRE AND CRADLE OF TRAVELERS UPON THE EARTH)
WHOA!
YOU'VE JUST BEEN PURIFIED. DON'T PUSH YOURSELF.
PERENAI!

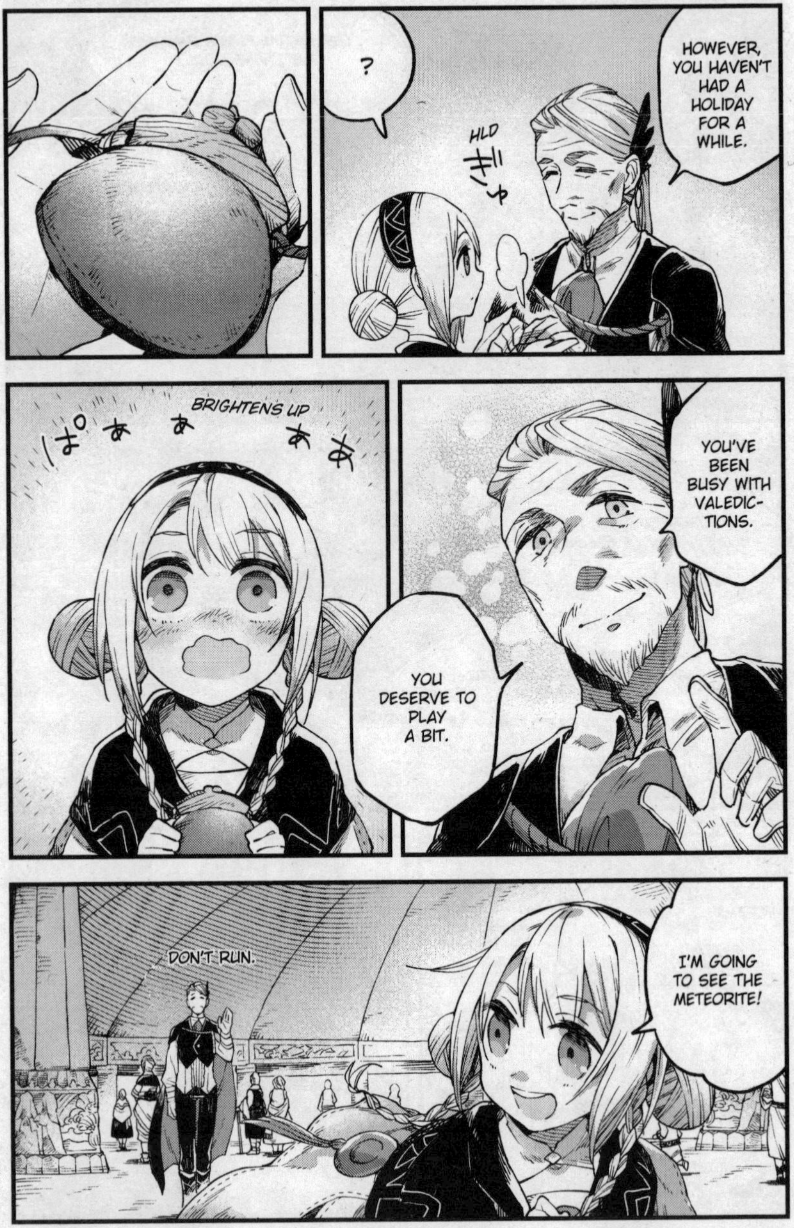
HOWEVER, YOU HAVEN'T HAD A HOLIDAY FOR A WHILE.
?
HLD
ぎゅ
YOU'VE BEEN BUSY WITH VALEDIC- TIONS.
YOU DESERVE TO PLAY A BIT.
BRIGHTENS UP
ぱあああ
I'M GOING TO SEE THE METEORITE!
DON'T RUN.

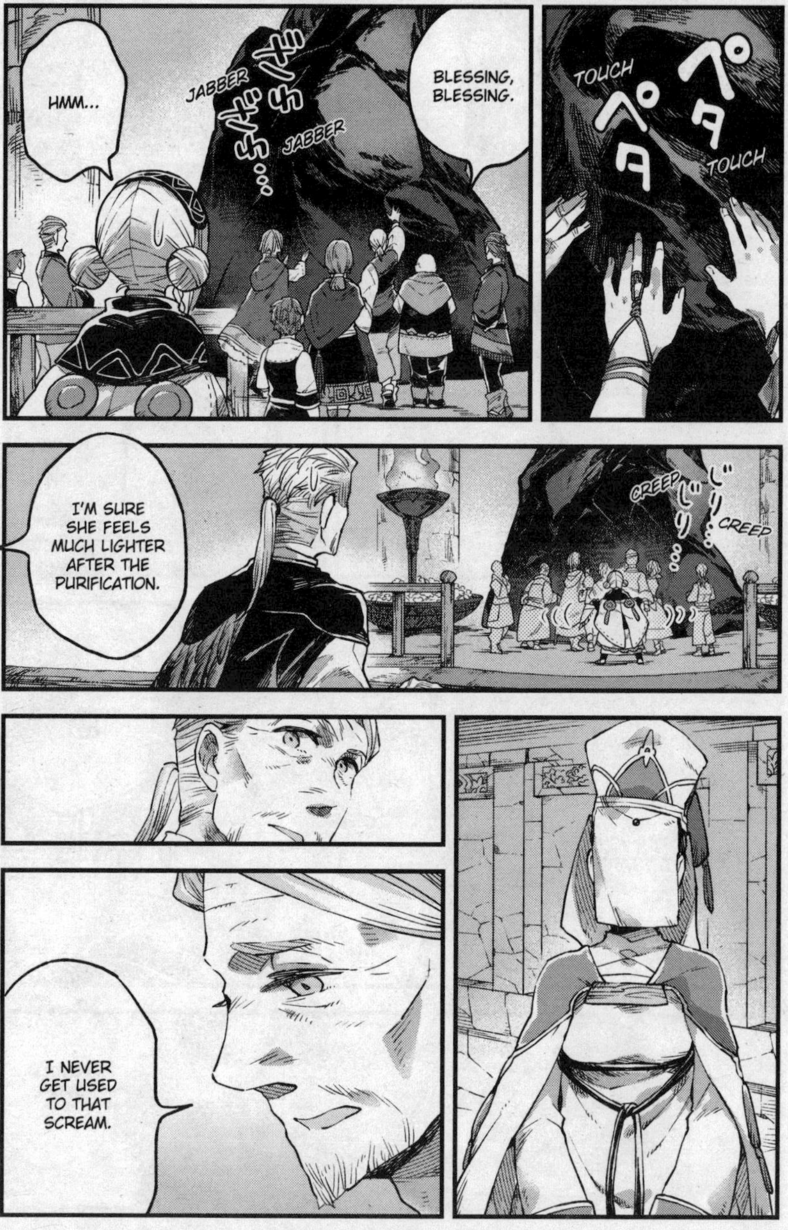
ペタ
TOUCH
ペタ
TOUCH
BLESSING, BLESSING.
JABBER
JABBER
HMM...
じりじり…
CREEP
CREEP
I'M SURE SHE FEELS MUCH LIGHTER AFTER THE PURIFICATION.
I NEVER GET USED TO THAT SCREAM.

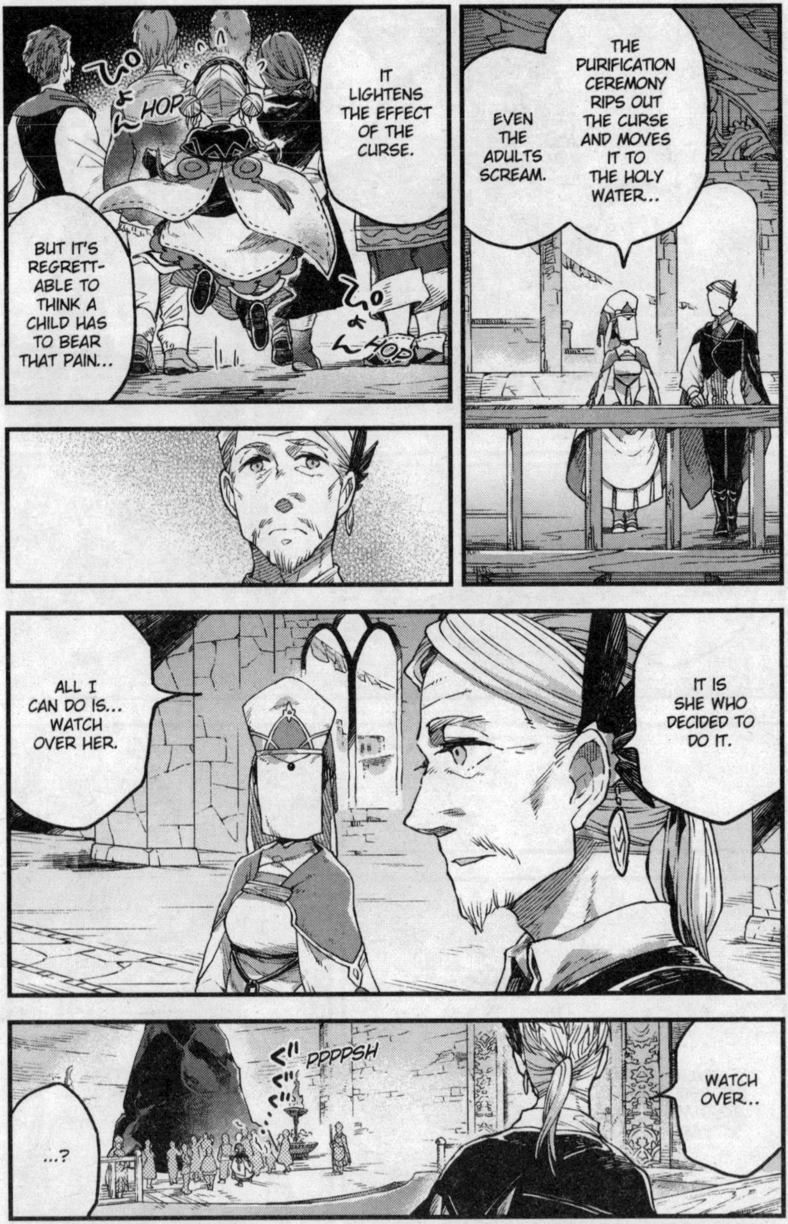
THE PURIFICATION CEREMONY RIPS OUT THE CURSE AND MOVES IT TO THE HOLY WATER..
EVEN THE ADULTS SCREAM.
IT LIGHTENS THE EFFECT OF THE CURSE.
HOP
BUT IT'S REGRETT-ABLE TO THINK A CHILD HAS TO BEAR THAT PAIN...
HOP
IT IS SHE WHO DECIDED TO DO IT.
ALL I CAN DO IS... WATCH OVER HER.
WATCH OVER..
PPPPSH
...?

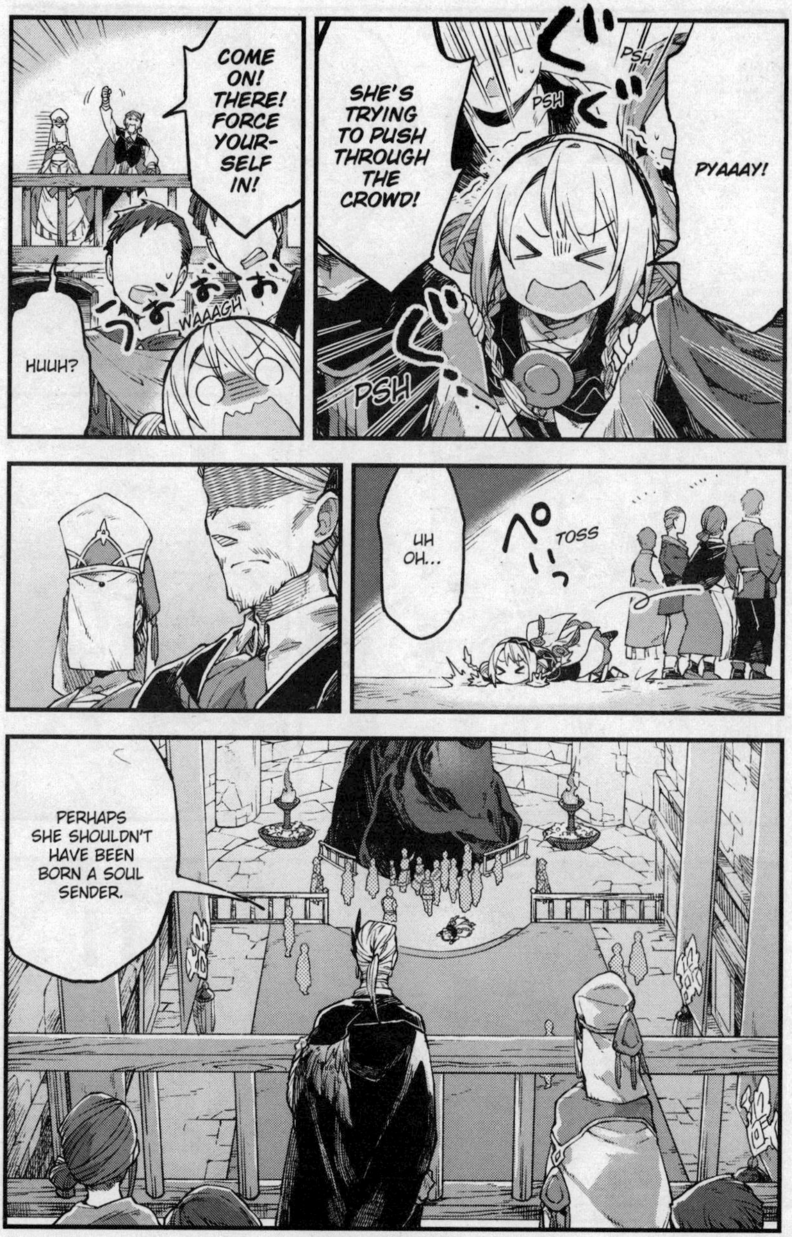

PSH
PSH
SHE'S TRYING TO PUSH THROUGH THE CROWD!
PYAAAY!
PSH
COME ON! THERE! FORCE YOURSELF IN!
WAAAGH
HUUH?
UH OH...
TOSS
PERHAPS SHE SHOULDN'T HAVE BEEN BORN A SOUL SENDER.

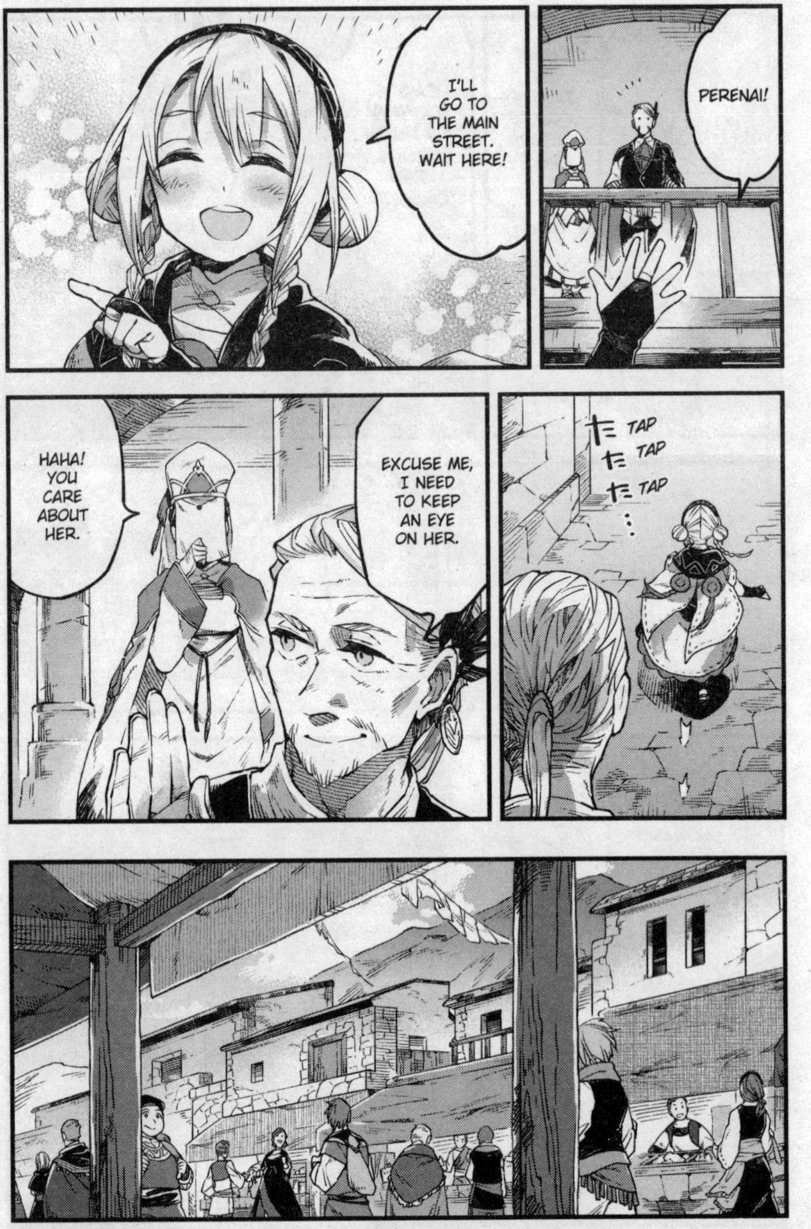
PERENAI!
I'LL GO TO THE MAIN STREET. WAIT HERE!
た TAP
た TAP
た TAP
...
EXCUSE ME, I NEED TO KEEP AN EYE ON HER.
HAHA! YOU CARE ABOUT HER.

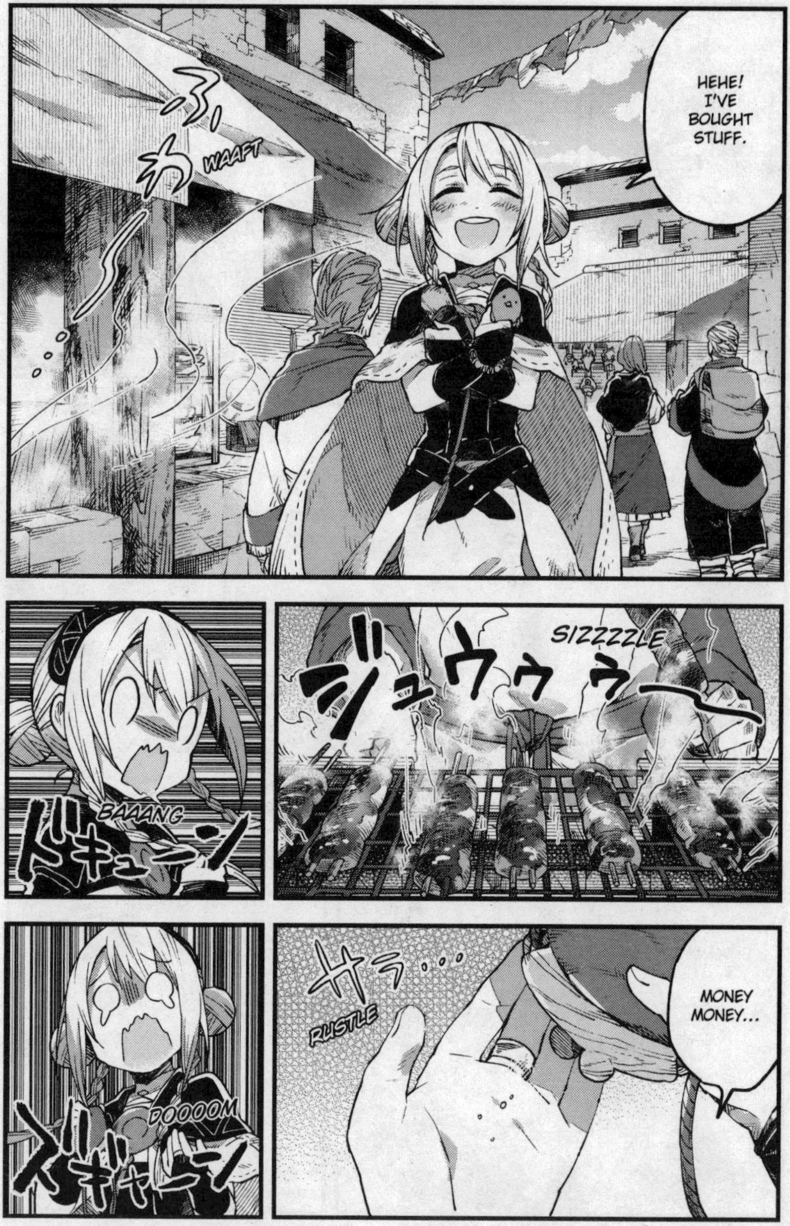
HEHE! I'VE BOUGHT STUFF.
WAAFT
SIZZZZLE
BAAANG
MONEY MONEY...
RUSTLE
DOOOOM

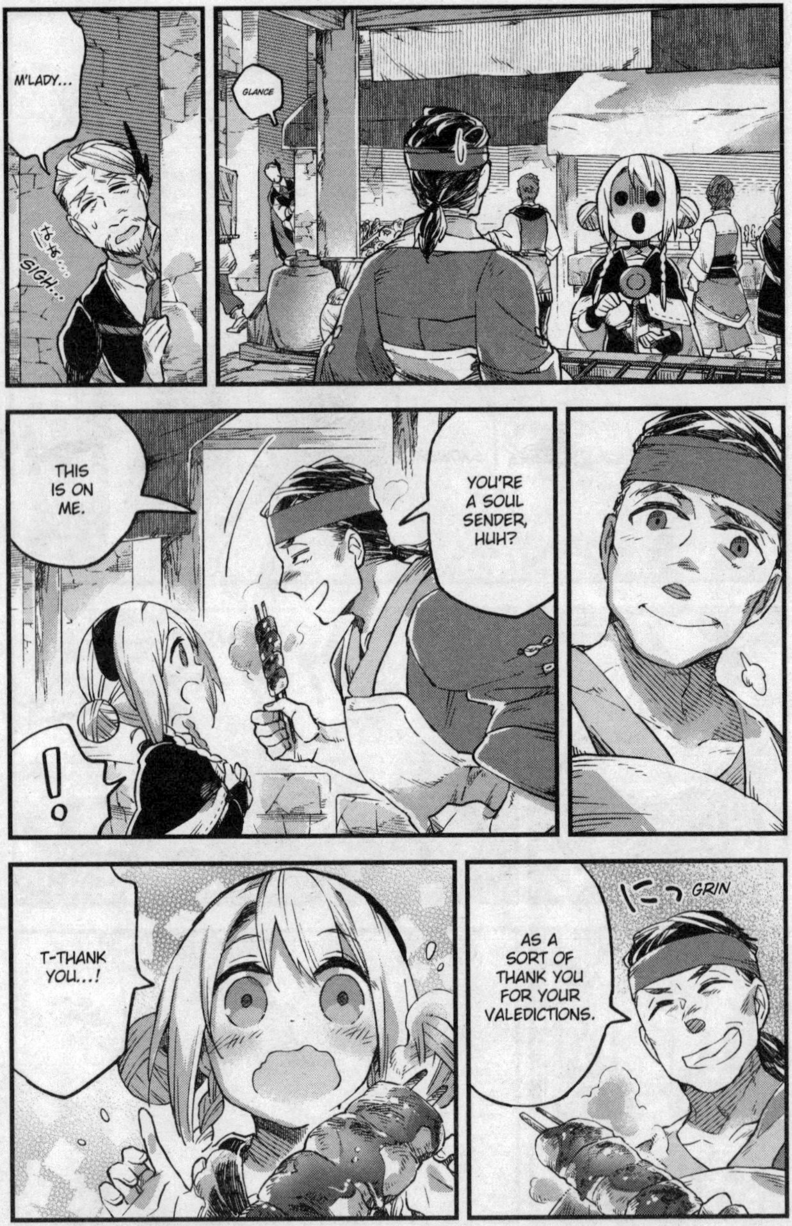
GLANCE
M'LADY...
SIGH...
YOU'RE A SOUL SENDER, HUH?
THIS IS ON ME.
!
GRIN
AS A SORT OF THANK YOU FOR YOUR VALEDICTIONS.
T-THANK YOU...!

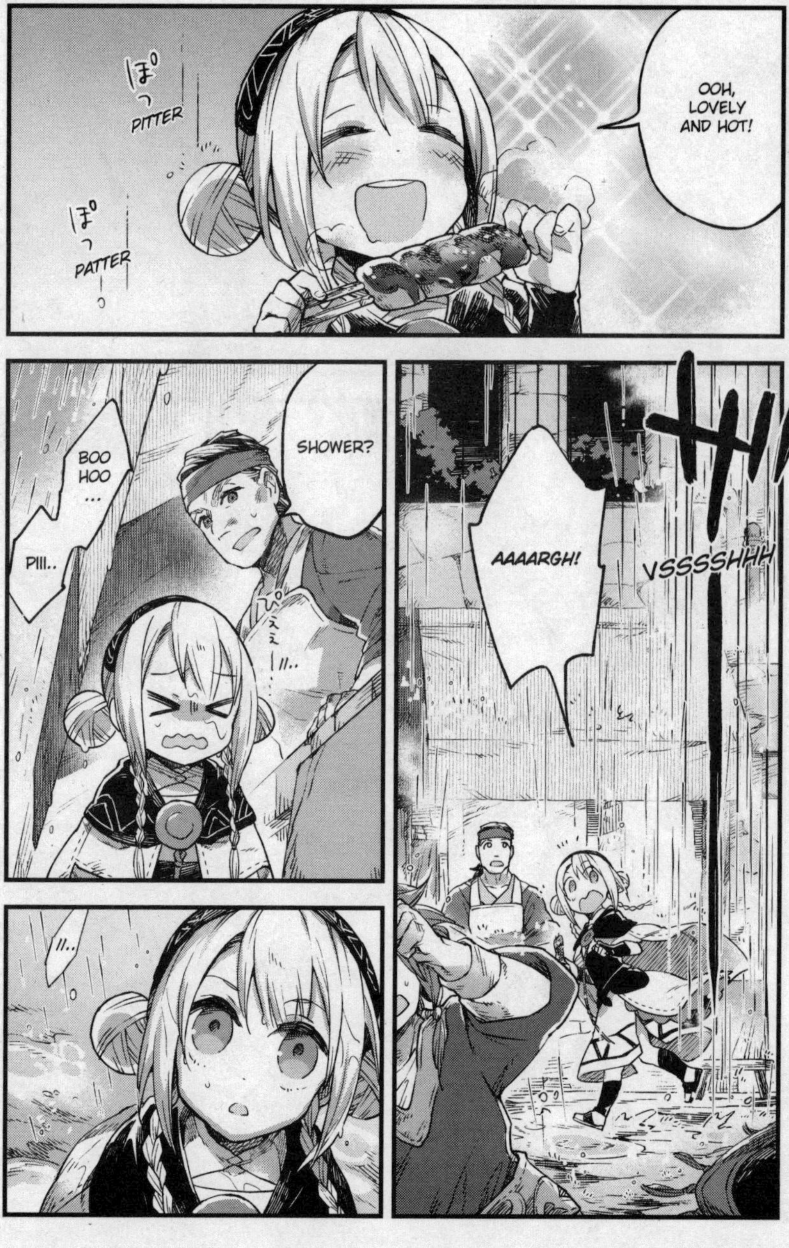
OOH, LOVELY AND HOT!
ぽっ
PITTER
ぽっ
PATTER
VSSSSHHH
AAAARGH!
SHOWER?
BOO HOO ...
PIII..

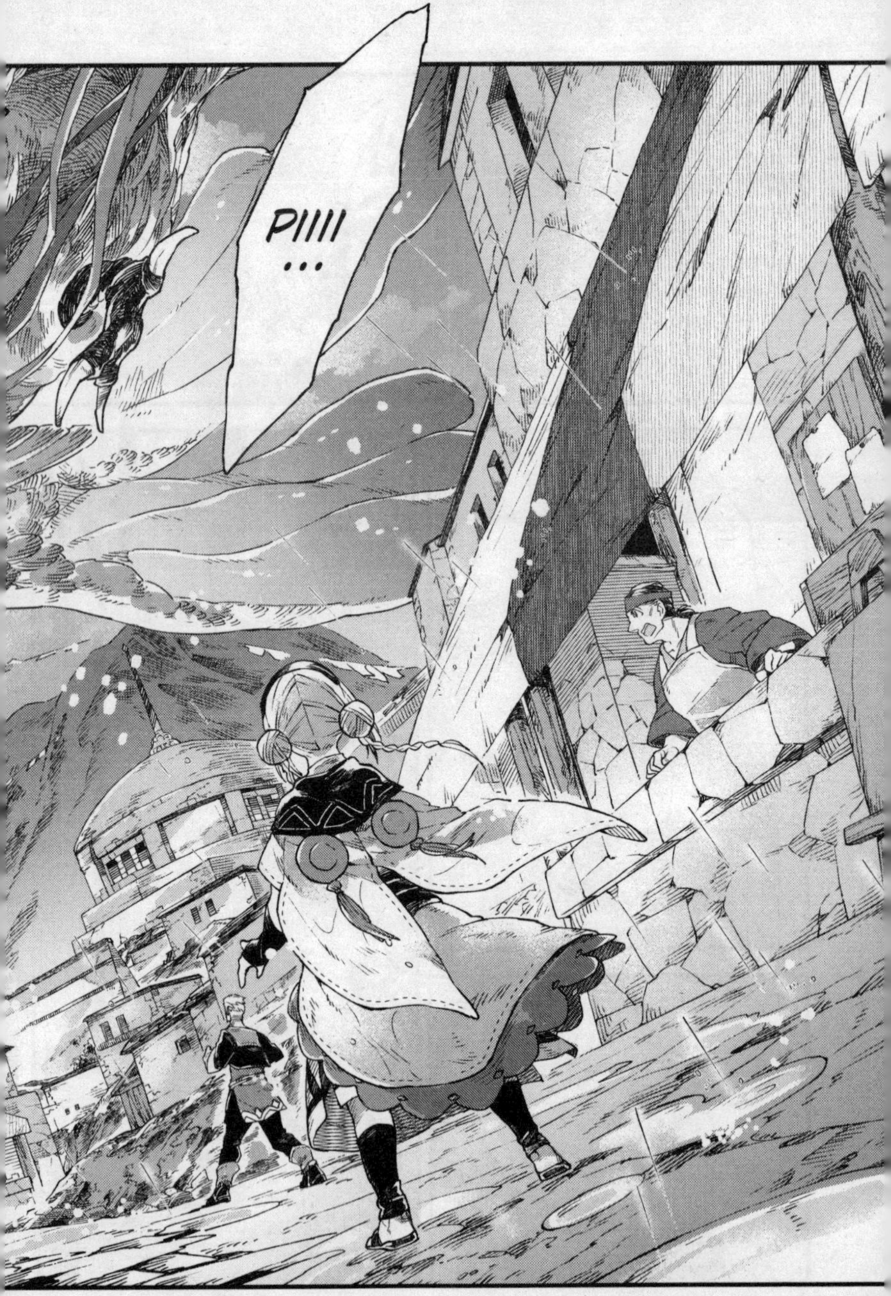
PIIII
...

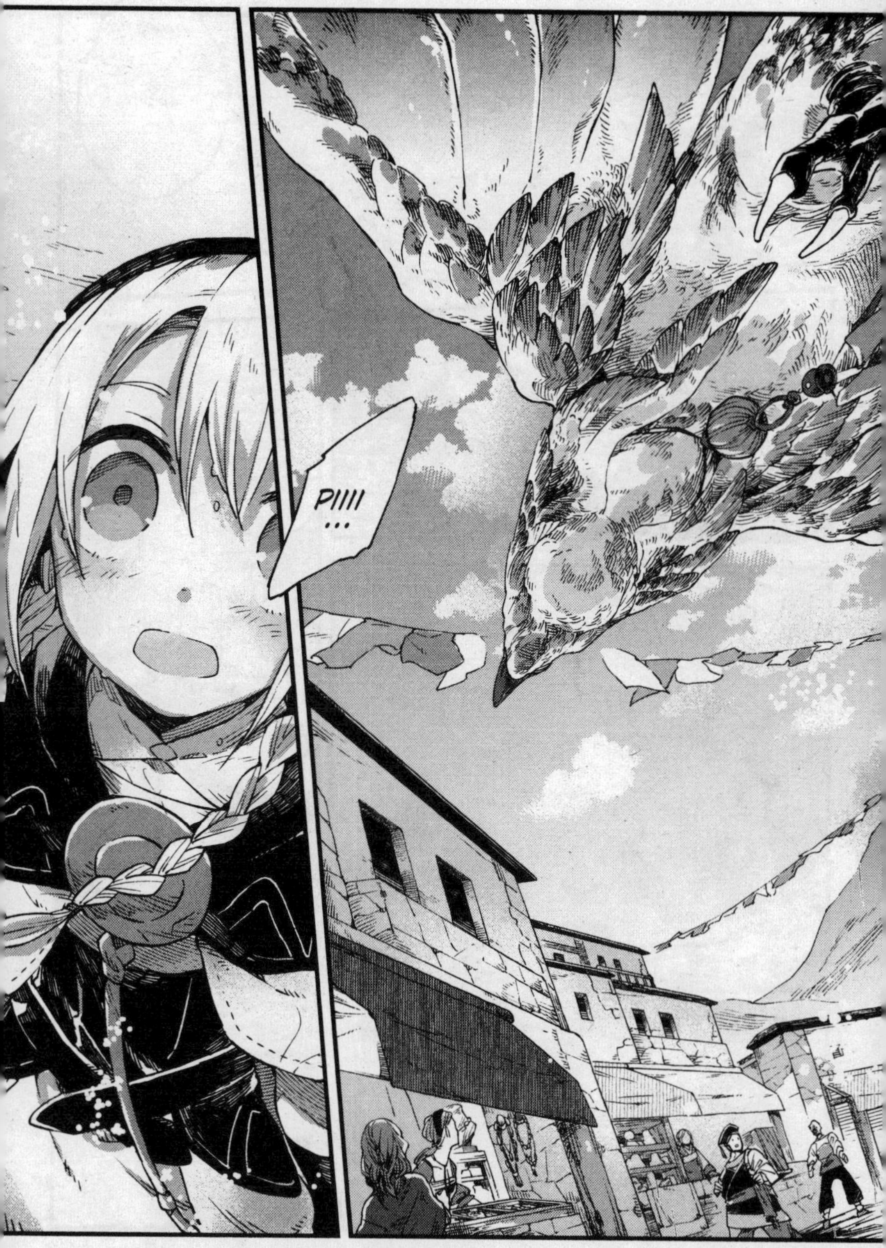
PI!!!
...

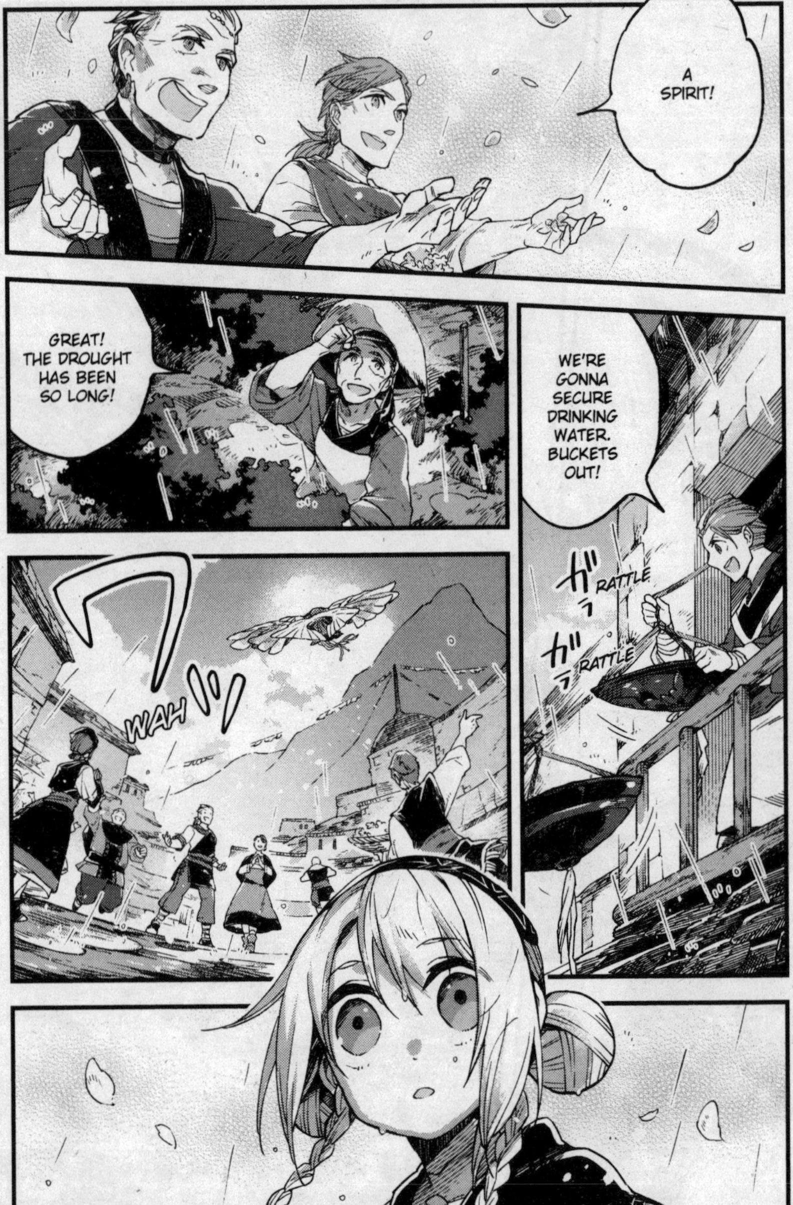
A SPIRIT!
WE'RE GONNA SECURE DRINKING WATER. BUCKETS OUT!
ガラ RATTLE
ガラ RATTLE
GREAT! THE DROUGHT HAS BEEN SO LONG!
WAH !!

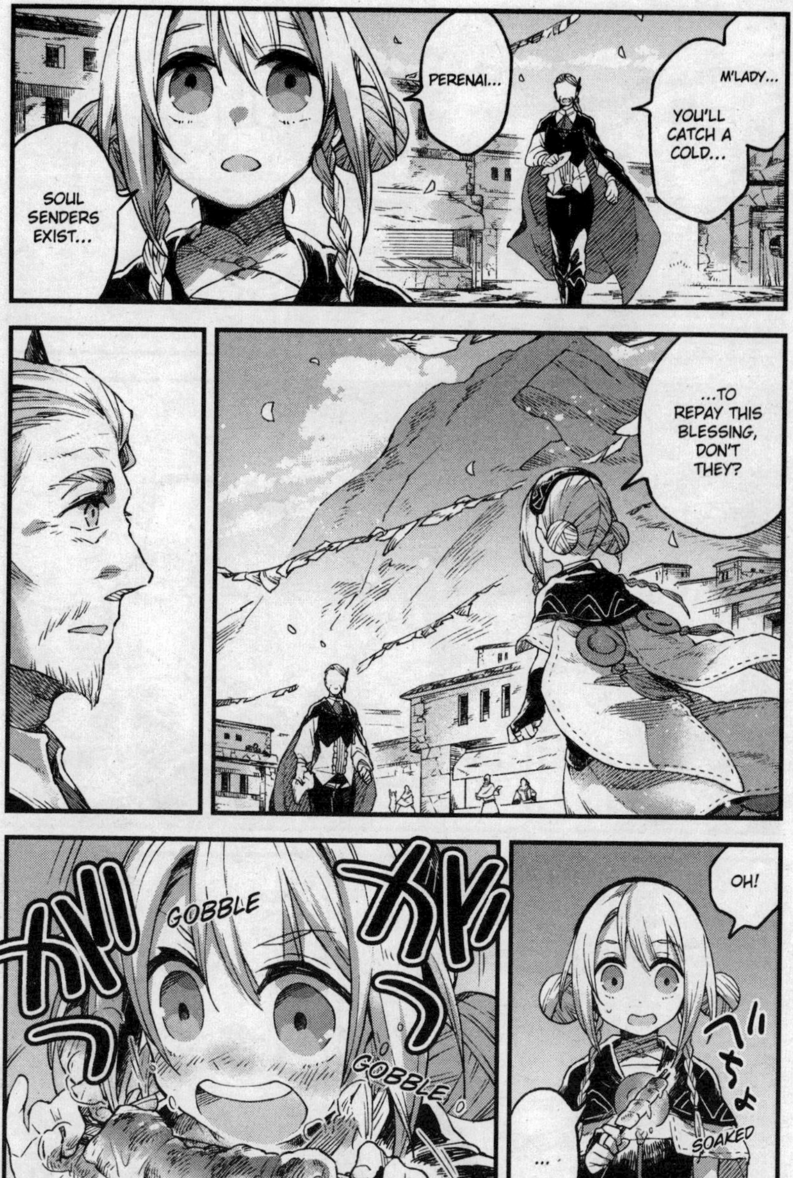
M'LADY...
YOU'LL CATCH A COLD...
PERENAI...
SOUL SENDERS EXIST...
...TO REPAY THIS BLESSING, DON'T THEY?
OH!
SOAKED
...
GOBBLE
GOBBLE

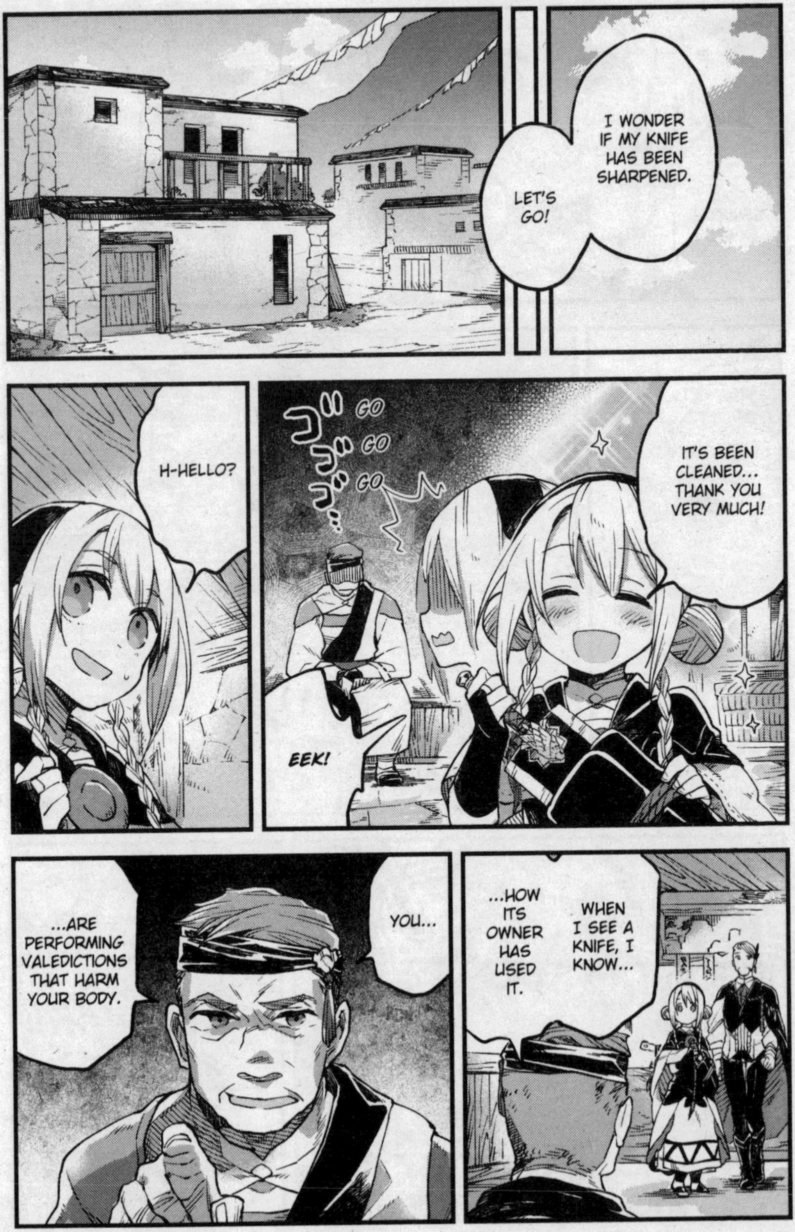
I WONDER IF MY KNIFE HAS BEEN SHARPENED.
LET'S GO!
ゴゴゴ GO GO GO
IT'S BEEN CLEANED... THANK YOU VERY MUCH!
EEK!
H-HELLO?
WHEN I SEE A KNIFE, I KNOW...
...HOW ITS OWNER HAS USED IT.
YOU...
...ARE PERFORMING VALEDICTIONS THAT HARM YOUR BODY.

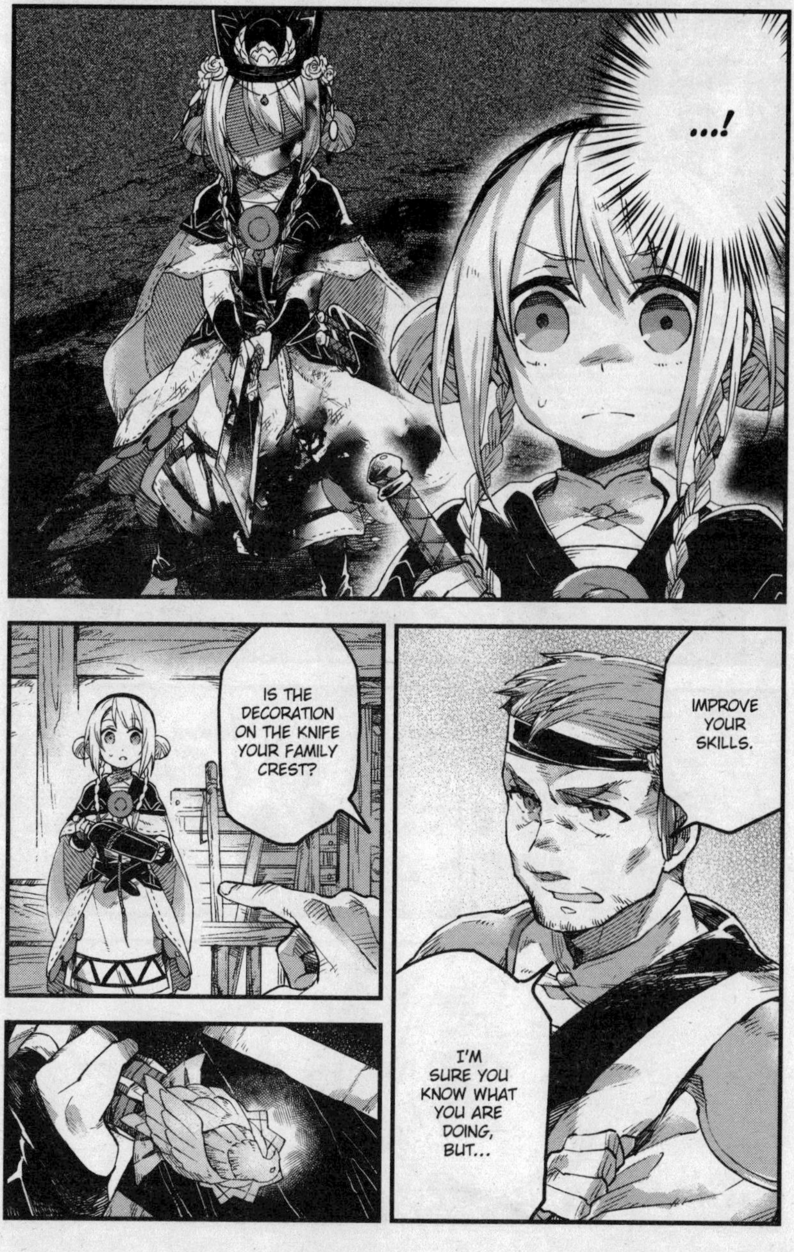
...!
IMPROVE YOUR SKILLS.
I'M SURE YOU KNOW WHAT YOU ARE DOING, BUT...
IS THE DECORATION ON THE KNIFE YOUR FAMILY CREST?

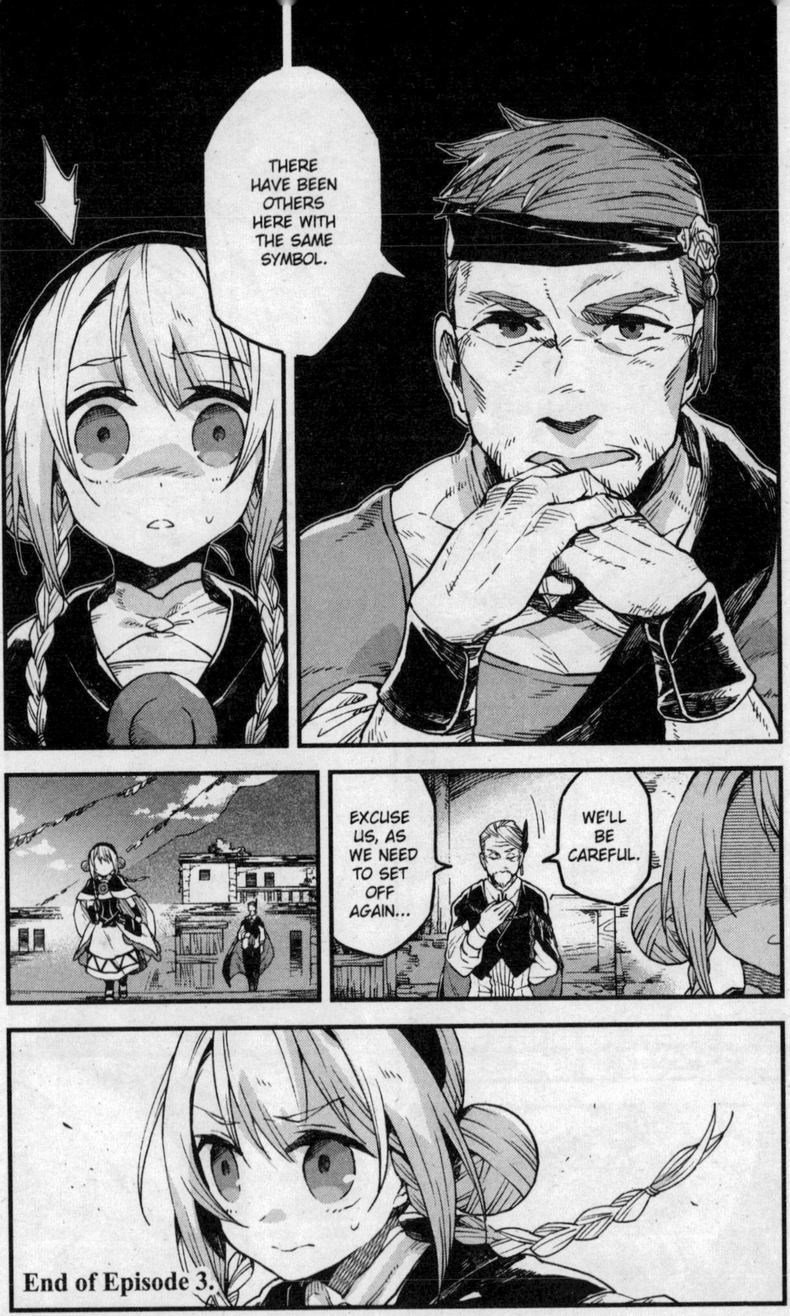
THERE HAVE BEEN OTHERS HERE WITH THE SAME SYMBOL.
WE'LL BE CAREFUL.
EXCUSE US, AS WE NEED TO SET OFF AGAIN...
End of Episode 3.

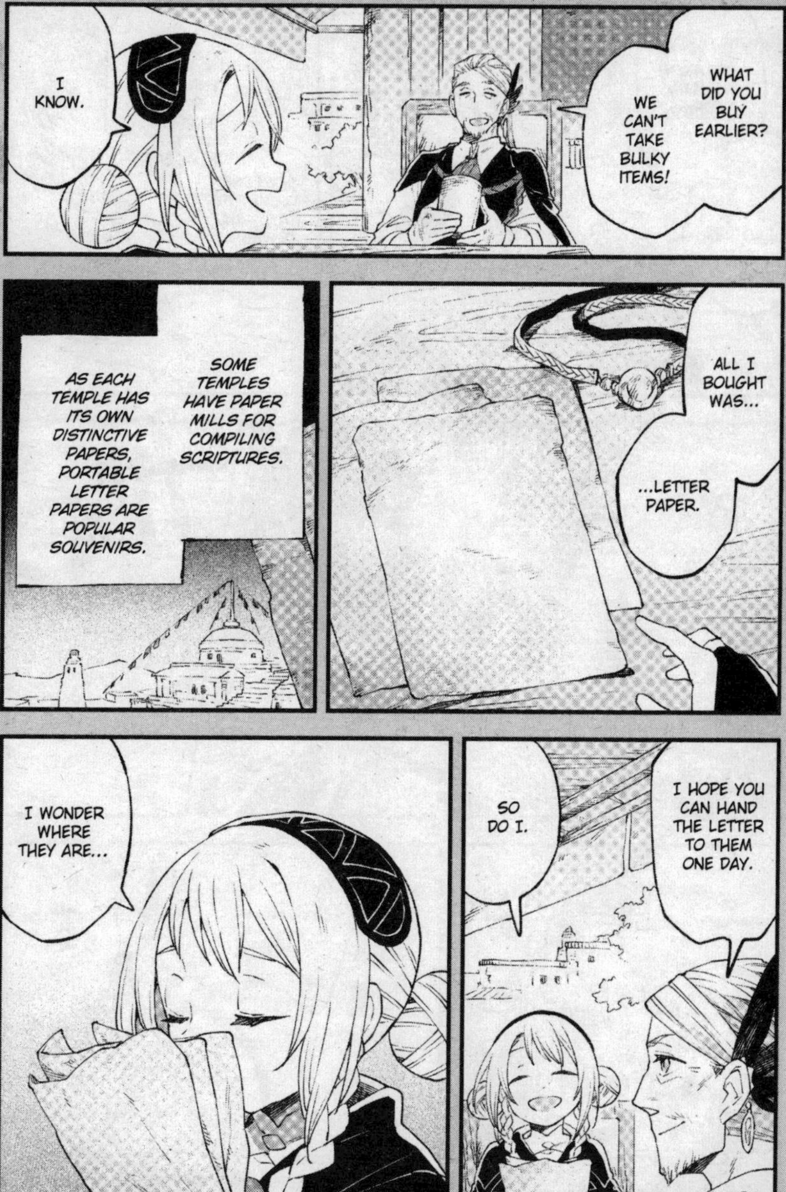
WHAT DID YOU BUY EARLIER?
WE CAN'T TAKE BULKY ITEMS!
I KNOW.
ALL I BOUGHT WAS...
...LETTER PAPER.
SOME TEMPLES HAVE PAPER MILLS FOR COMPILING SCRIPTURES.
AS EACH TEMPLE HAS ITS OWN DISTINCTIVE PAPERS, PORTABLE LETTER PAPERS ARE POPULAR SOUVENIRS.
I HOPE YOU CAN HAND THE LETTER TO THEM ONE DAY.
SO DO I.
I WONDER WHERE THEY ARE...

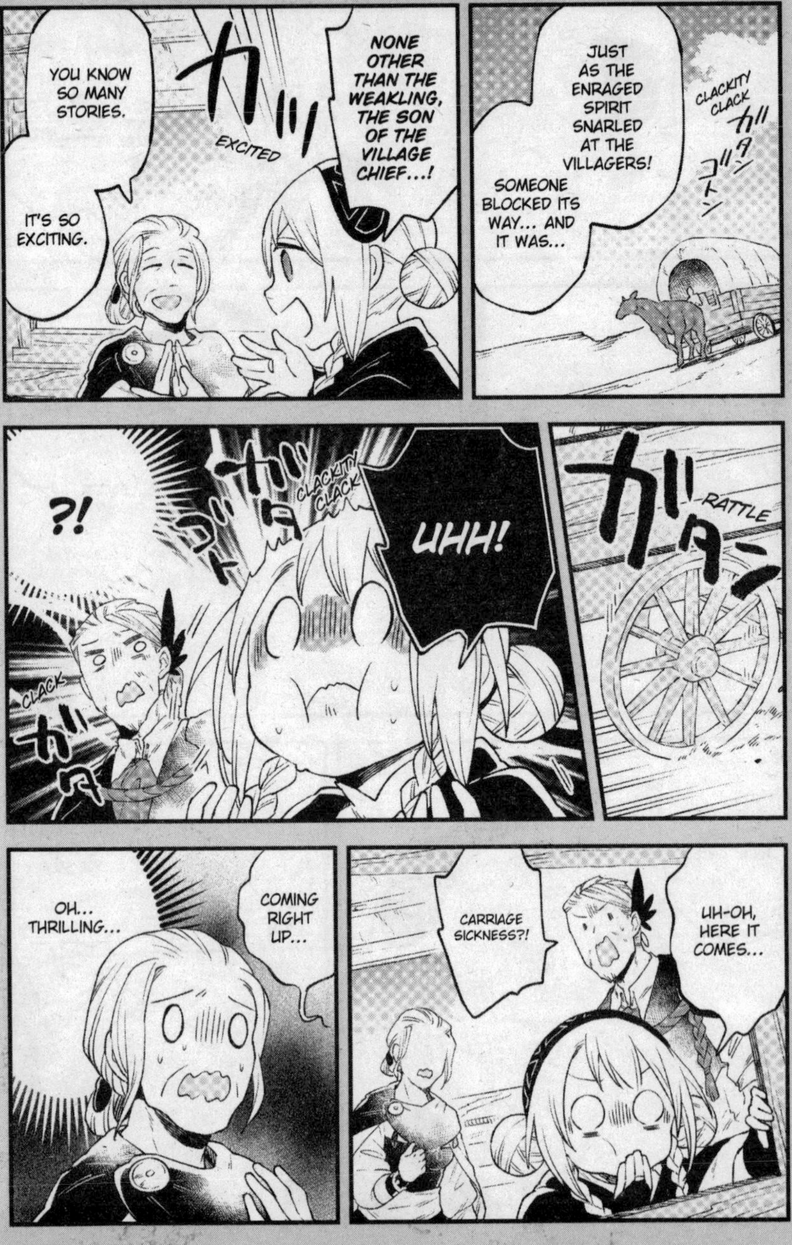
JUST AS THE ENRAGED SPIRIT SNARLED AT THE VILLAGERS!
SOMEONE BLOCKED ITS WAY... AND IT WAS...
CLACKITY CLACK
NONE OTHER THAN THE WEAKLING, THE SON OF THE VILLAGE CHIEF...!
EXCITED
YOU KNOW SO MANY STORIES.
IT'S SO EXCITING.
RATTLE
UHH!
CLACKITY CLACK
?!
CLACK
UH-OH, HERE IT COMES...
CARRIAGE SICKNESS?!
COMING RIGHT UP...
OH... THRILLING...

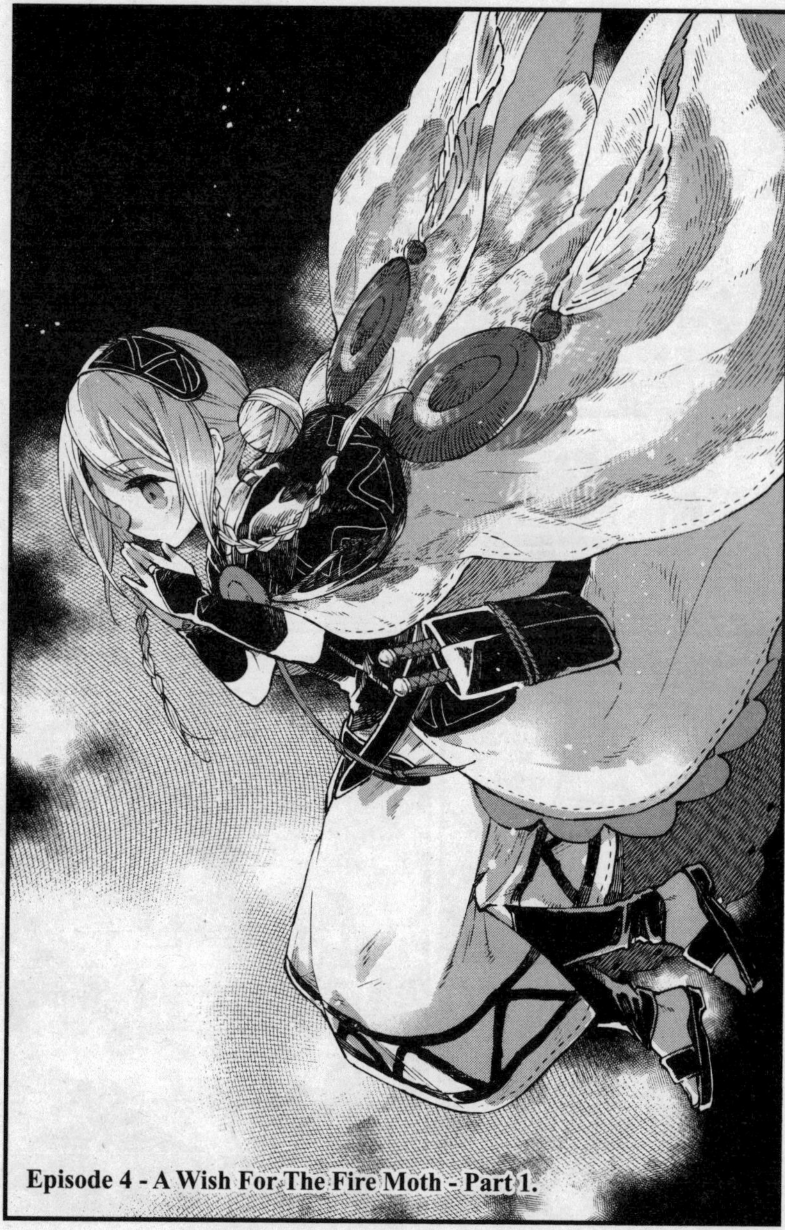

Episode 4 - A Wish For The Fire Moth - Part 1.

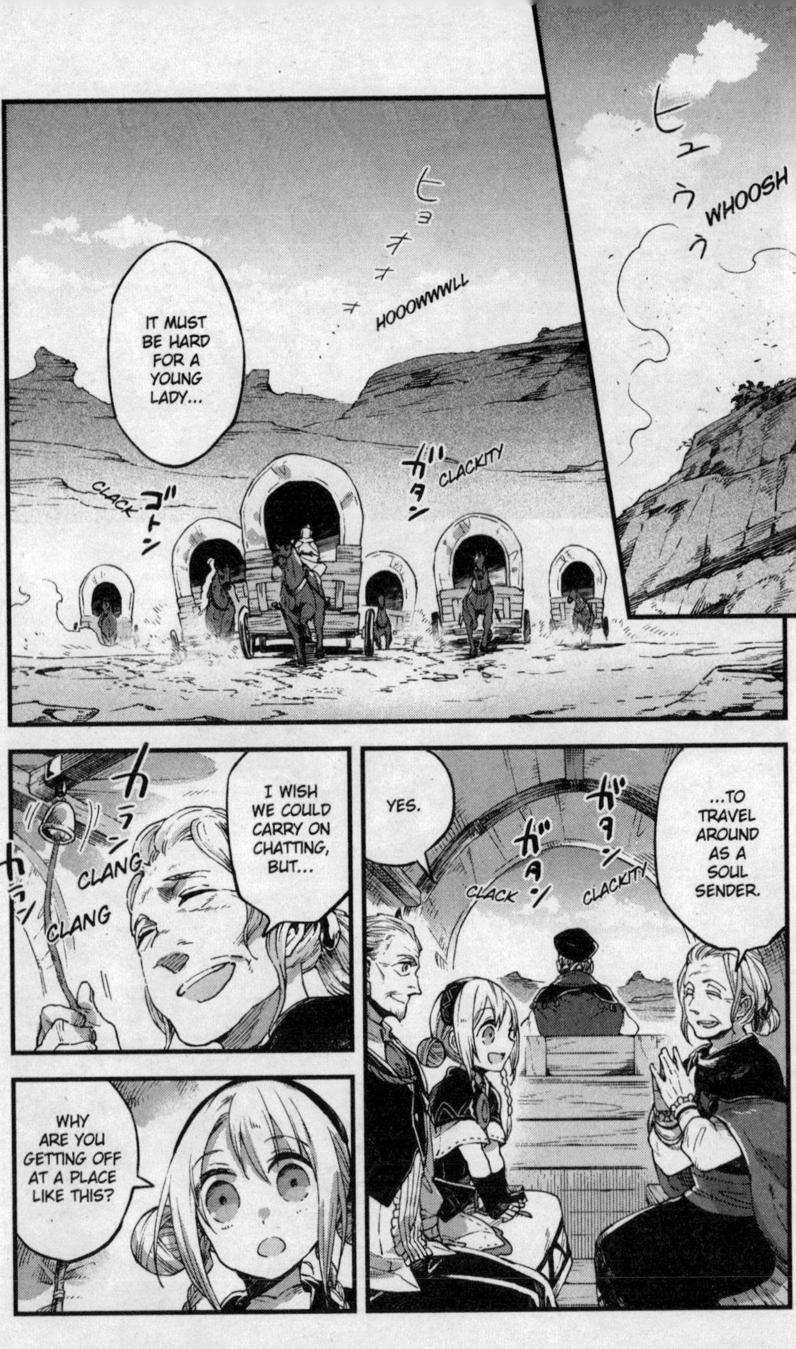
ヒュウウ
WHOOSH
ヒョオオォ
HOOOWWWLL
IT MUST BE HARD FOR A YOUNG LADY...
ガタン
CLACKITY
ゴトン
CLACK
...TO TRAVEL AROUND AS A SOUL SENDER.
ガタン
CLACKITY
YES.
ガタン
CLACK
I WISH WE COULD CARRY ON CHATTING, BUT...
カラン
CLANG
カラン
CLANG
WHY ARE YOU GETTING OFF AT A PLACE LIKE THIS?

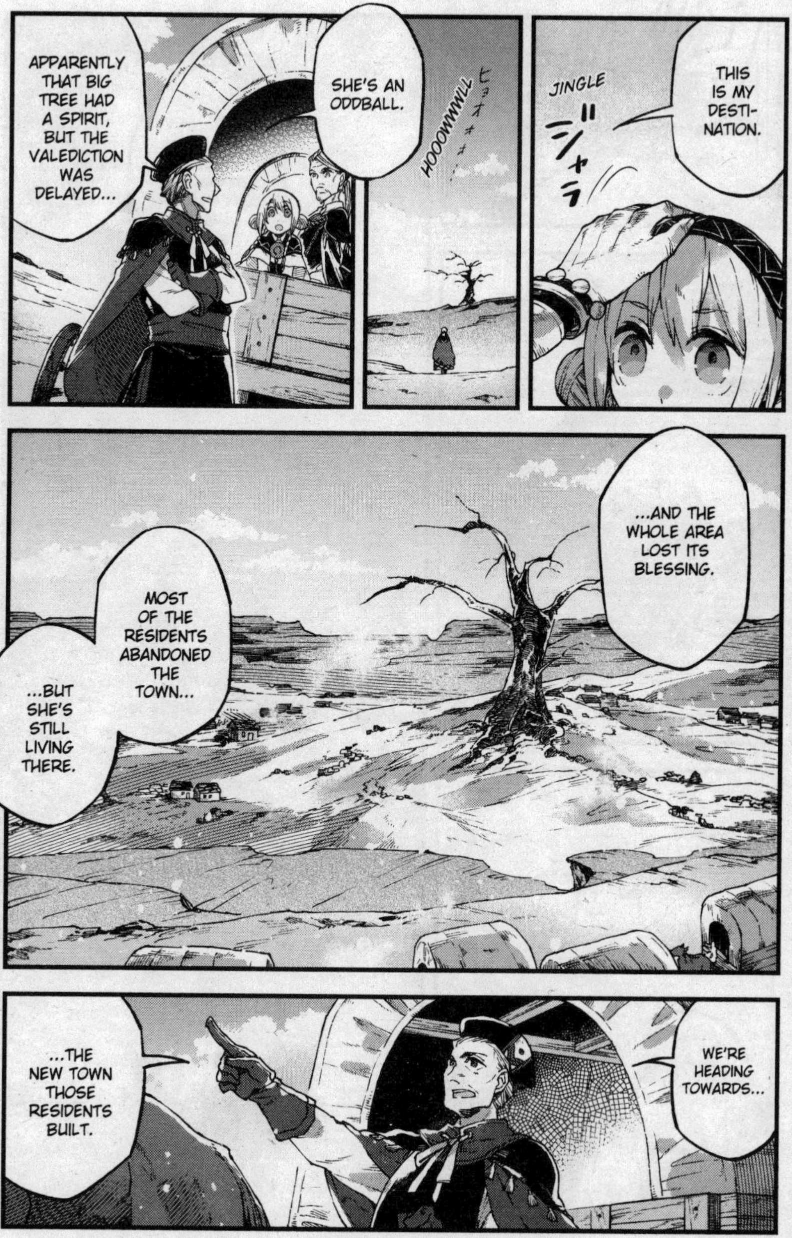
THIS IS MY DESTINATION.
JINGLE
HOOOWWWL
SHE'S AN ODDBALL.
APPARENTLY THAT BIG TREE HAD A SPIRIT, BUT THE VALEDICTION WAS DELAYED...
...AND THE WHOLE AREA LOST ITS BLESSING.
MOST OF THE RESIDENTS ABANDONED THE TOWN...
...BUT SHE'S STILL LIVING THERE.
WE'RE HEADING TOWARDS...
...THE NEW TOWN THOSE RESIDENTS BUILT.

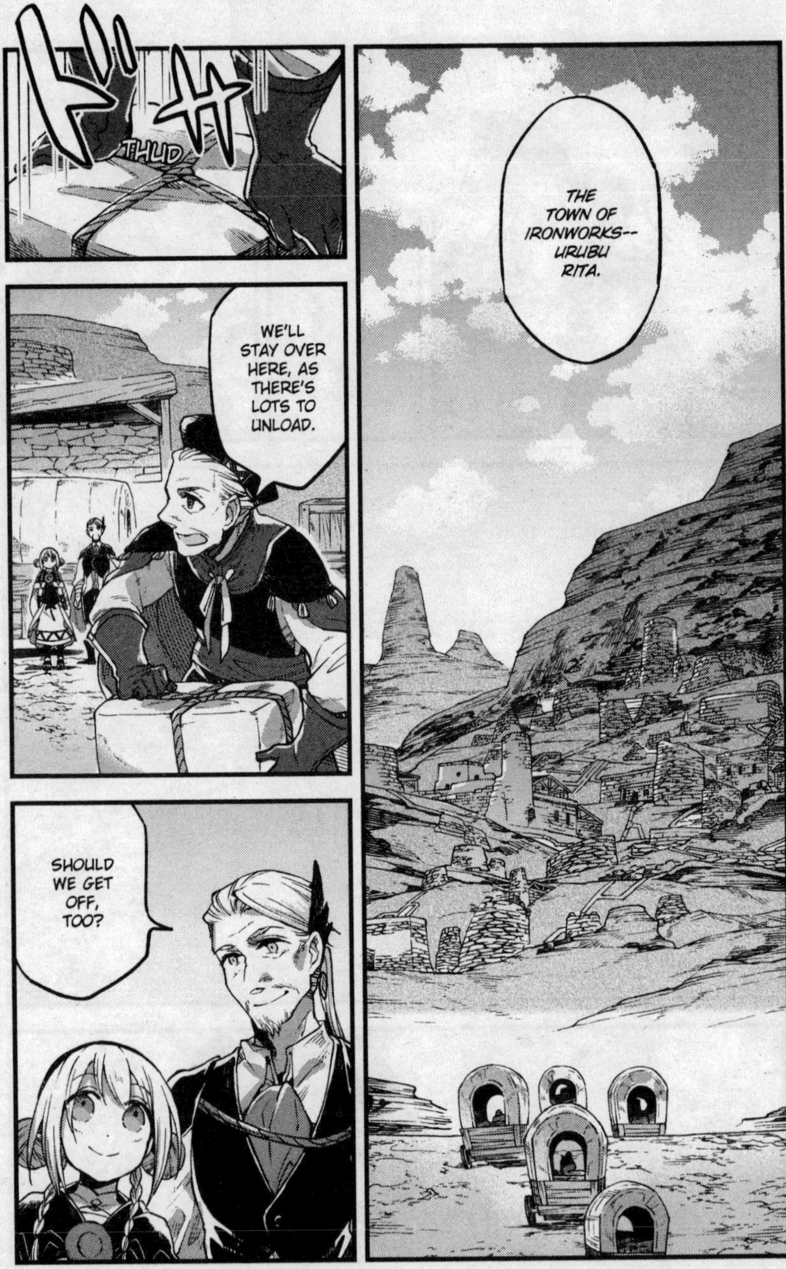
THE TOWN OF IRONWORKS-- URUBU RITA.
THUD
WE'LL STAY OVER HERE, AS THERE'S LOTS TO UNLOAD.
SHOULD WE GET OFF, TOO?

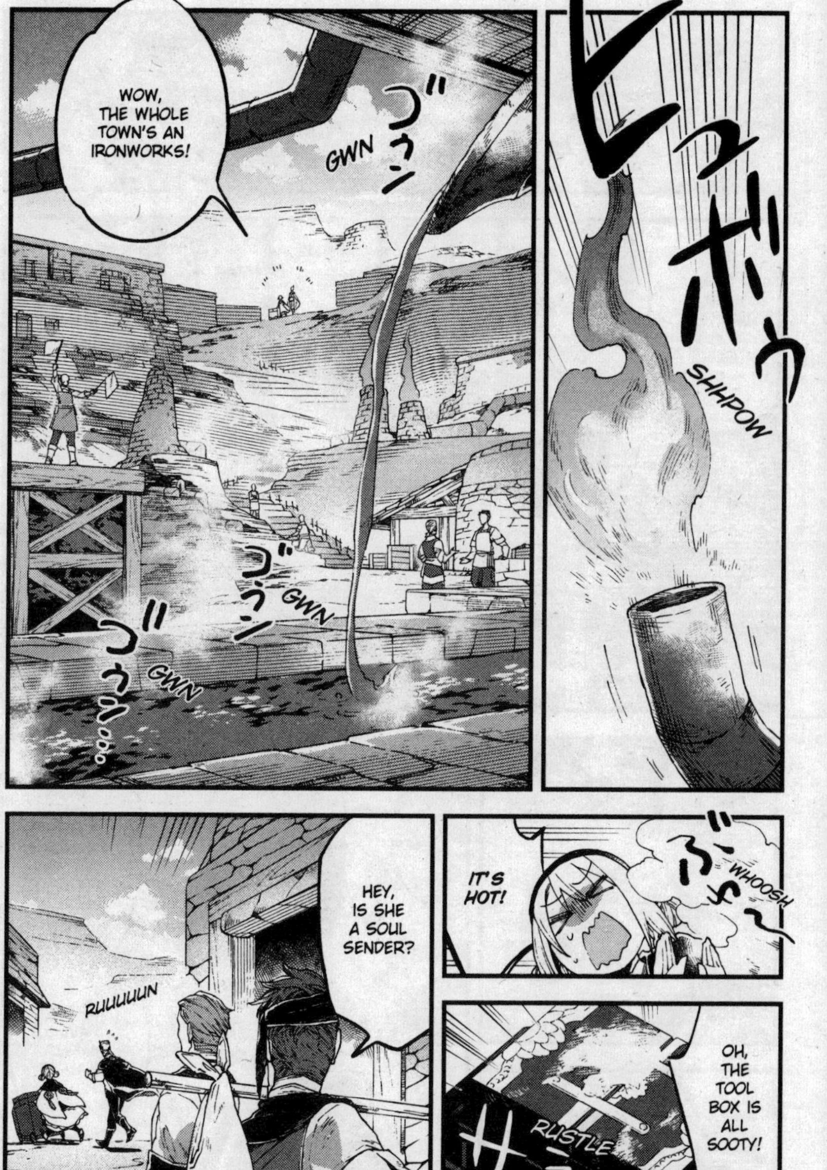
SHHPOW
WOW, THE WHOLE TOWN'S AN IRONWORKS!
GWN
GWN
GWN
WHOOSH
IT'S HOT!
OH, THE TOOL BOX IS ALL SOOTY!
RUSTLE
HEY, IS SHE A SOUL SENDER?
RUUUUUN

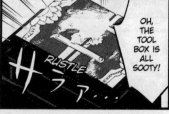

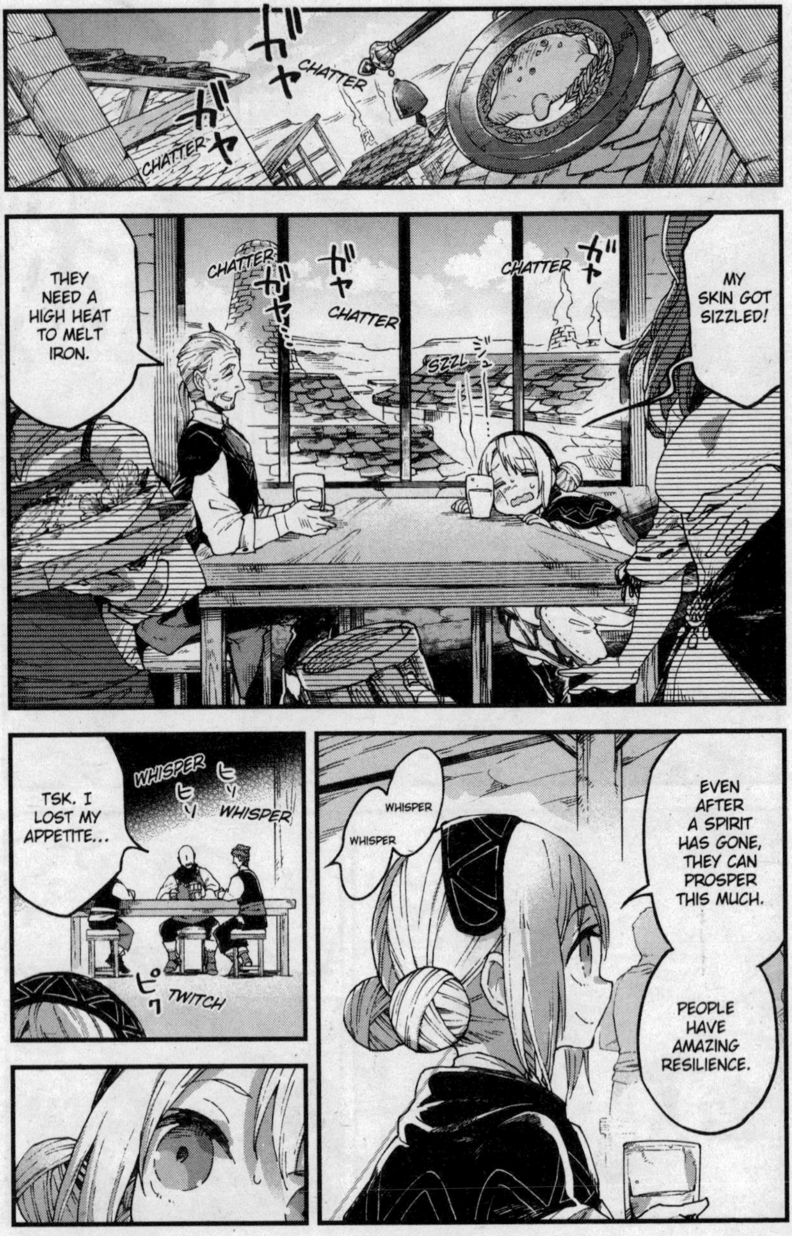
ガヤ
CHATTER
ガヤ
CHATTER
ガヤ
CHATTER
SZZL
ジュ
MY SKIN GOT SIZZLED!
ガヤ
CHATTER
ガヤ
CHATTER
THEY NEED A HIGH HEAT TO MELT IRON.
EVEN AFTER A SPIRIT HAS GONE, THEY CAN PROSPER THIS MUCH.
WHISPER
WHISPER
PEOPLE HAVE AMAZING RESILIENCE.
ヒソ
WHISPER
ヒソ
WHISPER
TSK. I LOST MY APPETITE...
ピク
TWITCH

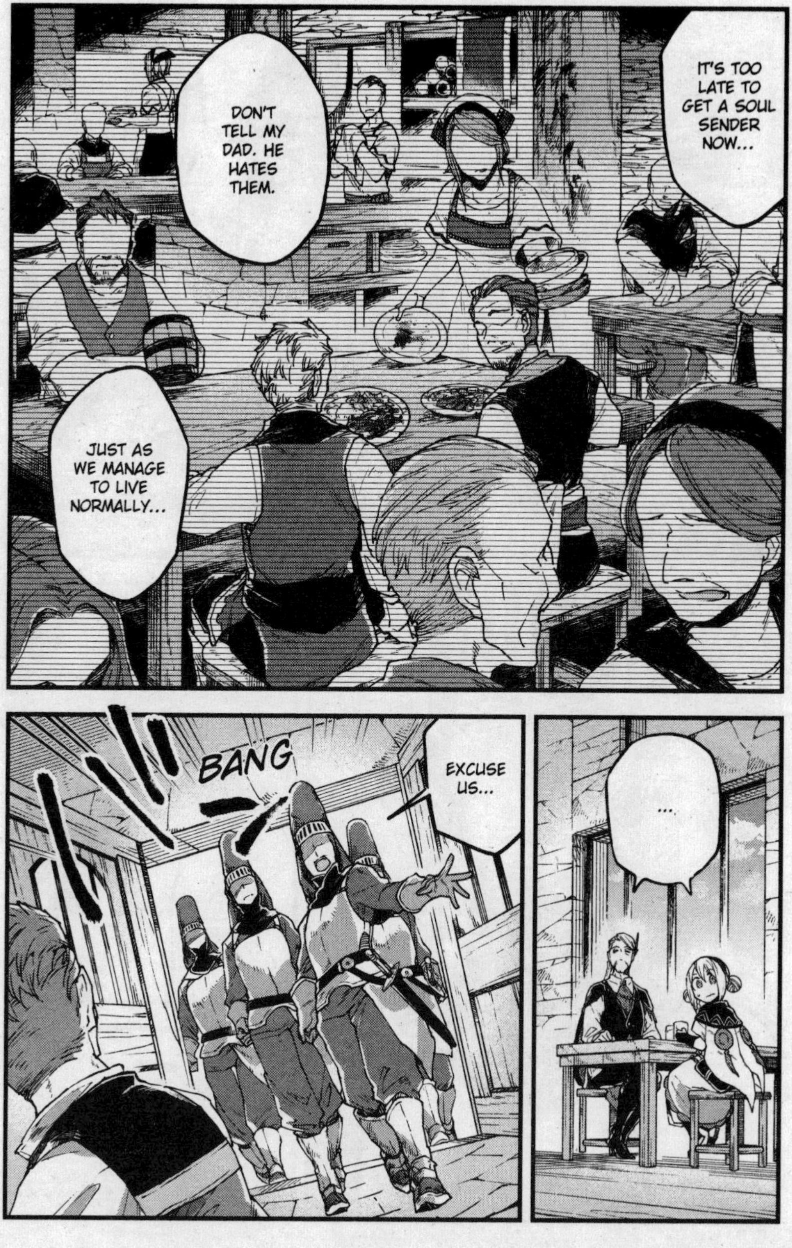
IT'S TOO LATE TO GET A SOUL SENDER NOW...
DON'T TELL MY DAD. HE HATES THEM.
JUST AS WE MANAGE TO LIVE NORMALLY...
...
EXCUSE US...
BANG

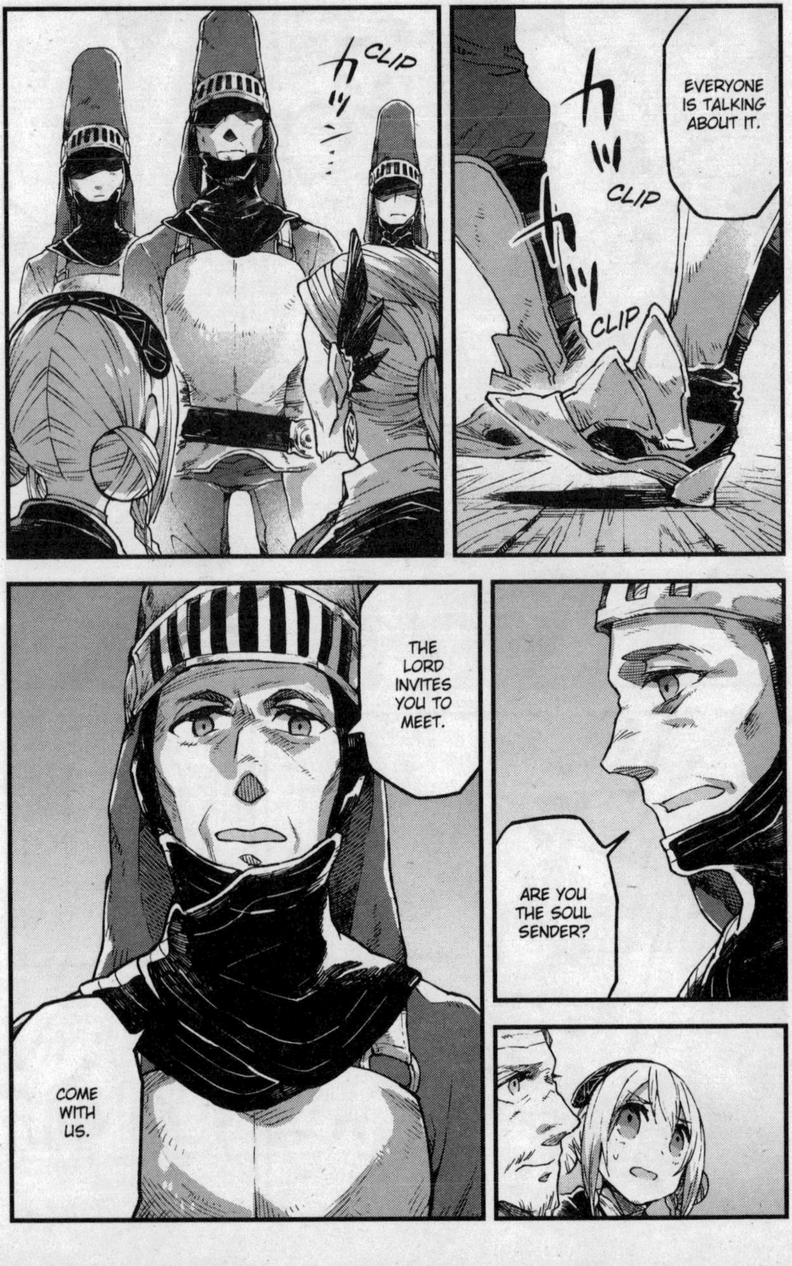
EVERYONE IS TALKING ABOUT IT.
カッ
CLIP
カッ
CLIP
カッ
CLIP
ARE YOU THE SOUL SENDER?
THE LORD INVITES YOU TO MEET.
COME WITH US.

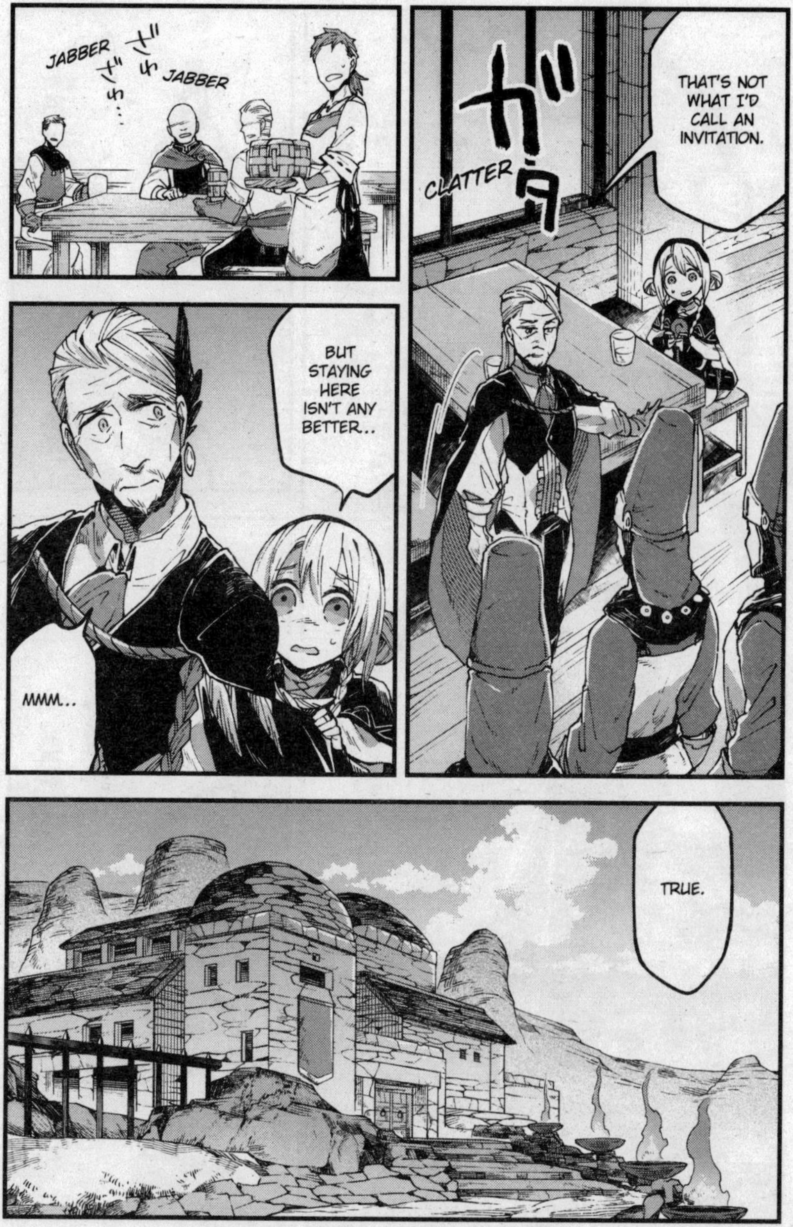
THAT'S NOT WHAT I'D CALL AN INVITATION.
ガタ
CLATTER
ざわざわ…
JABBER
JABBER
BUT STAYING HERE ISN'T ANY BETTER..
MMM..
TRUE.

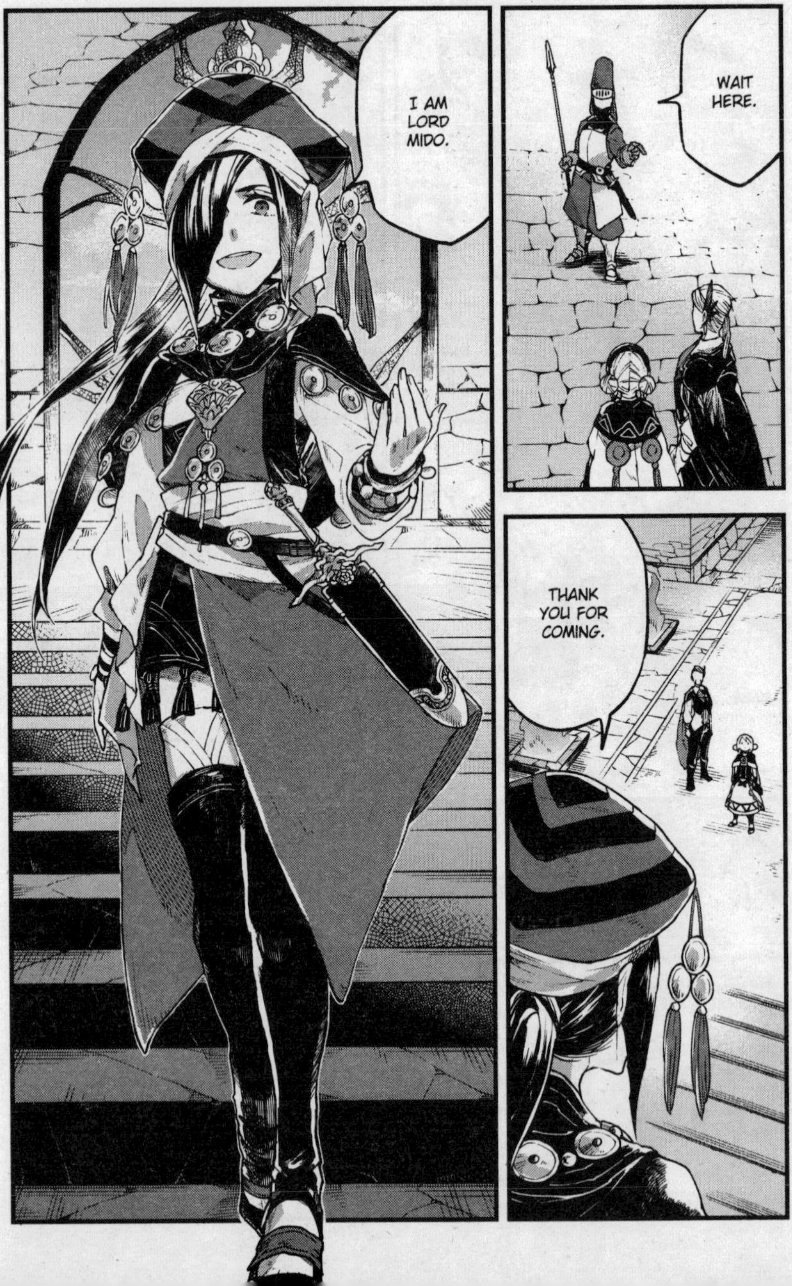
WAIT HERE.
THANK YOU FOR COMING.
I AM LORD MIDO.

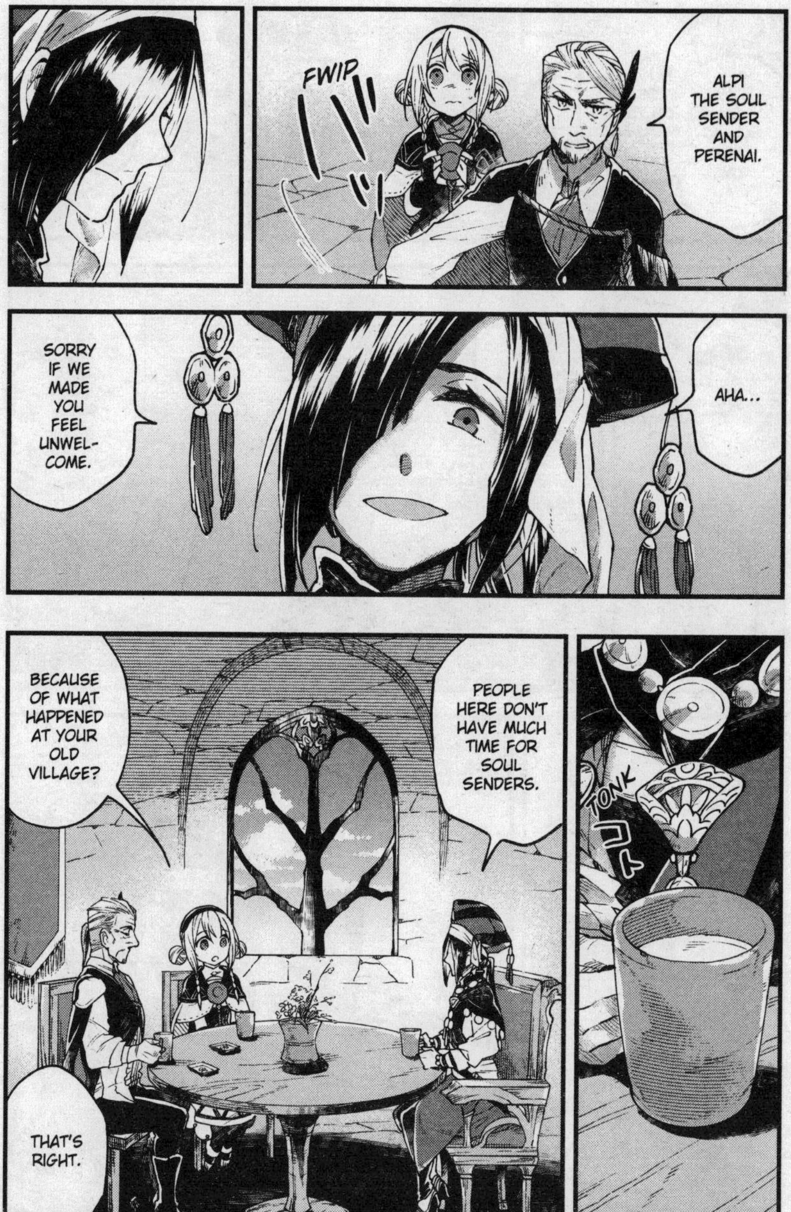
ALPI THE SOUL SENDER AND PERENAI.
FWIP
AHA...
SORRY IF WE MADE YOU FEEL UNWEL-COME.
TONK
PEOPLE HERE DON'T HAVE MUCH TIME FOR SOUL SENDERS.
BECAUSE OF WHAT HAPPENED AT YOUR OLD VILLAGE?
THAT'S RIGHT.

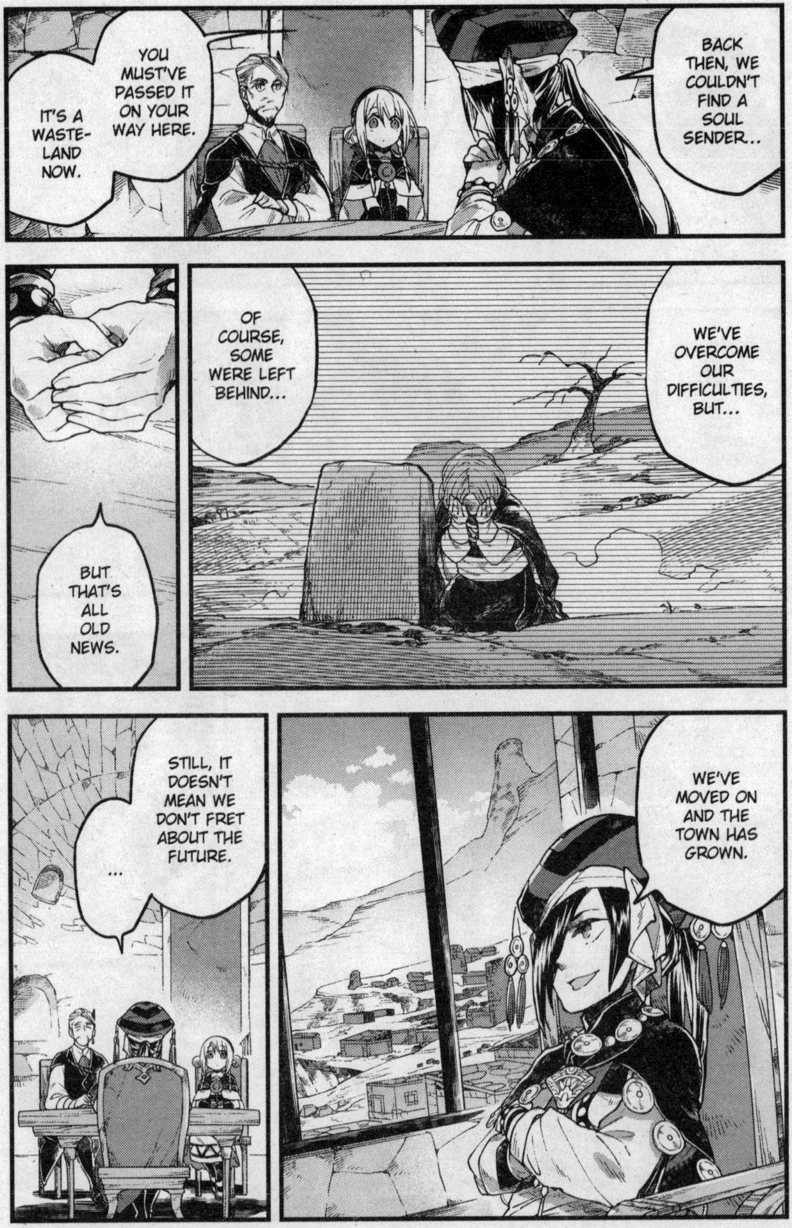
BACK THEN, WE COULDN'T FIND A SOUL SENDER...
YOU MUST'VE PASSED IT ON YOUR WAY HERE.
IT'S A WASTE-LAND NOW.
WE'VE OVERCOME OUR DIFFICULTIES, BUT...
OF COURSE, SOME WERE LEFT BEHIND...
BUT THAT'S ALL OLD NEWS.
WE'VE MOVED ON AND THE TOWN HAS GROWN.
STILL, IT DOESN'T MEAN WE DON'T FRET ABOUT THE FUTURE.
...

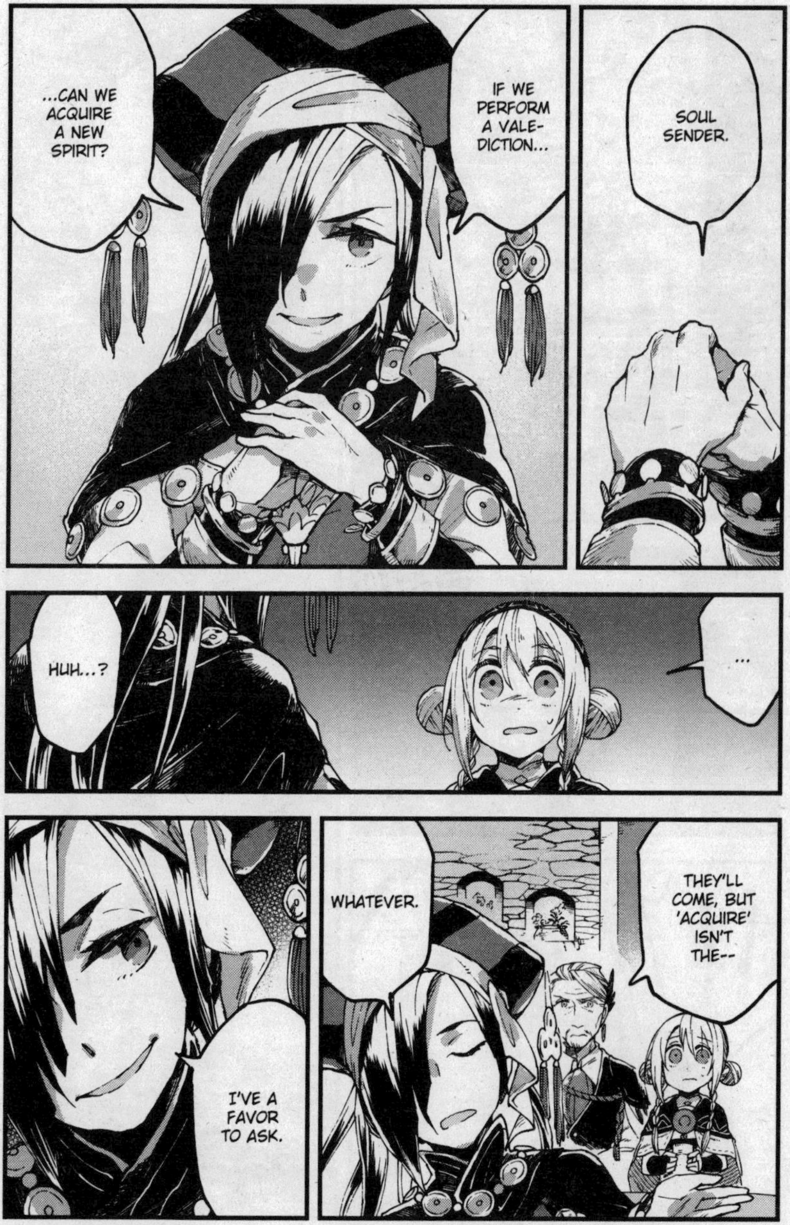
SOUL SENDER.
IF WE PERFORM A VALE-DICTION...
...CAN WE ACQUIRE A NEW SPIRIT?
...
HUH...?
THEY'LL COME, BUT 'ACQUIRE' ISN'T THE--
WHATEVER.
I'VE A FAVOR TO ASK.

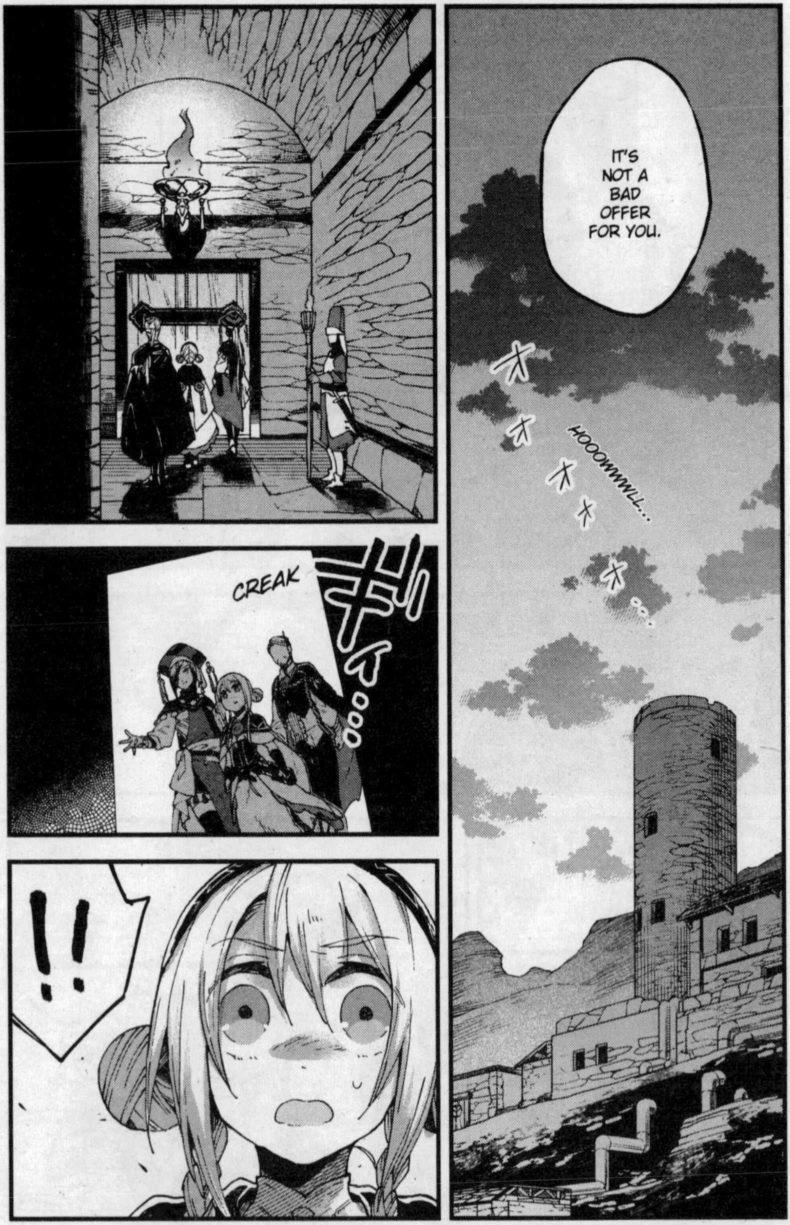
IT'S NOT A BAD OFFER FOR YOU.
HOOOWWWLL...
CREAK
!!

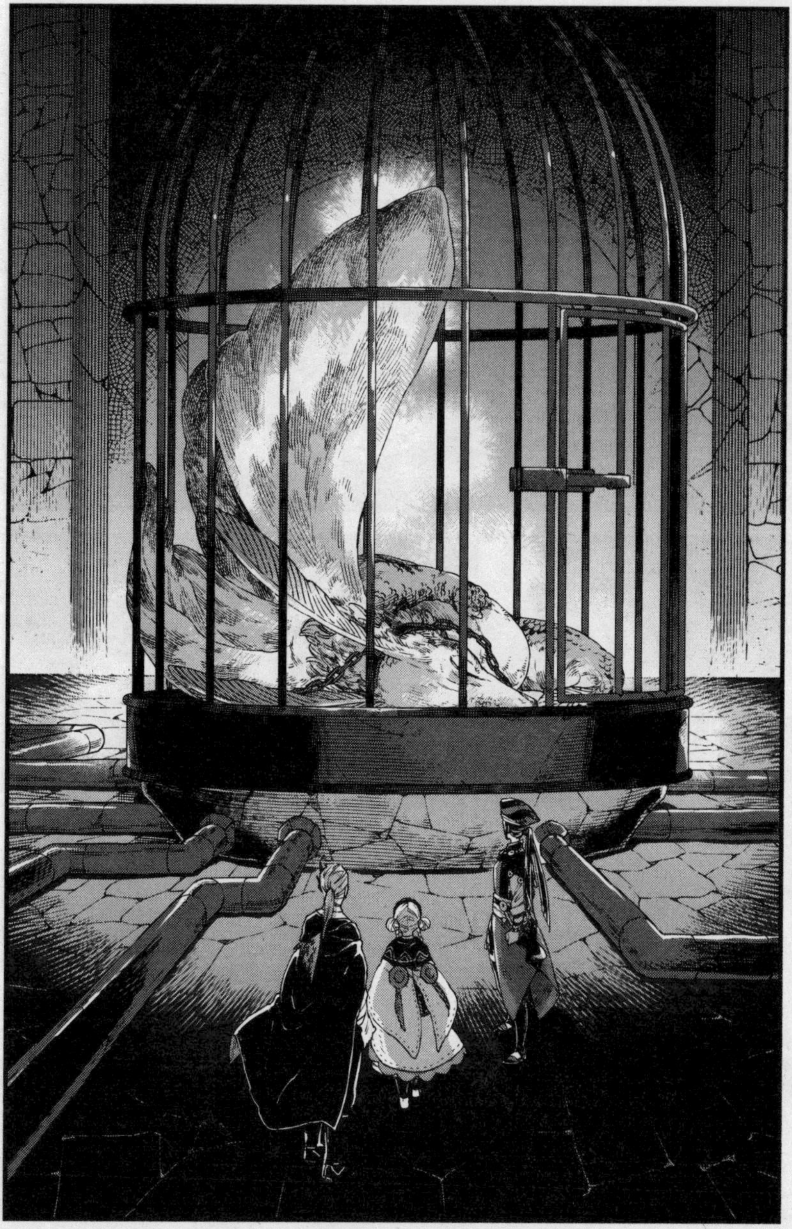

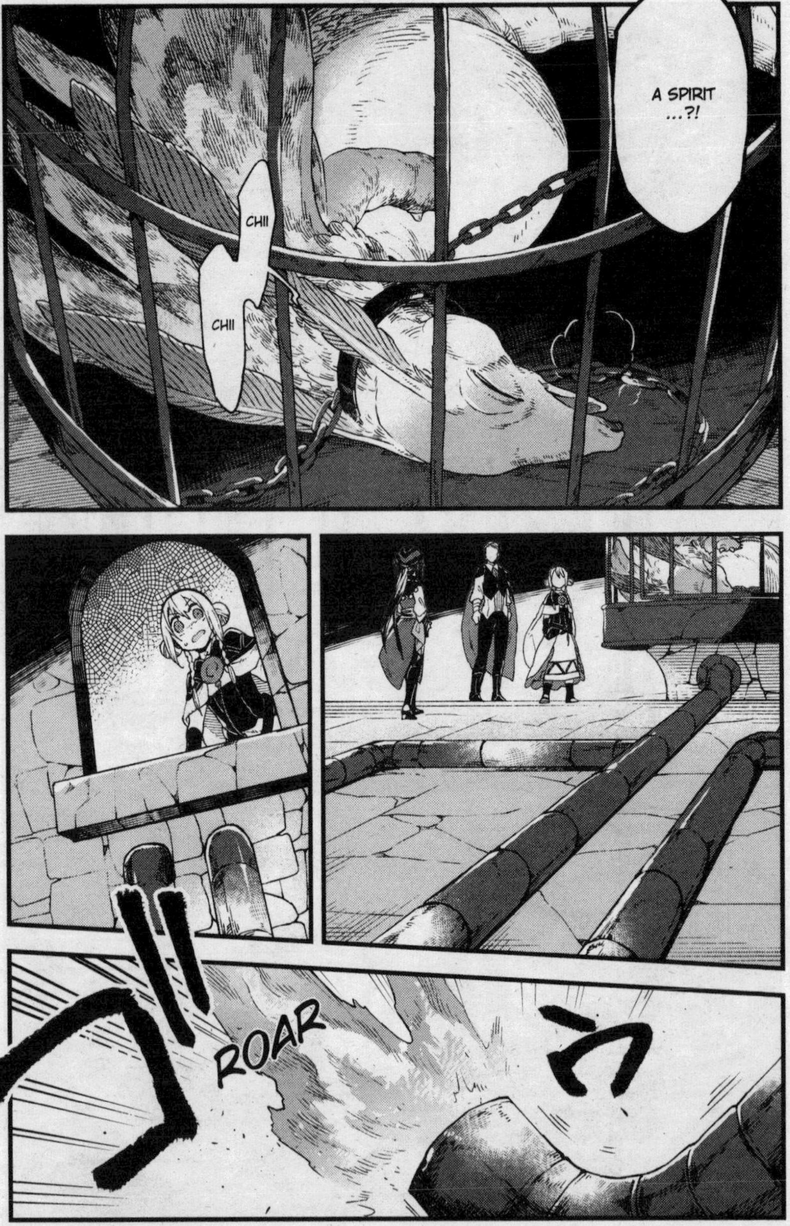
A SPIRIT ...?!
CHII
CHII
ROAR

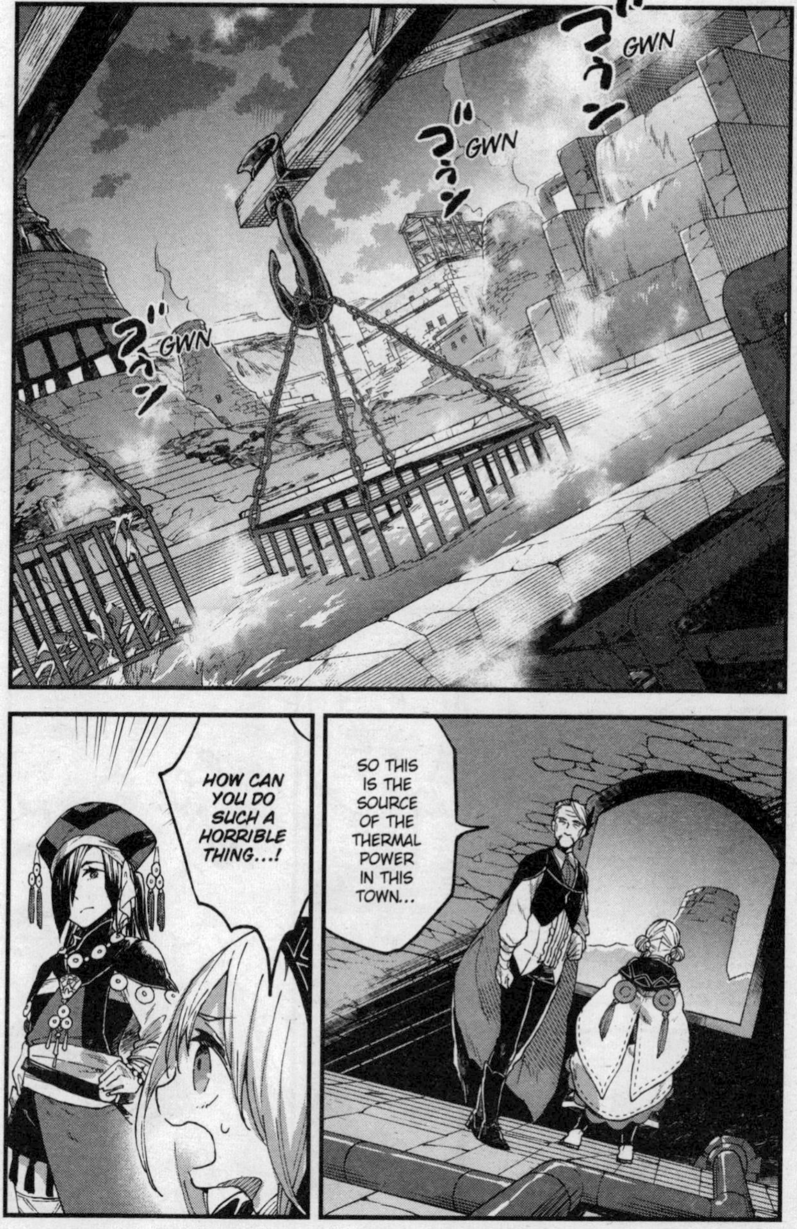
ゴウン
GWN
ゴウン
GWN
ゴウン
GWN
SO THIS IS THE SOURCE OF THE THERMAL POWER IN THIS TOWN...
HOW CAN YOU DO SUCH A HORRIBLE THING...!

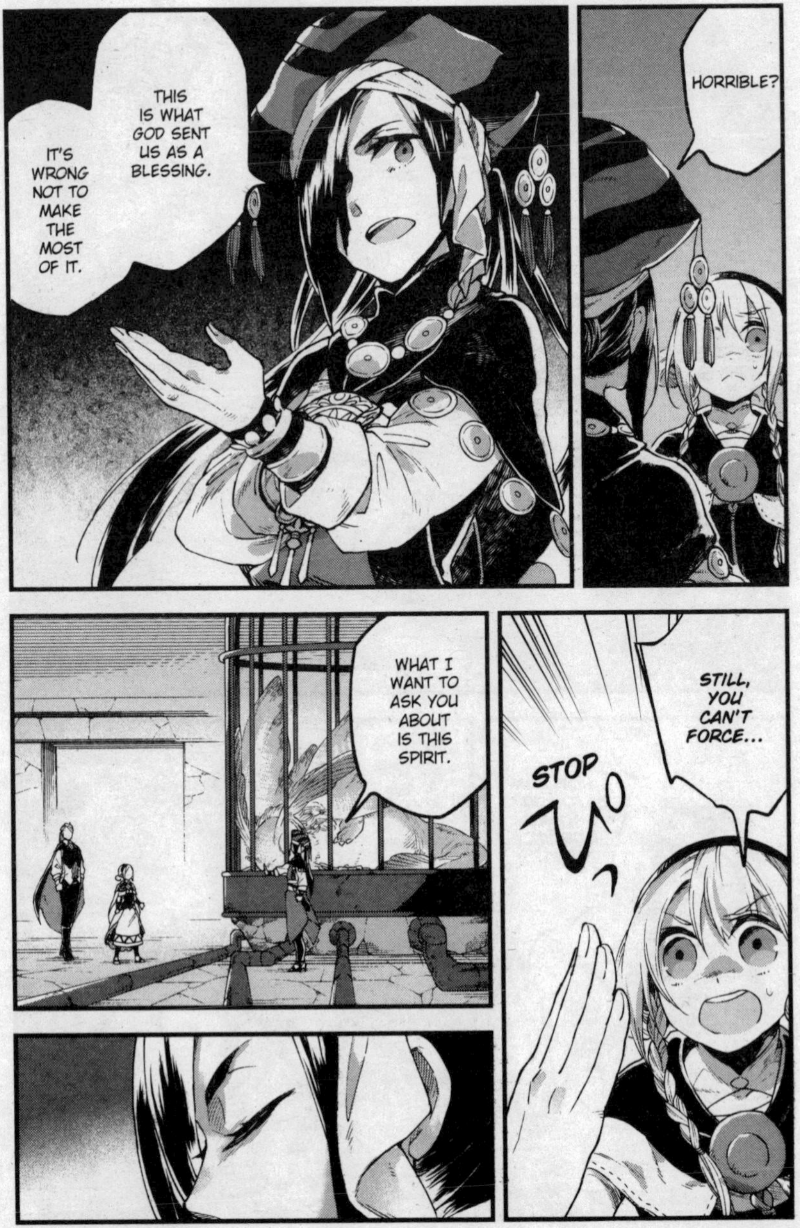
HORRIBLE?
THIS IS WHAT GOD SENT US AS A BLESSING.
IT'S WRONG NOT TO MAKE THE MOST OF IT.
STILL, YOU CAN'T FORCE...
STOP
WHAT I WANT TO ASK YOU ABOUT IS THIS SPIRIT.

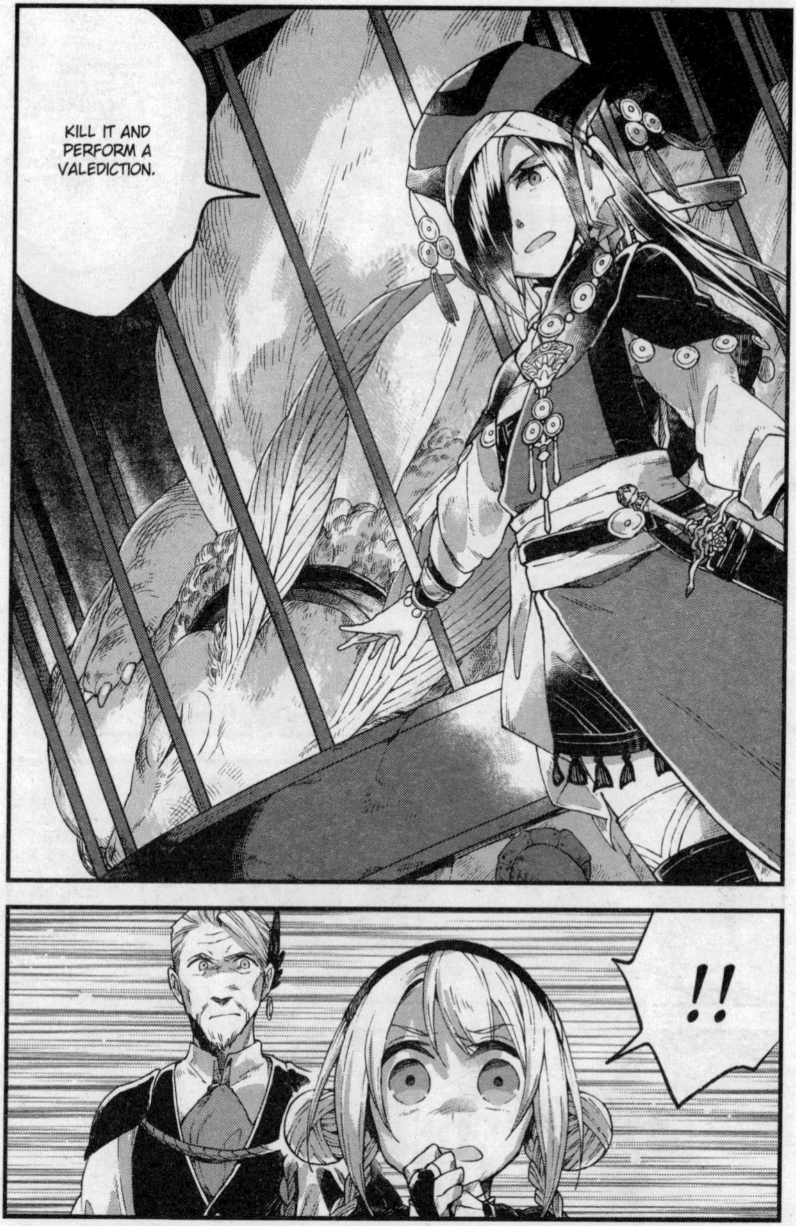
KILL IT AND PERFORM A VALEDICTION.
!!

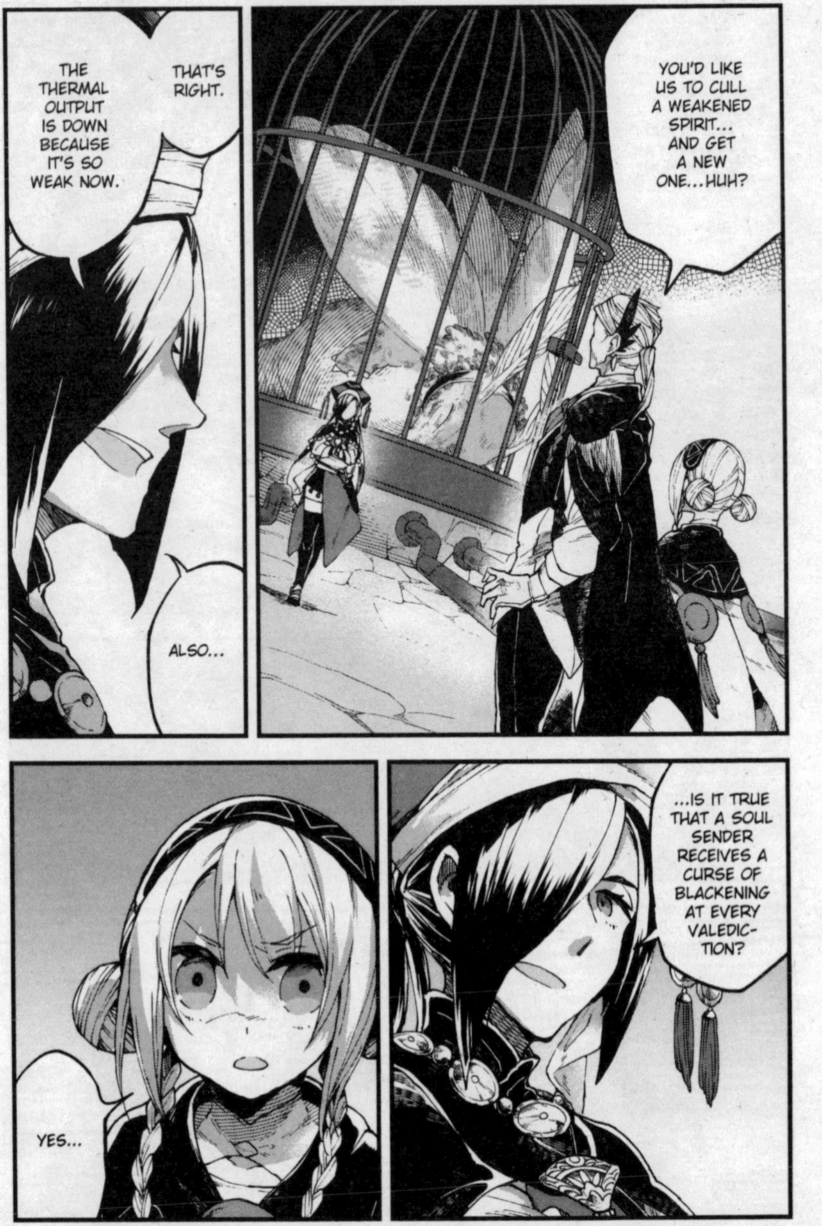
YOU'D LIKE US TO CULL A WEAKENED SPIRIT... AND GET A NEW ONE...HUH?
THAT'S RIGHT.
THE THERMAL OUTPUT IS DOWN BECAUSE IT'S SO WEAK NOW.
ALSO...
...IS IT TRUE THAT A SOUL SENDER RECEIVES A CURSE OF BLACKENING AT EVERY VALEDIC-TION?
YES...

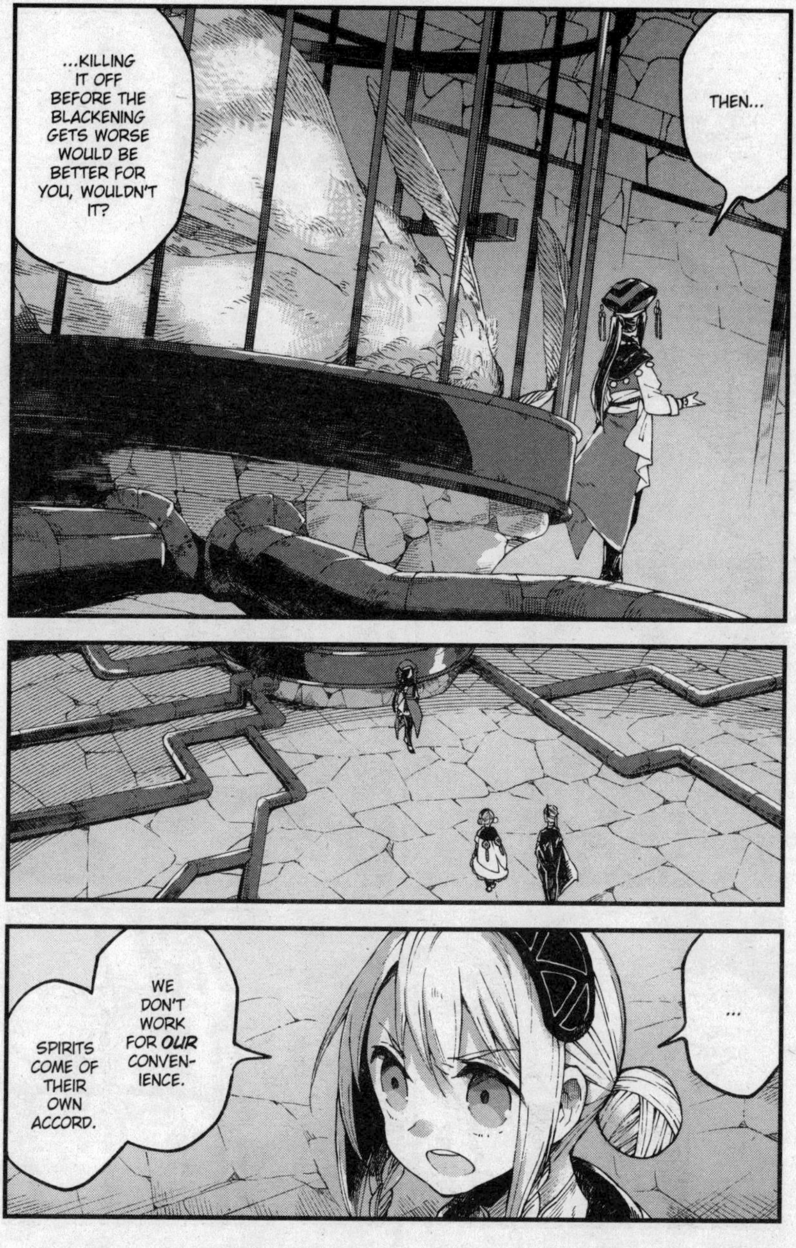
THEN...
...KILLING IT OFF BEFORE THE BLACKENING GETS WORSE WOULD BE BETTER FOR YOU, WOULDN'T IT?
...
WE DON'T WORK FOR *OUR* CONVENIENCE.
SPIRITS COME OF THEIR OWN ACCORD.

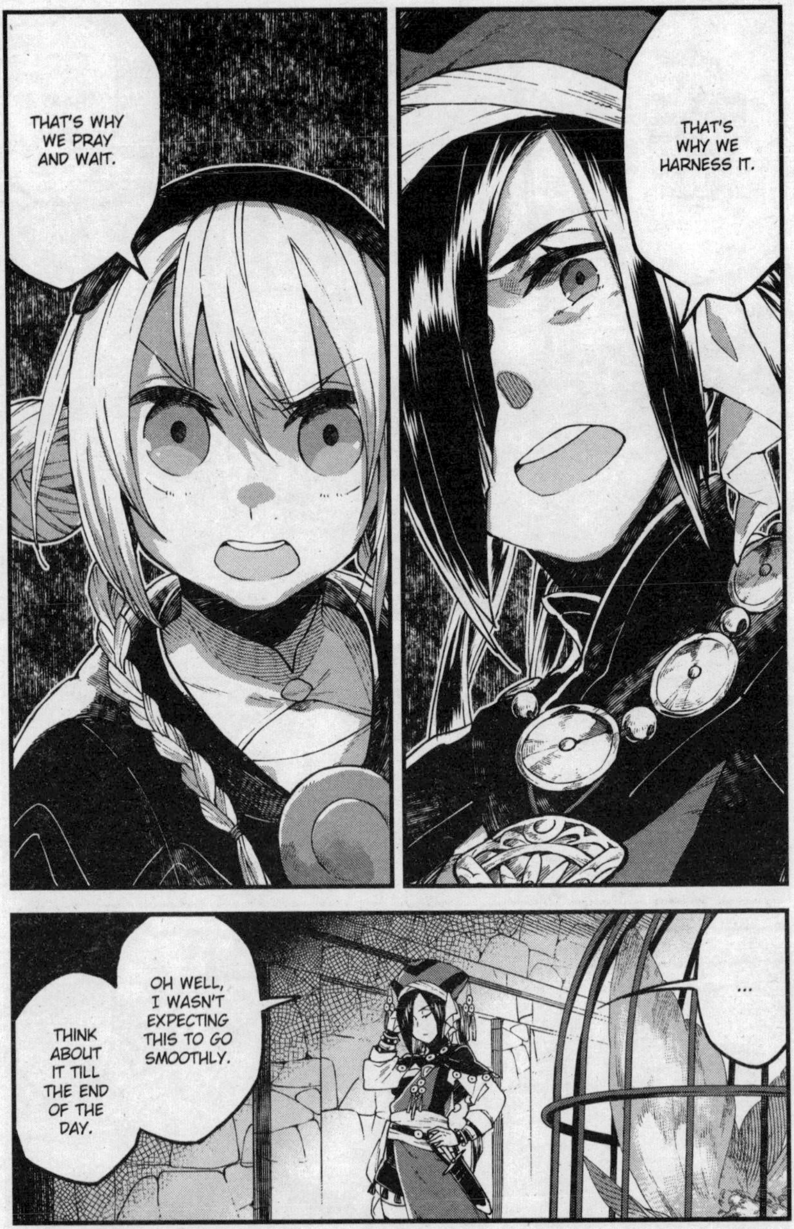
THAT'S WHY WE HARNESS IT.
THAT'S WHY WE PRAY AND WAIT.
...
OH WELL, I WASN'T EXPECTING THIS TO GO SMOOTHLY.
THINK ABOUT IT TILL THE END OF THE DAY.

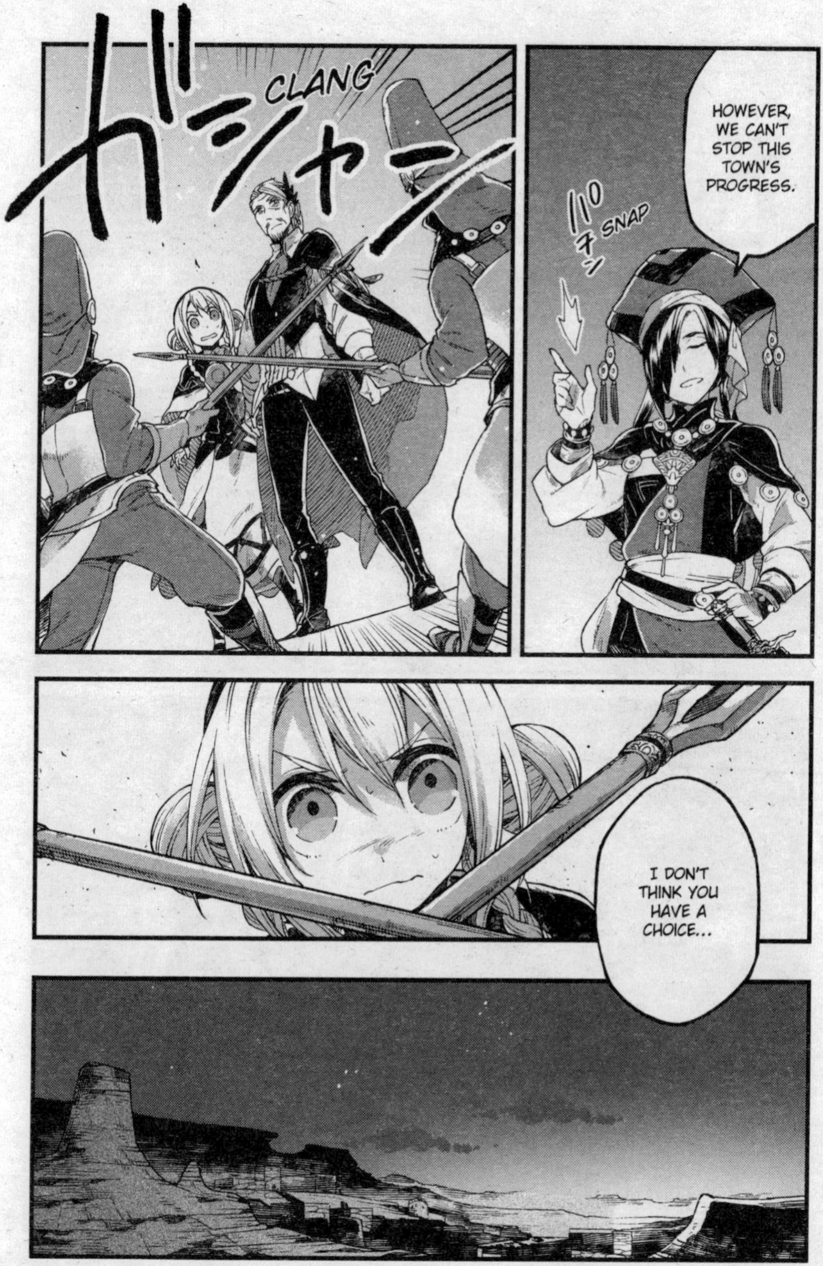
HOWEVER, WE CAN'T STOP THIS TOWN'S PROGRESS.
パチン
SNAP
ガシャーン
CLANG
I DON'T THINK YOU HAVE A CHOICE...

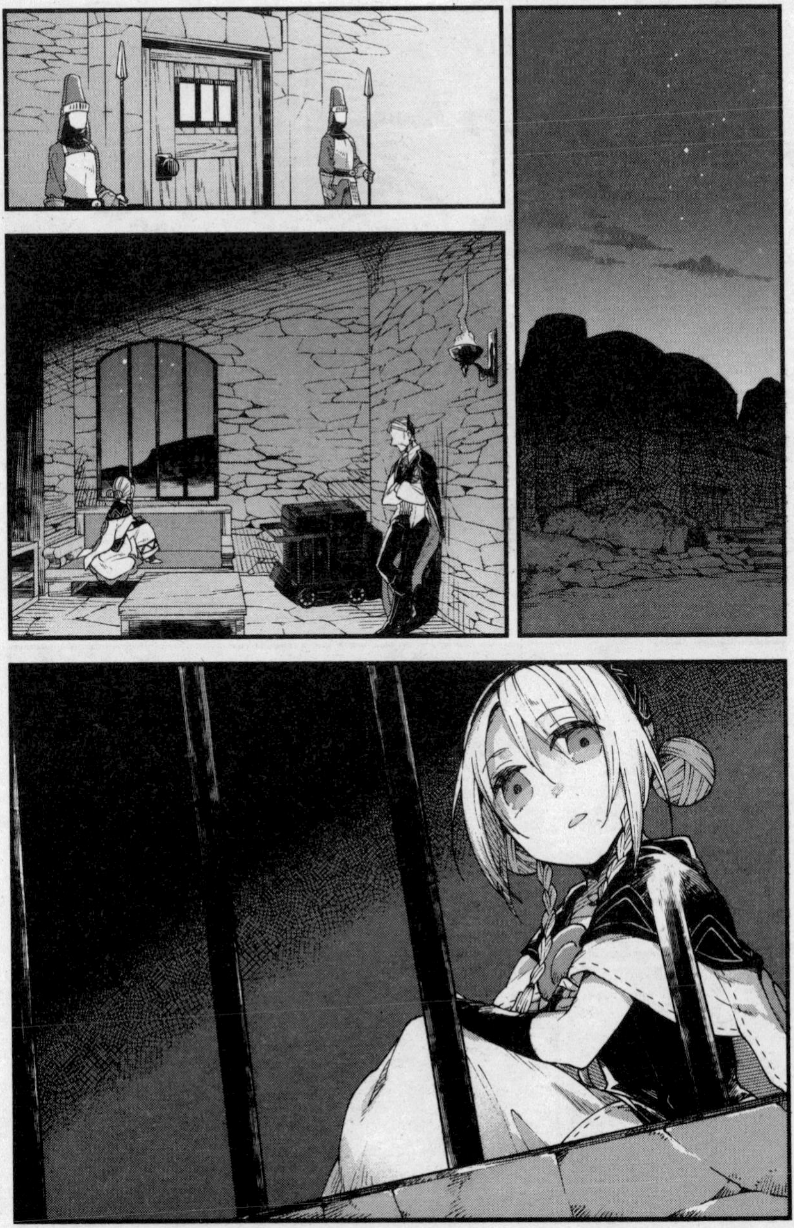

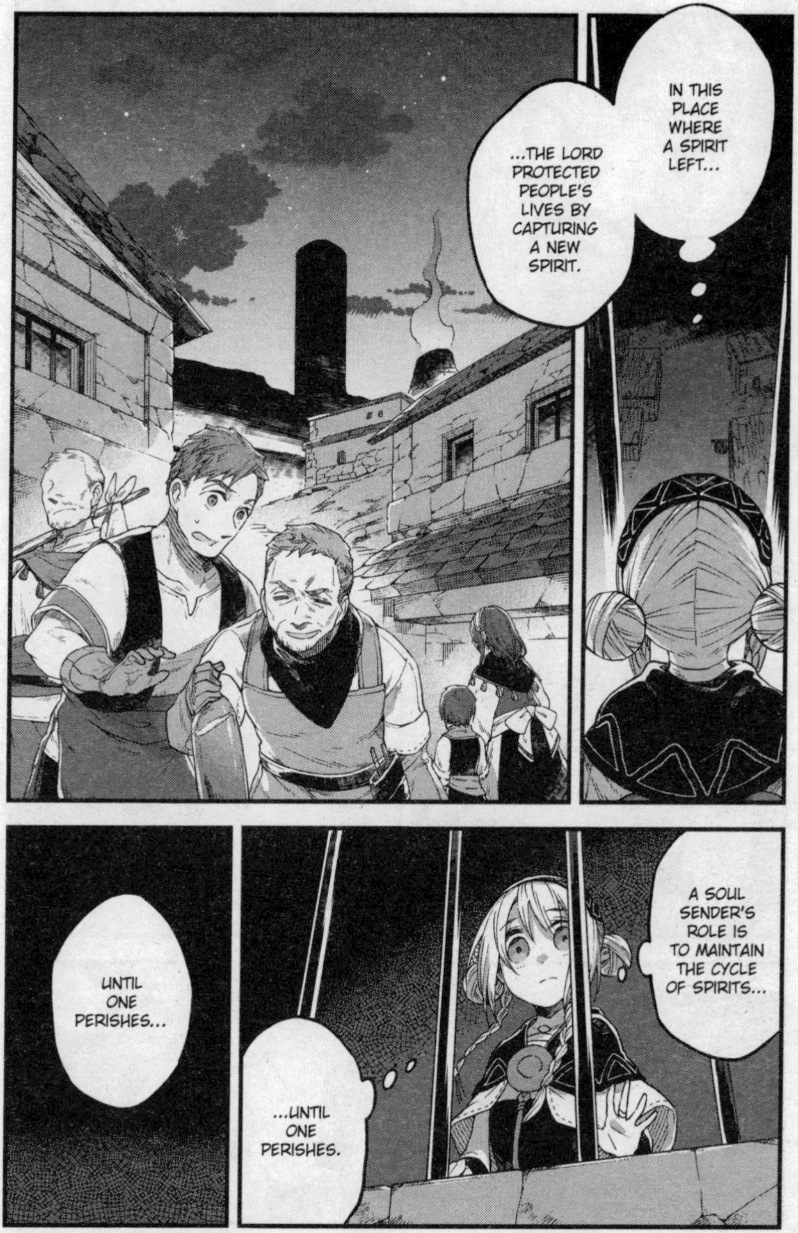
IN THIS PLACE WHERE A SPIRIT LEFT...
...THE LORD PROTECTED PEOPLE'S LIVES BY CAPTURING A NEW SPIRIT.
A SOUL SENDER'S ROLE IS TO MAINTAIN THE CYCLE OF SPIRITS...
...UNTIL ONE PERISHES.
UNTIL ONE PERISHES...

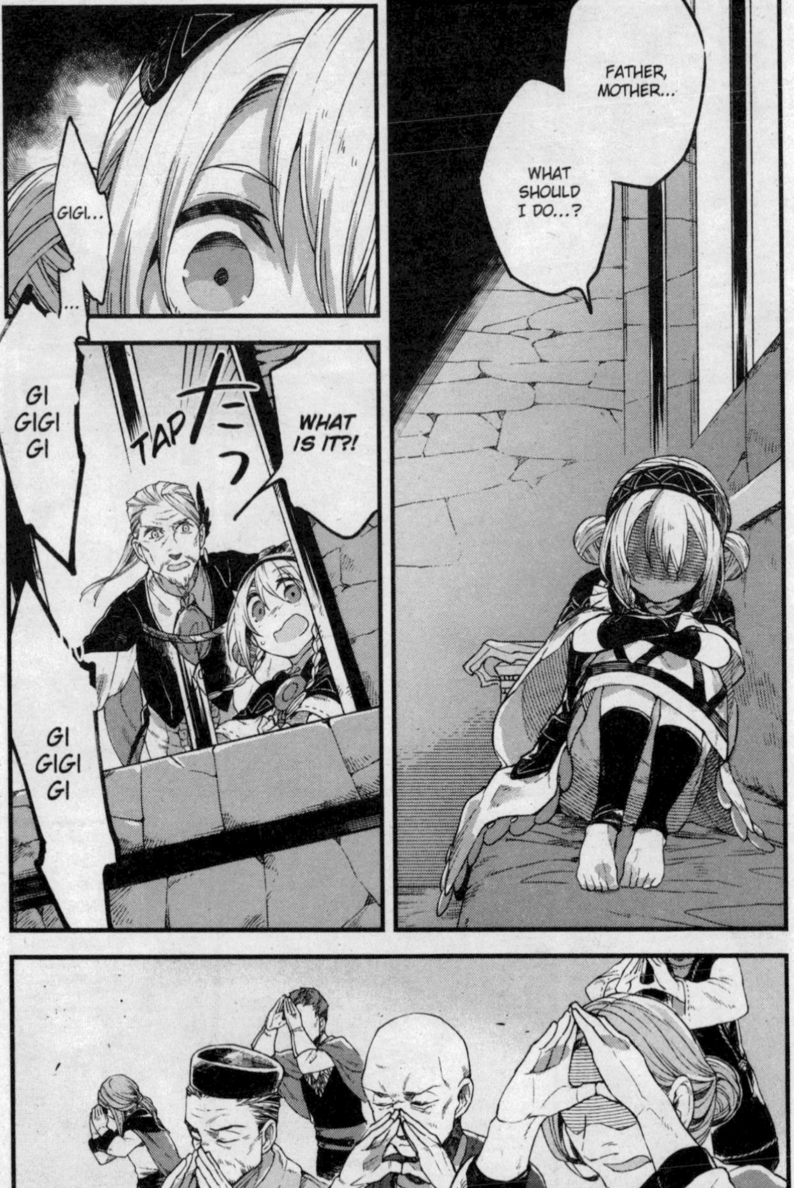
FATHER, MOTHER...
WHAT SHOULD I DO...?
GIGI...
...
TAP
WHAT IS IT?!
GI GIGI GI
GI GIGI GI

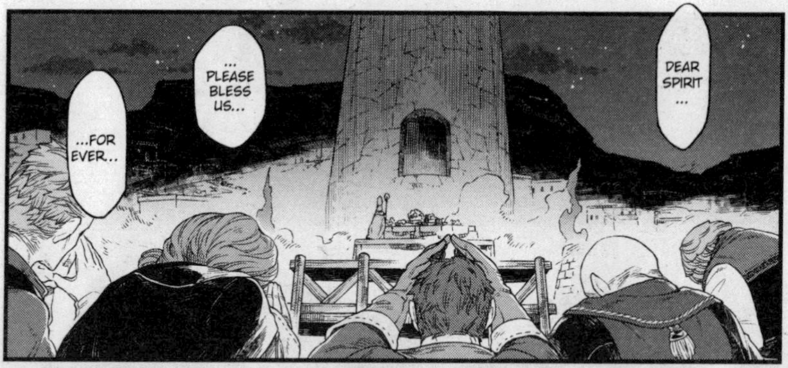
DEAR SPIRIT ...
... PLEASE BLESS US...
...FOR EVER...

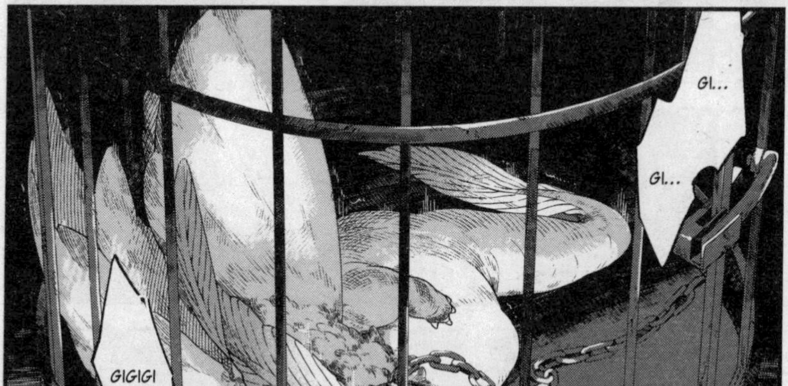
GI...
GI...
GIGIGI

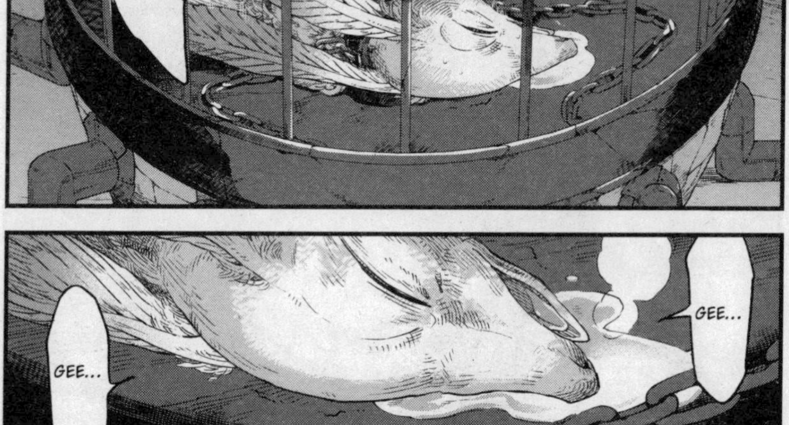
GEE...
GEE...

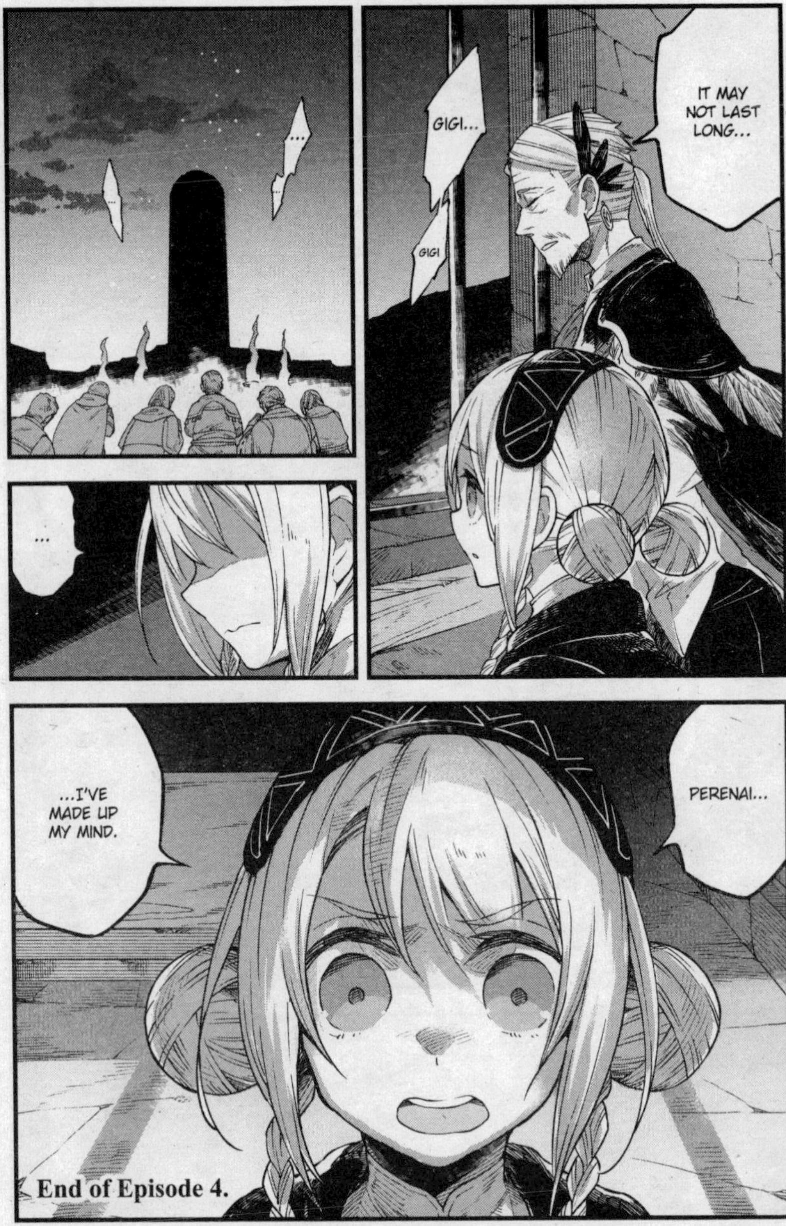
IT MAY NOT LAST LONG...
GIGI...
GIGI
...
...
...
PERENAI...
...I'VE MADE UP MY MIND.
End of Episode 4.

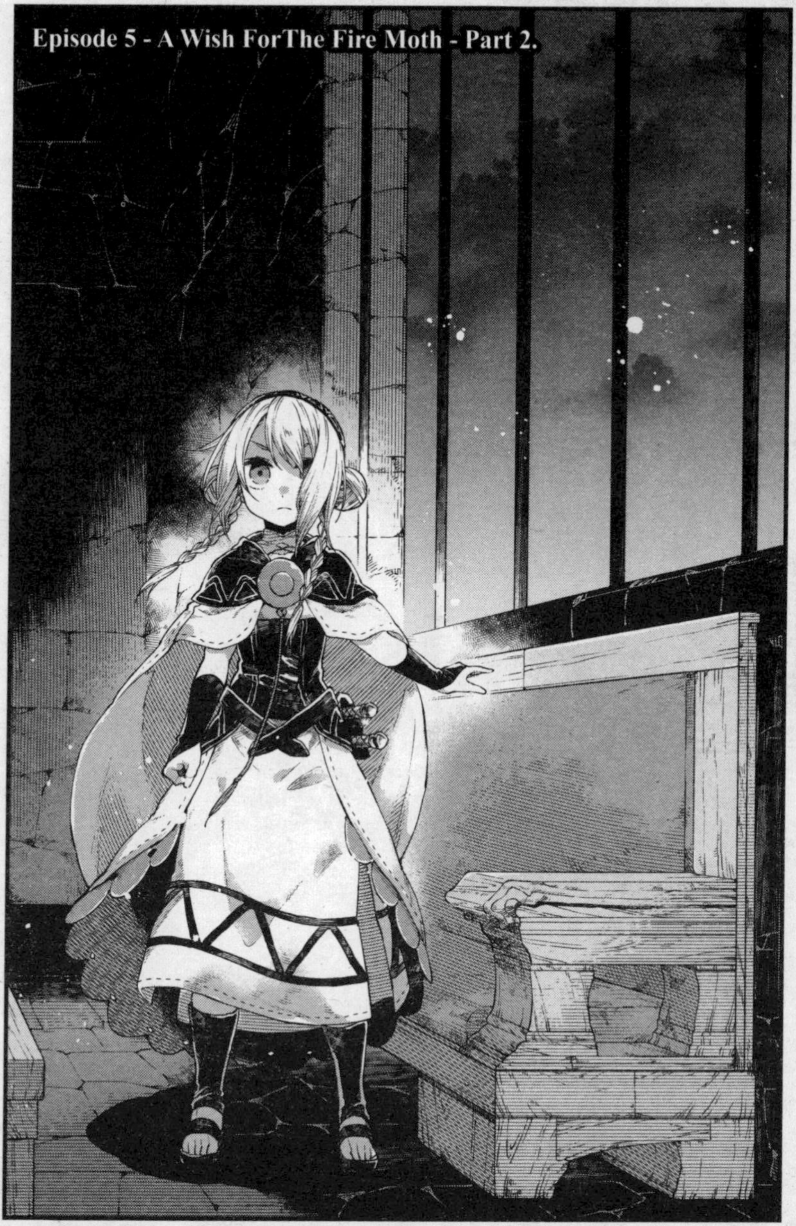
Episode 5 - A Wish ForThe Fire Moth - Part 2.

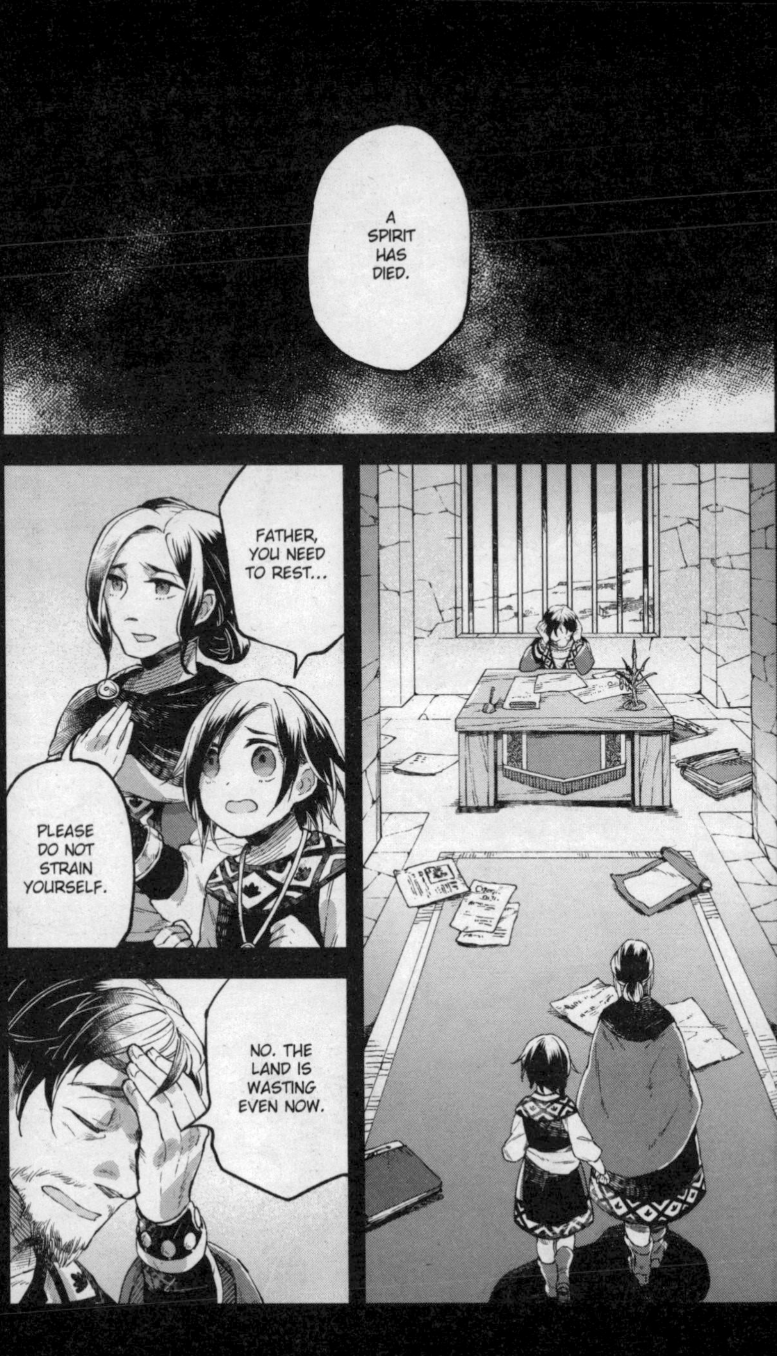
A SPIRIT HAS DIED.
FATHER, YOU NEED TO REST...
PLEASE DO NOT STRAIN YOURSELF.
NO. THE LAND IS WASTING EVEN NOW.

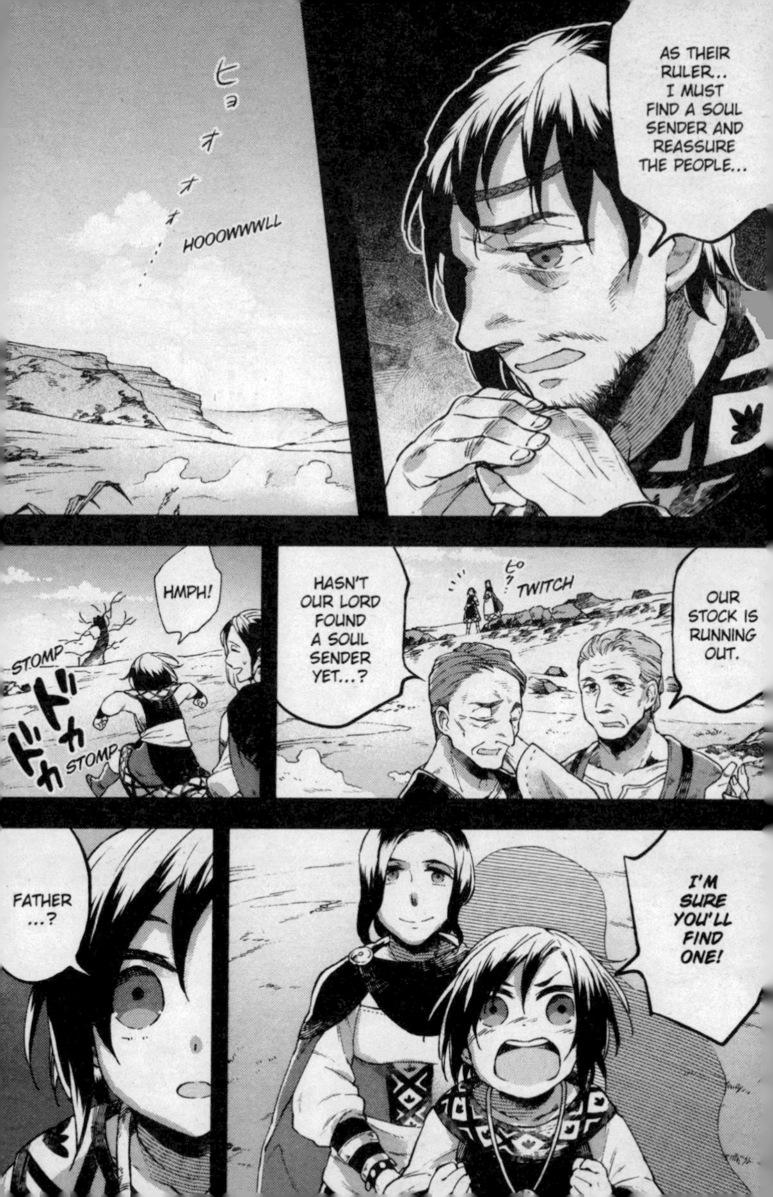
AS THEIR RULER... I MUST FIND A SOUL SENDER AND REASSURE THE PEOPLE...
ヒョオオオ…
HOOOWWWLL
OUR STOCK IS RUNNING OUT.
ピク
TWITCH
HASN'T OUR LORD FOUND A SOUL SENDER YET...?
HMPH!
ドカ
STOMP
ドカ
STOMP
I'M SURE YOU'LL FIND ONE!
FATHER ...?

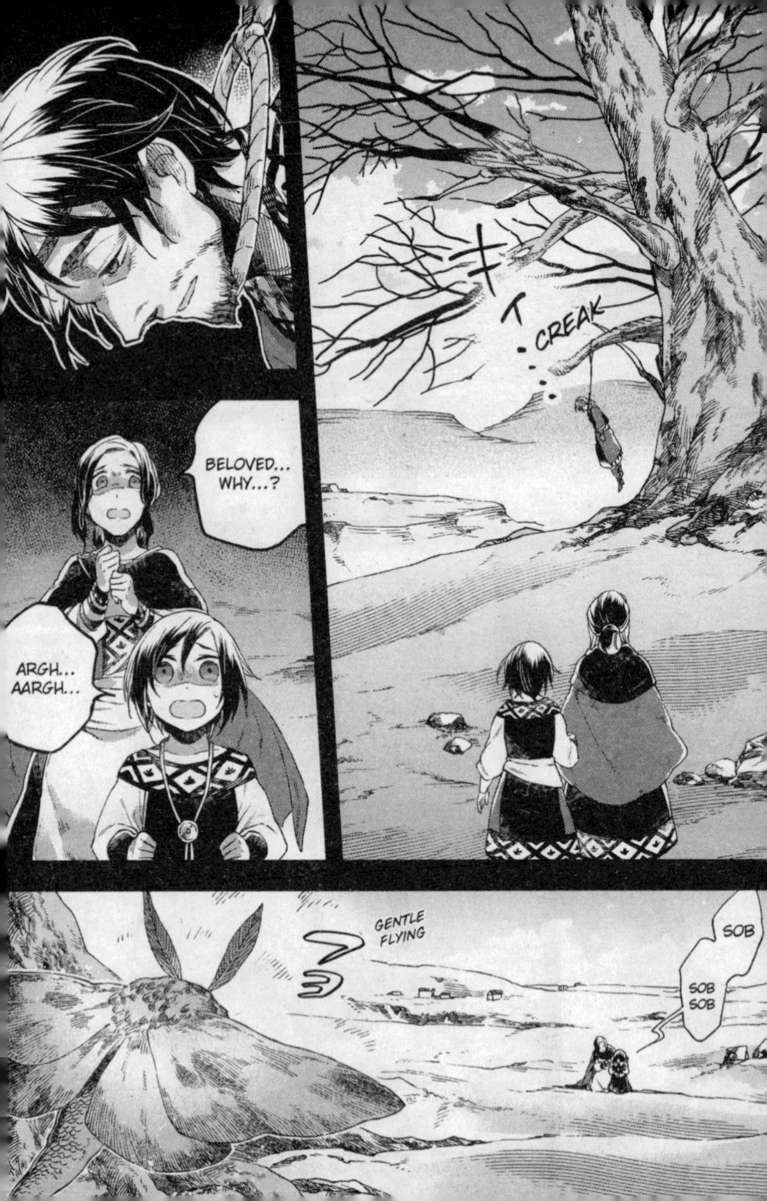
CREAK
BELOVED... WHY...?
ARGH... AARGH...
SOB
SOB SOB
GENTLE FLYING

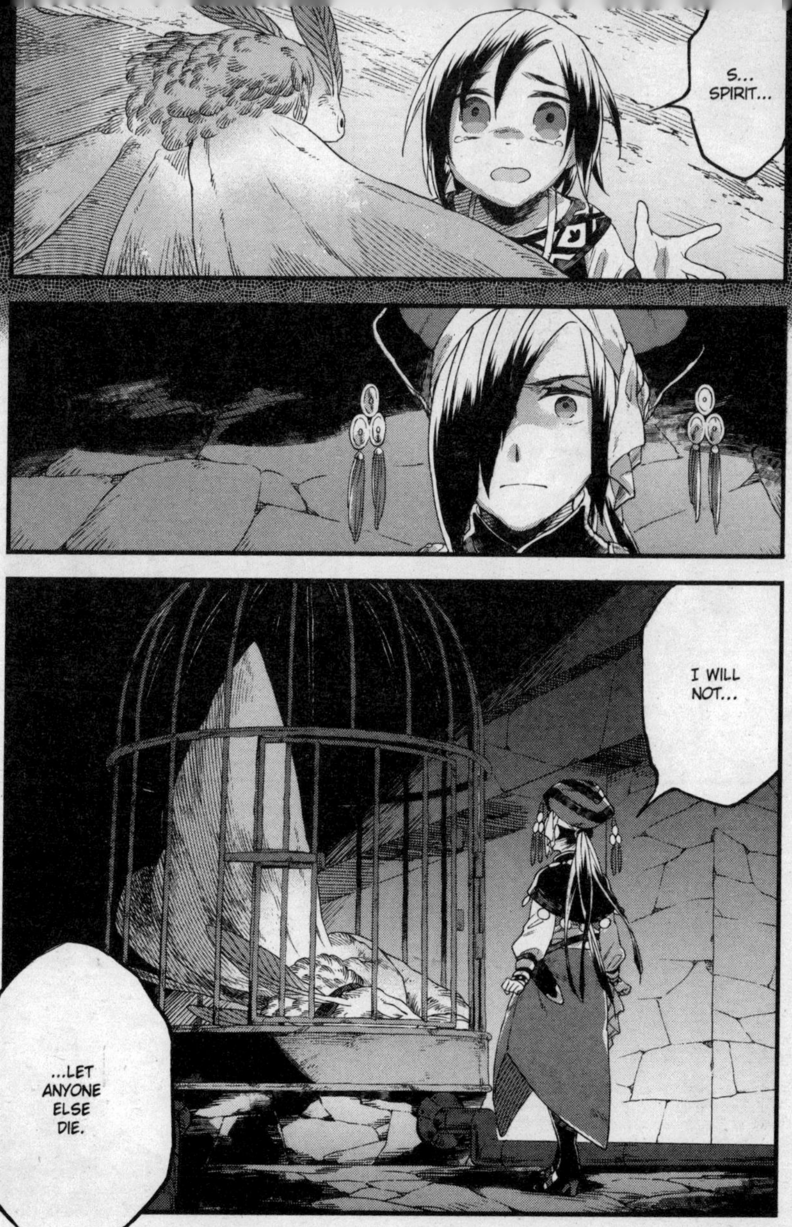
S... SPIRIT...
I WILL NOT...
...LET ANYONE ELSE DIE.

SOUL SENDER.

CLIP

SO, YOU'RE DOING IT.

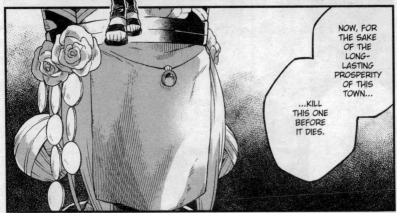

NOW, FOR THE SAKE OF THE LONG-LASTING PROSPERITY OF THIS TOWN...

...KILL THIS ONE BEFORE IT DIES.

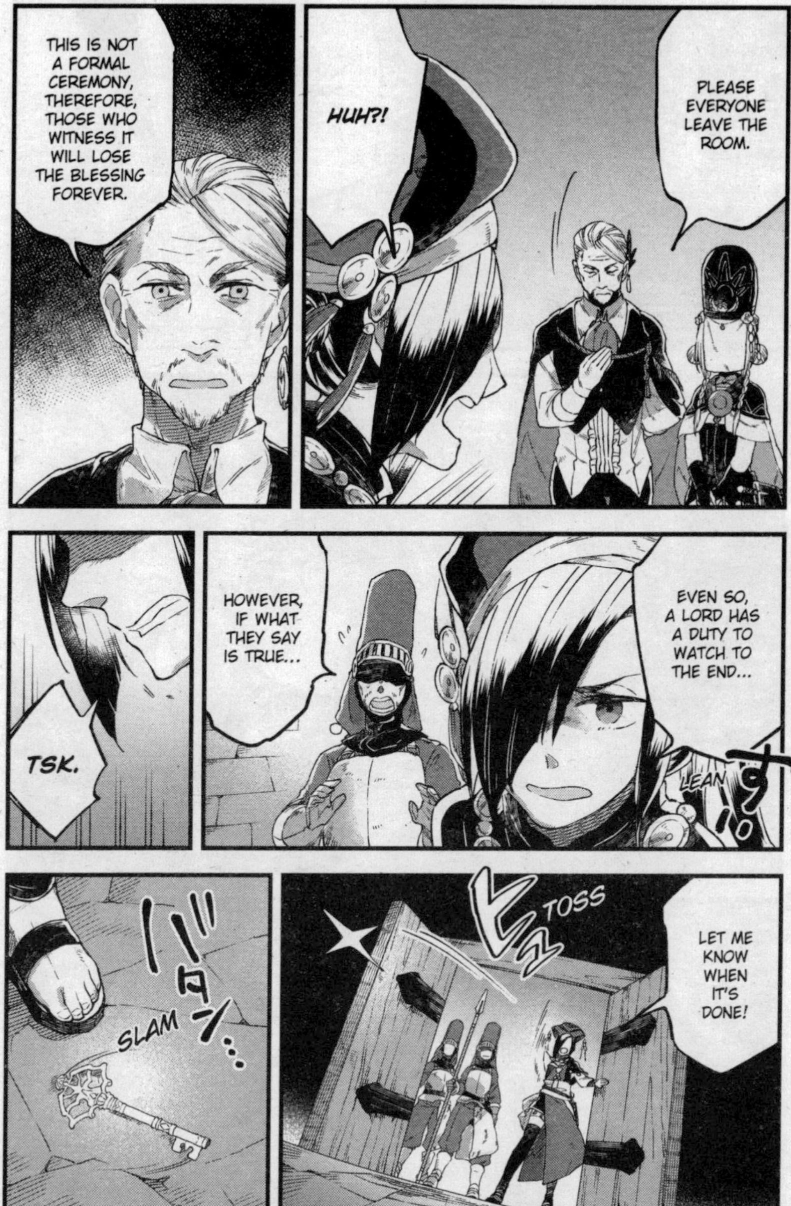
PLEASE EVERYONE LEAVE THE ROOM.
HUH?!
THIS IS NOT A FORMAL CEREMONY, THEREFORE, THOSE WHO WITNESS IT WILL LOSE THE BLESSING FOREVER.
EVEN SO, A LORD HAS A DUTY TO WATCH TO THE END...
LEAN
HOWEVER, IF WHAT THEY SAY IS TRUE...
TSK.
TOSS
LET ME KNOW WHEN IT'S DONE!
SLAM

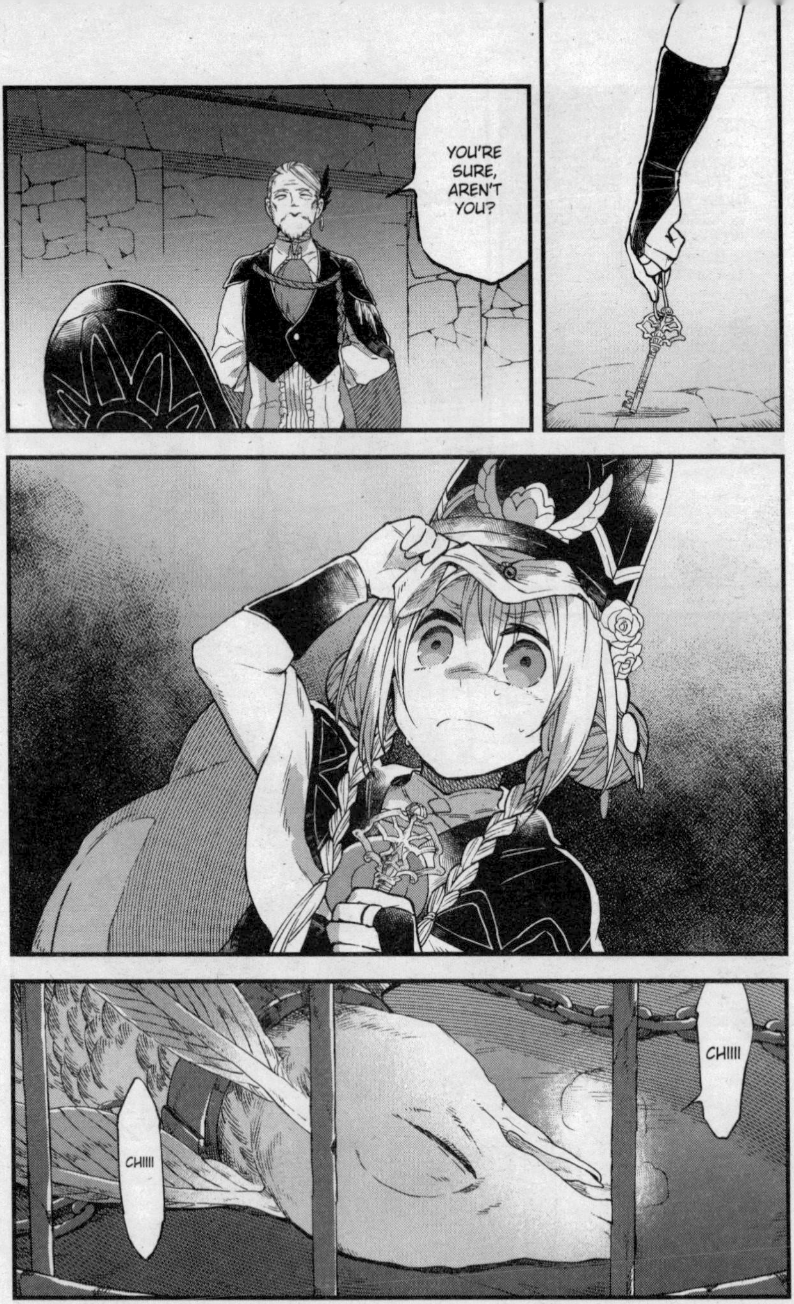
YOU'RE SURE, AREN'T YOU?
CHIIII
CHIIII

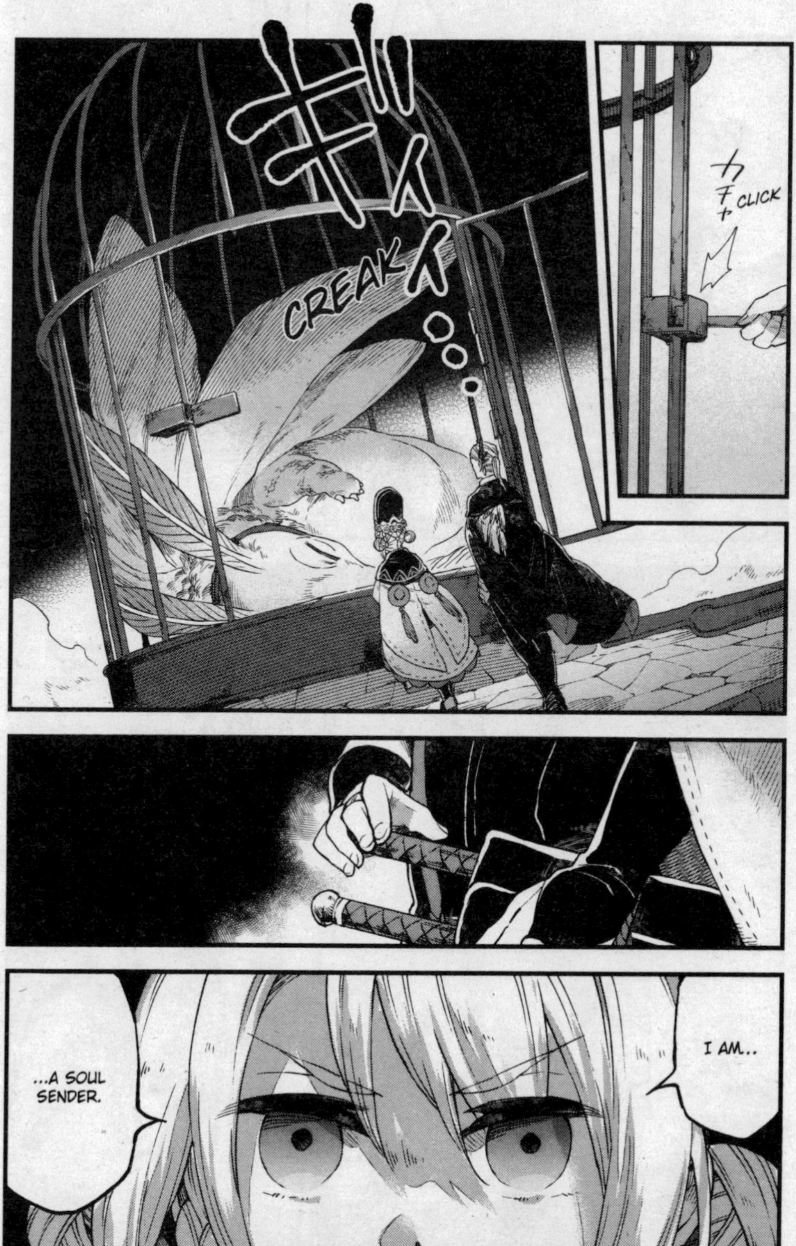

カチャ CLICK
ギイイ
CREAK
...
I AM...
...A SOUL SENDER.

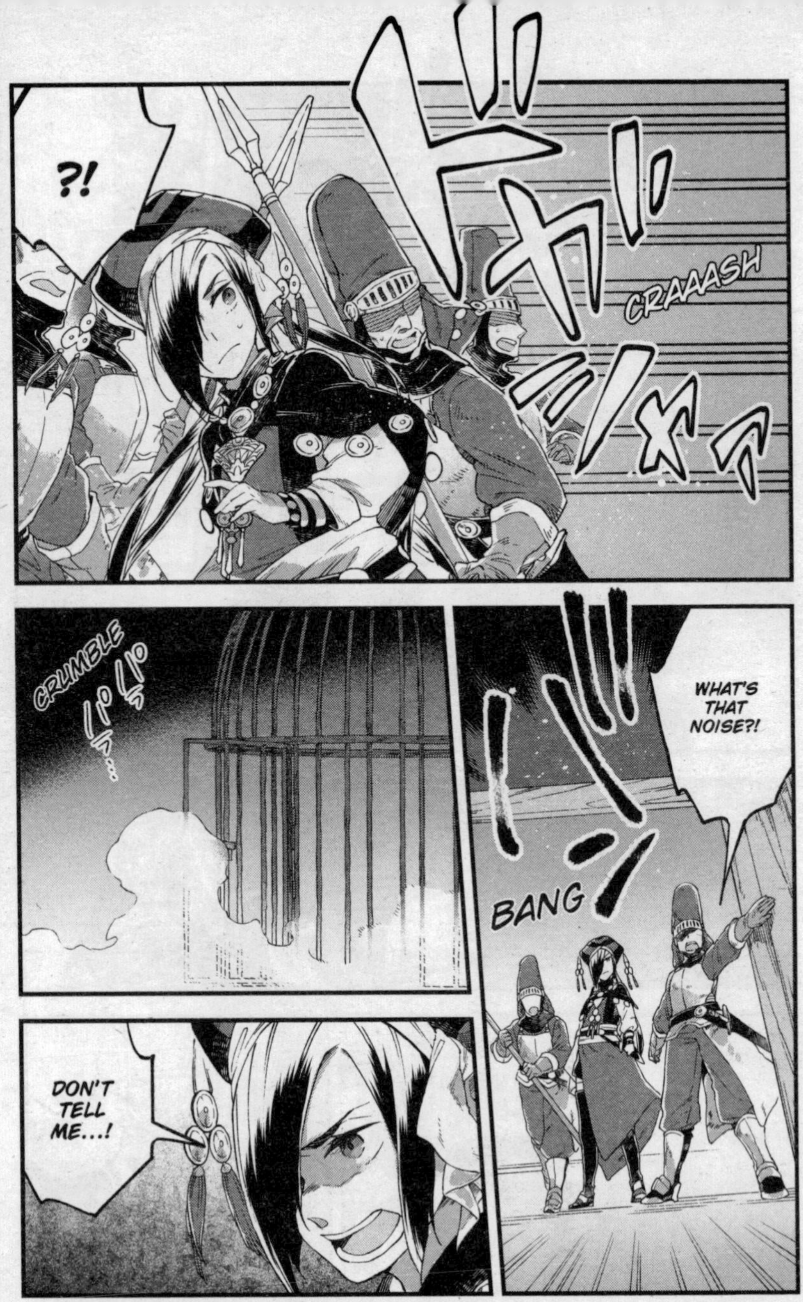
?!
CRAAASH
WHAT'S THAT NOISE?!
BANG
CRUMBLE
DON'T TELL ME...!

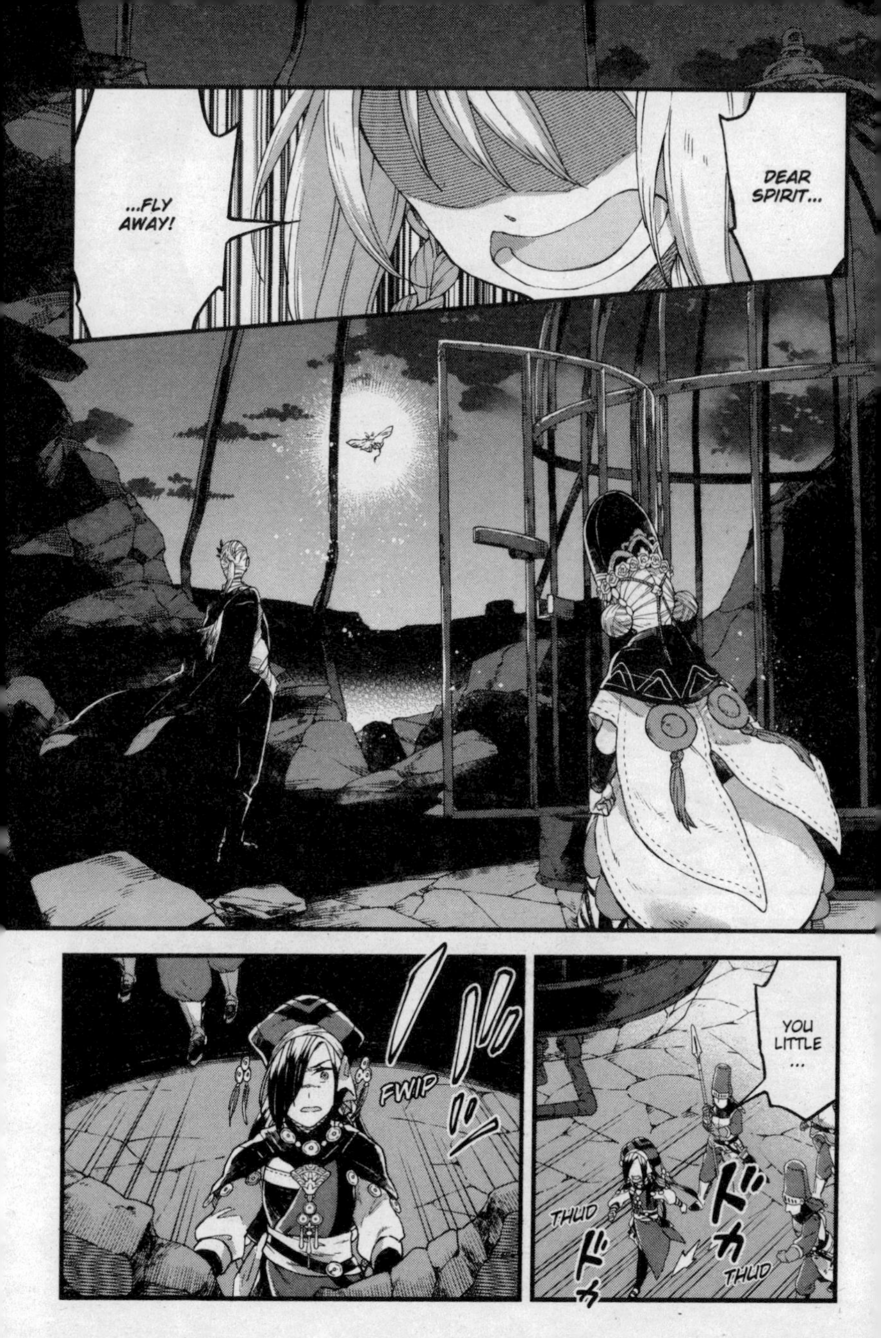
DEAR SPIRIT...
...FLY AWAY!
YOU LITTLE ...
THUD
ドカ
THUD
ドカ
FWIP

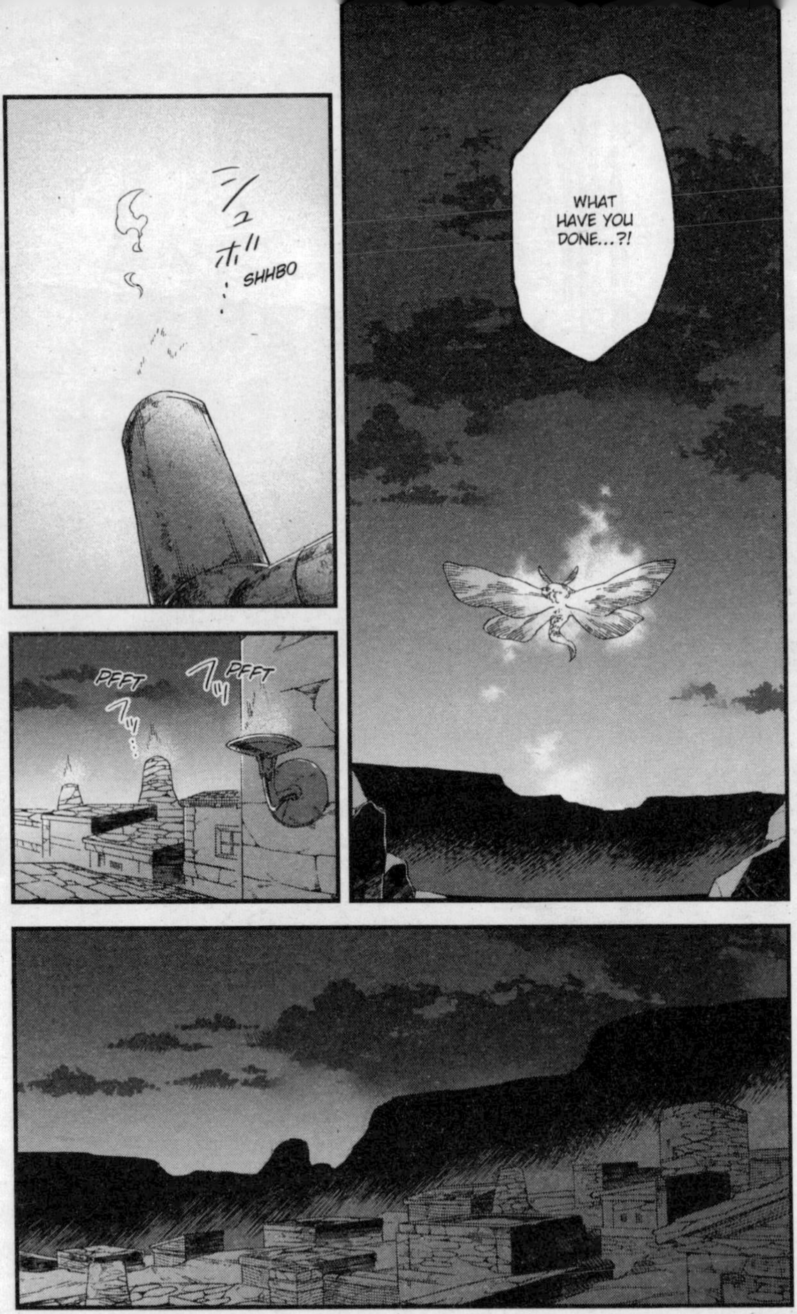
WHAT HAVE YOU DONE...?!
シュボ…
SHHBO
ヘッ
PFFT
ヘッ…
PFFT

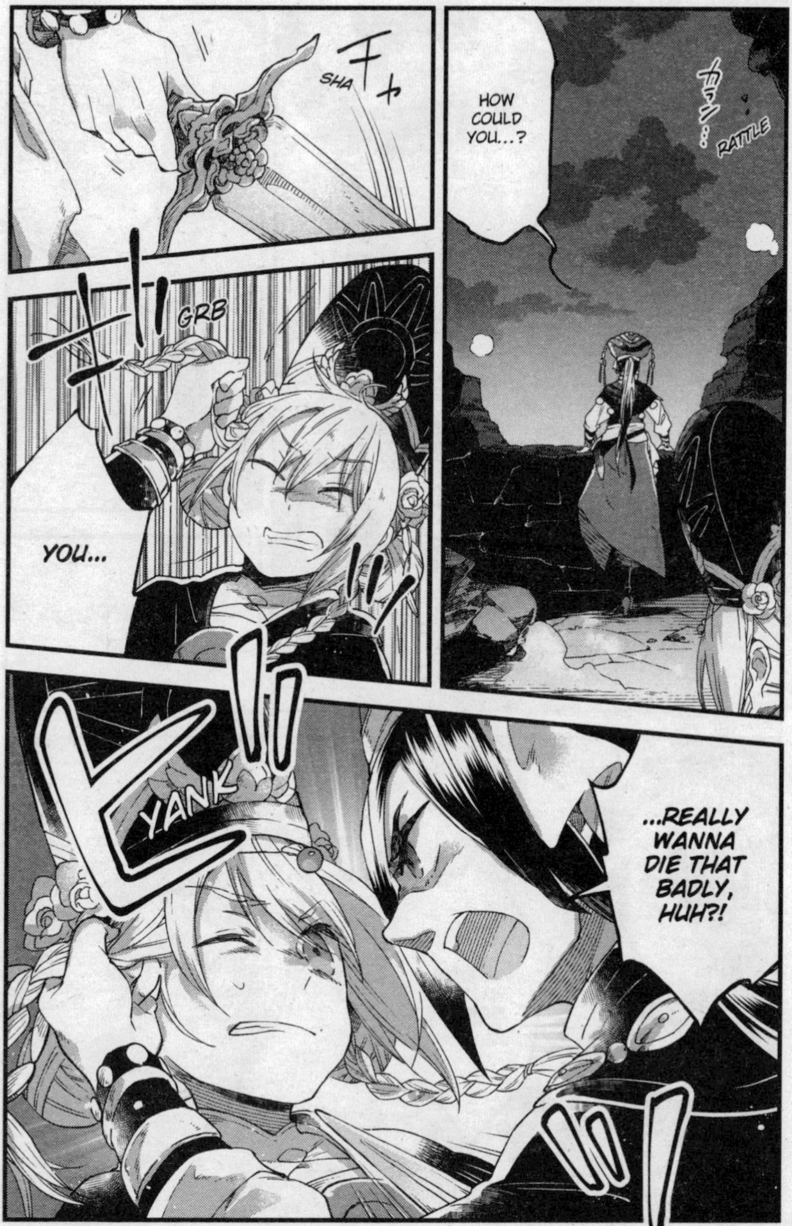
HOW COULD YOU...?
RATTLE
SHA
GRB
YOU...
YANK
...REALLY WANNA DIE THAT BADLY, HUH?!

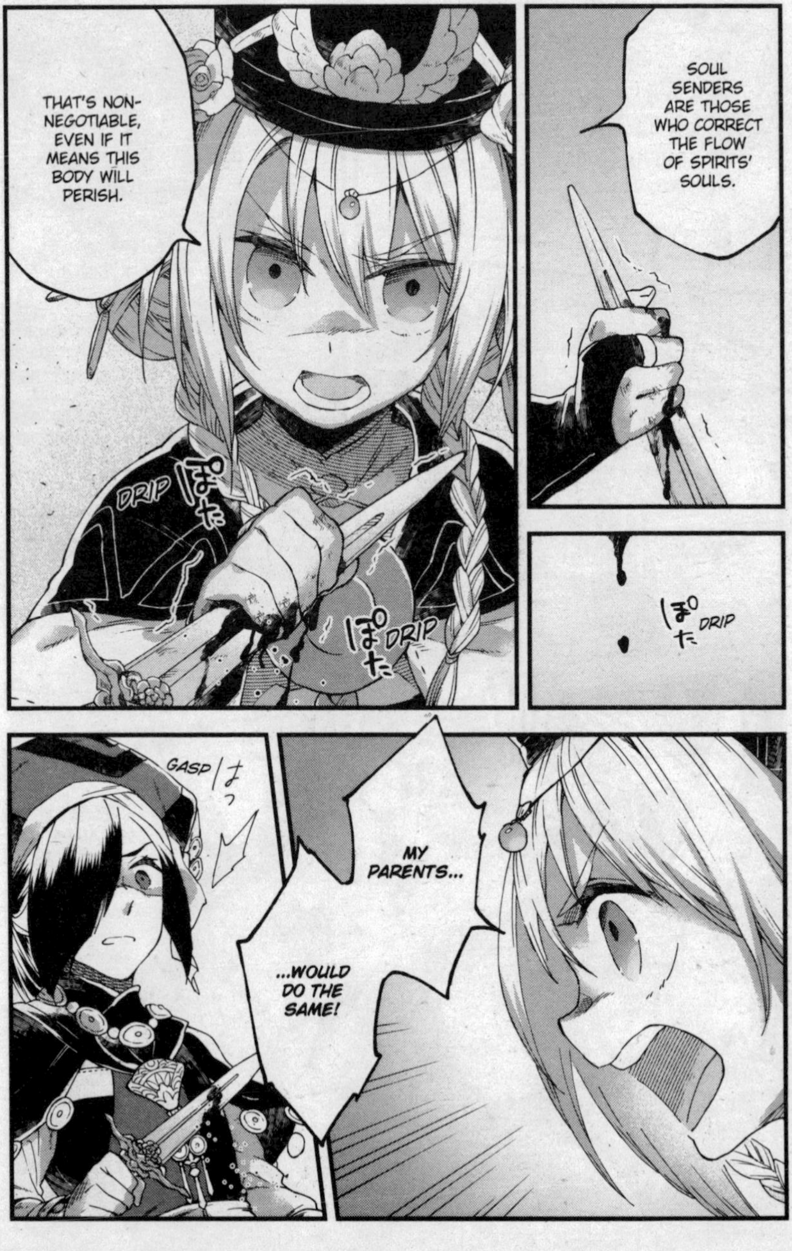
SOUL SENDERS ARE THOSE WHO CORRECT THE FLOW OF SPIRITS' SOULS.
ぽた DRIP
THAT'S NON-NEGOTIABLE, EVEN IF IT MEANS THIS BODY WILL PERISH.
ぽた DRIP
ぽた DRIP
MY PARENTS...
...WOULD DO THE SAME!
GASP はっ

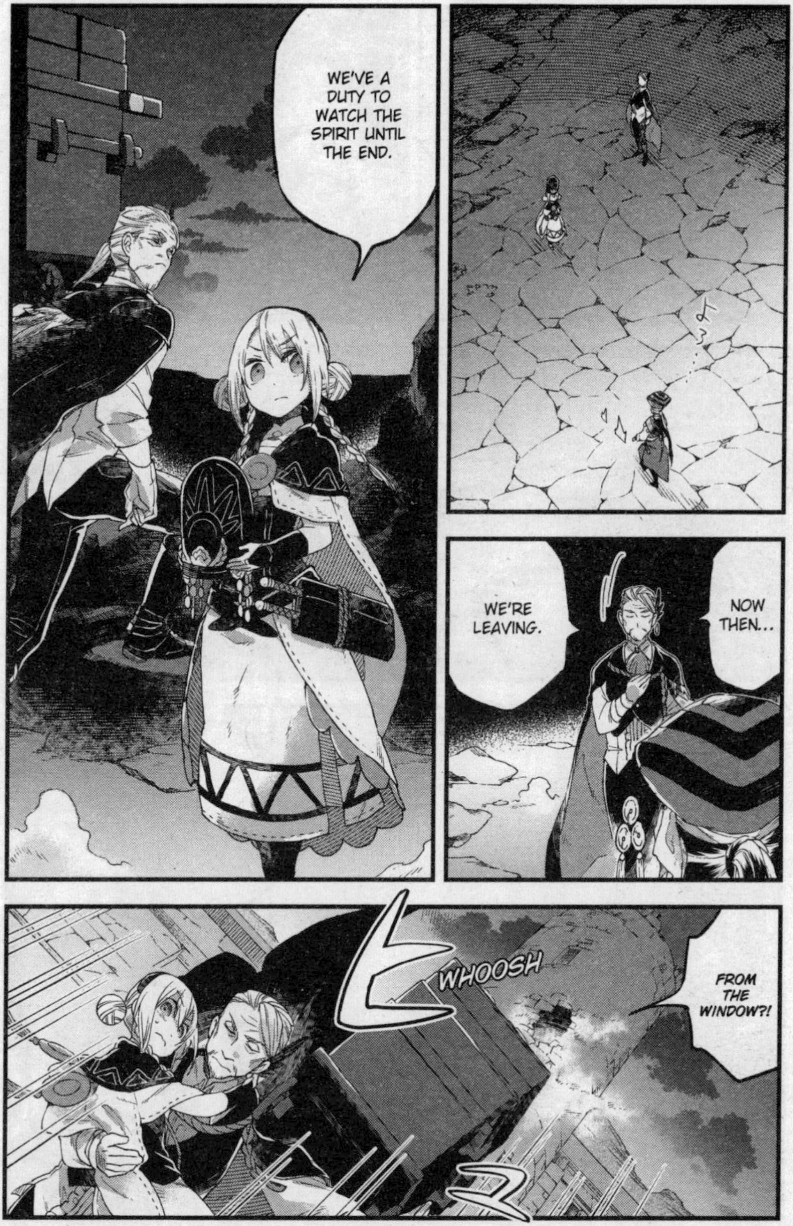
NOW THEN...
WE'RE LEAVING.
WE'VE A DUTY TO WATCH THE SPIRIT UNTIL THE END.
FROM THE WINDOW?!
WHOOSH

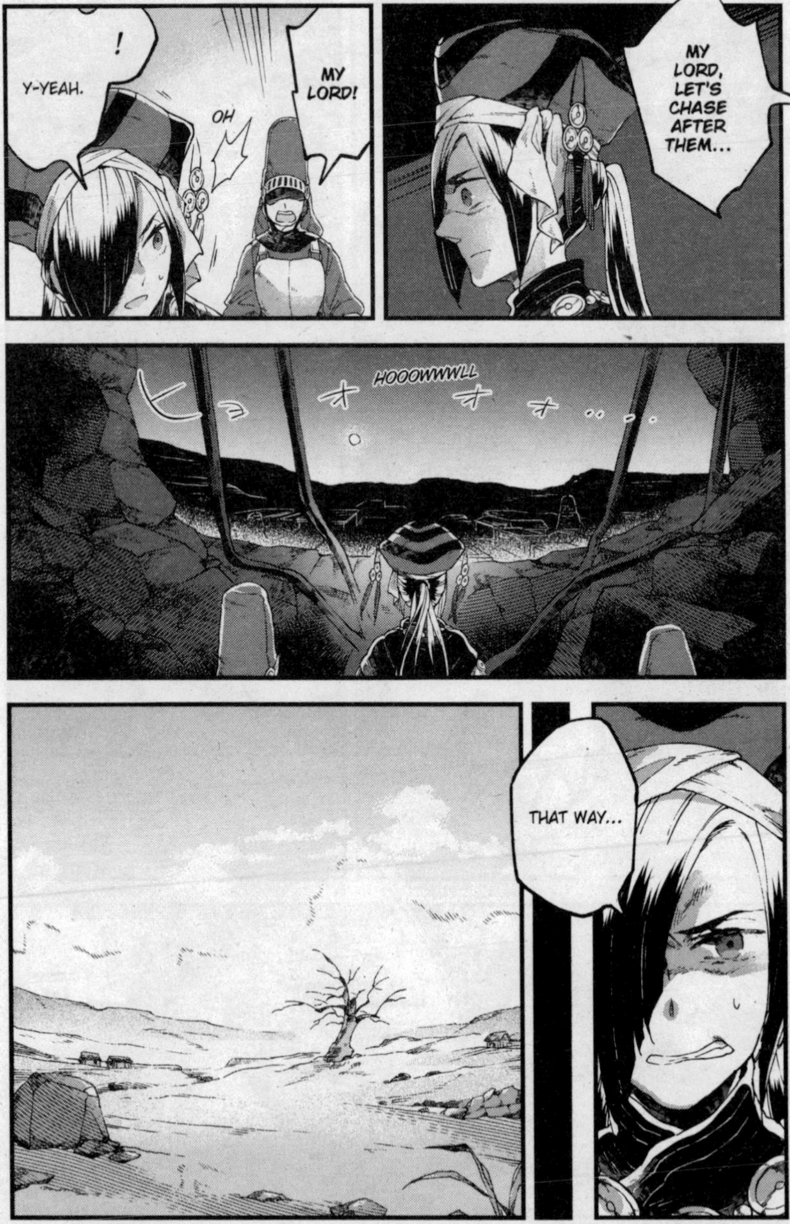
MY LORD, LET'S CHASE AFTER THEM...
MY LORD!
!
Y-YEAH.
OH
HOOOWWWLL
THAT WAY...

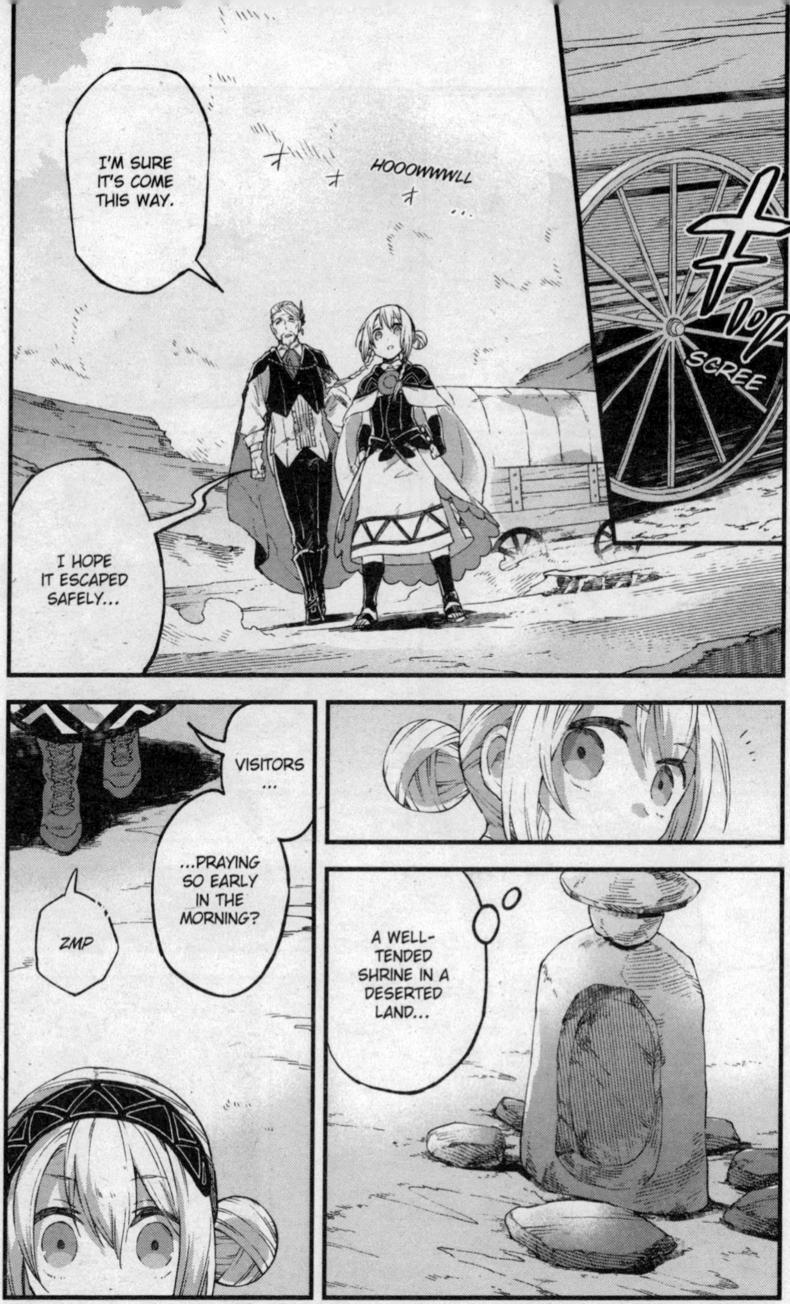
SCREE
HOOOWWWLL
I'M SURE IT'S COME THIS WAY.
I HOPE IT ESCAPED SAFELY...
A WELL-TENDED SHRINE IN A DESERTED LAND...
VISITORS...
...PRAYING SO EARLY IN THE MORNING?
ZMP

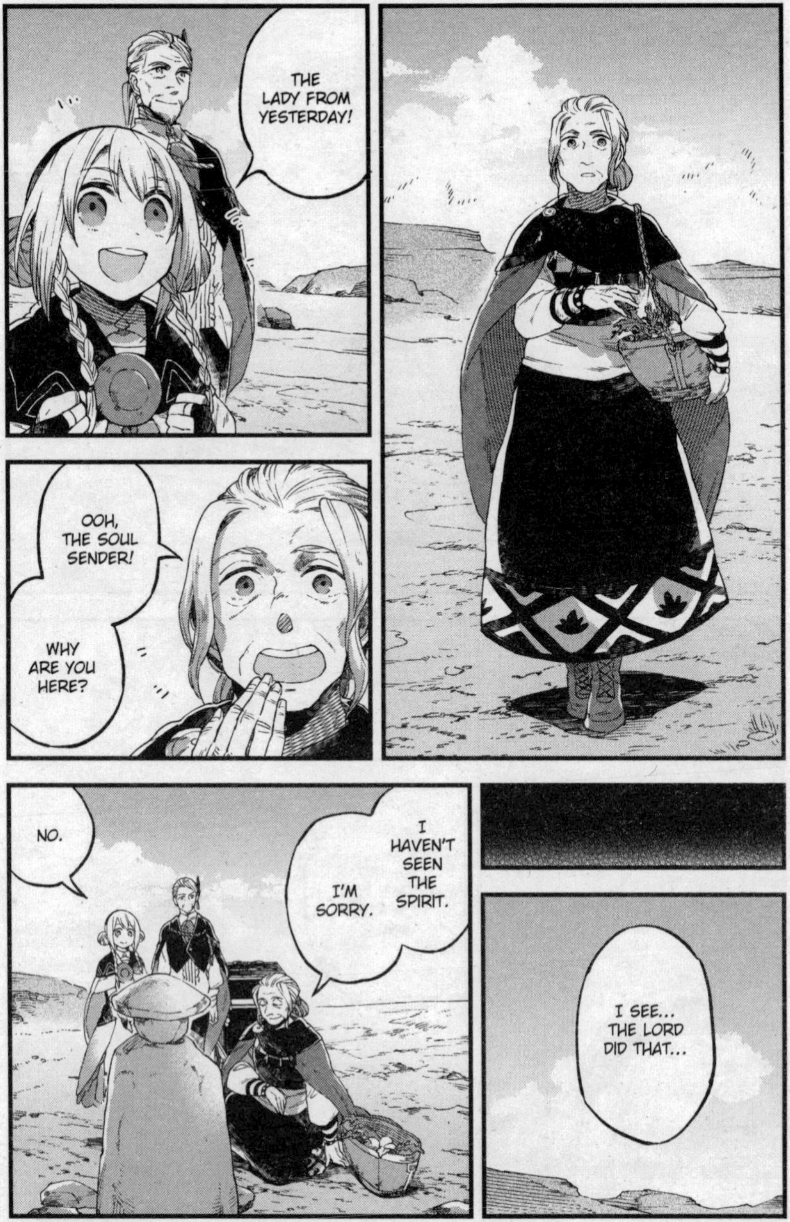
THE LADY FROM YESTERDAY!
OOH, THE SOUL SENDER!
WHY ARE YOU HERE?
I SEE... THE LORD DID THAT...
I HAVEN'T SEEN THE SPIRIT.
I'M SORRY.
NO.

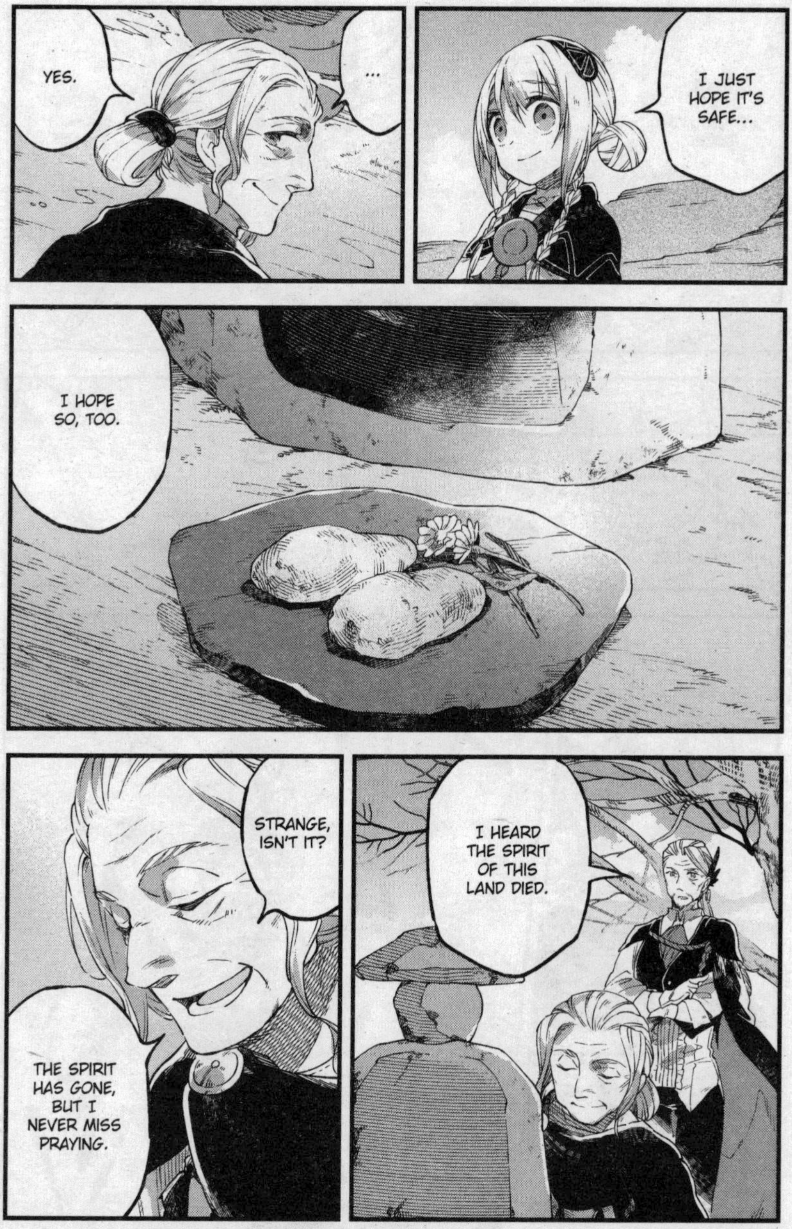
I JUST HOPE IT'S SAFE...
...
YES.
I HOPE SO, TOO.
I HEARD THE SPIRIT OF THIS LAND DIED.
STRANGE, ISN'T IT?
THE SPIRIT HAS GONE, BUT I NEVER MISS PRAYING.

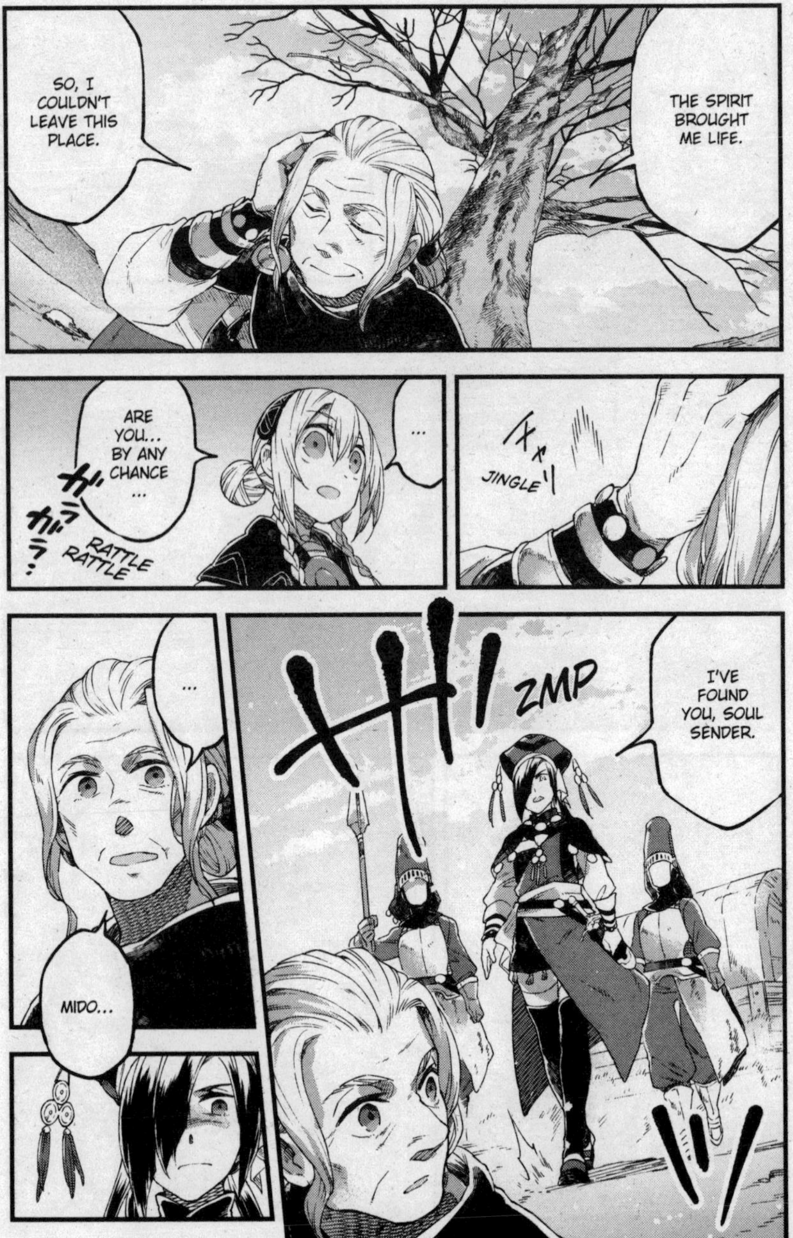
THE SPIRIT BROUGHT ME LIFE.
SO, I COULDN'T LEAVE THIS PLACE.
チャリ
JINGLE
...
ARE YOU... BY ANY CHANCE ...
ガラガラ
RATTLE RATTLE
ザッ
ZMP
I'VE FOUND YOU, SOUL SENDER.
...
MIDO...

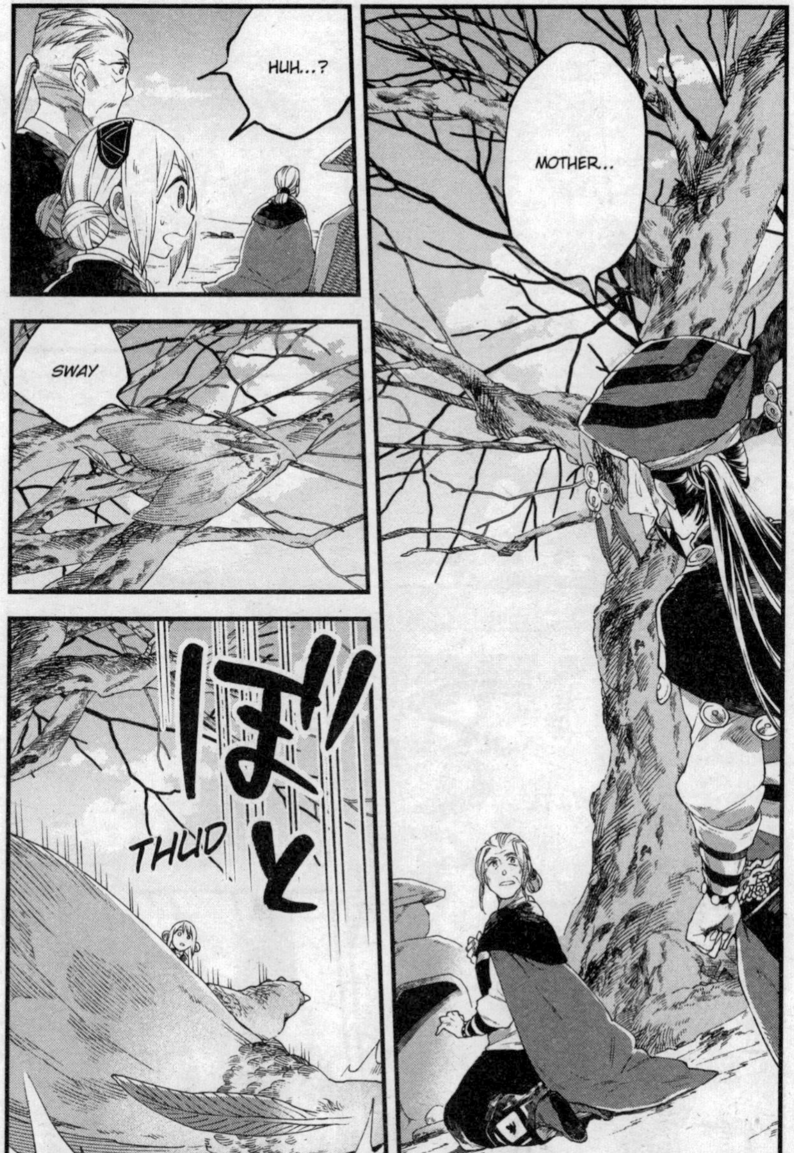
MOTHER..
HUH...?
SWAY
ぼと
THUD

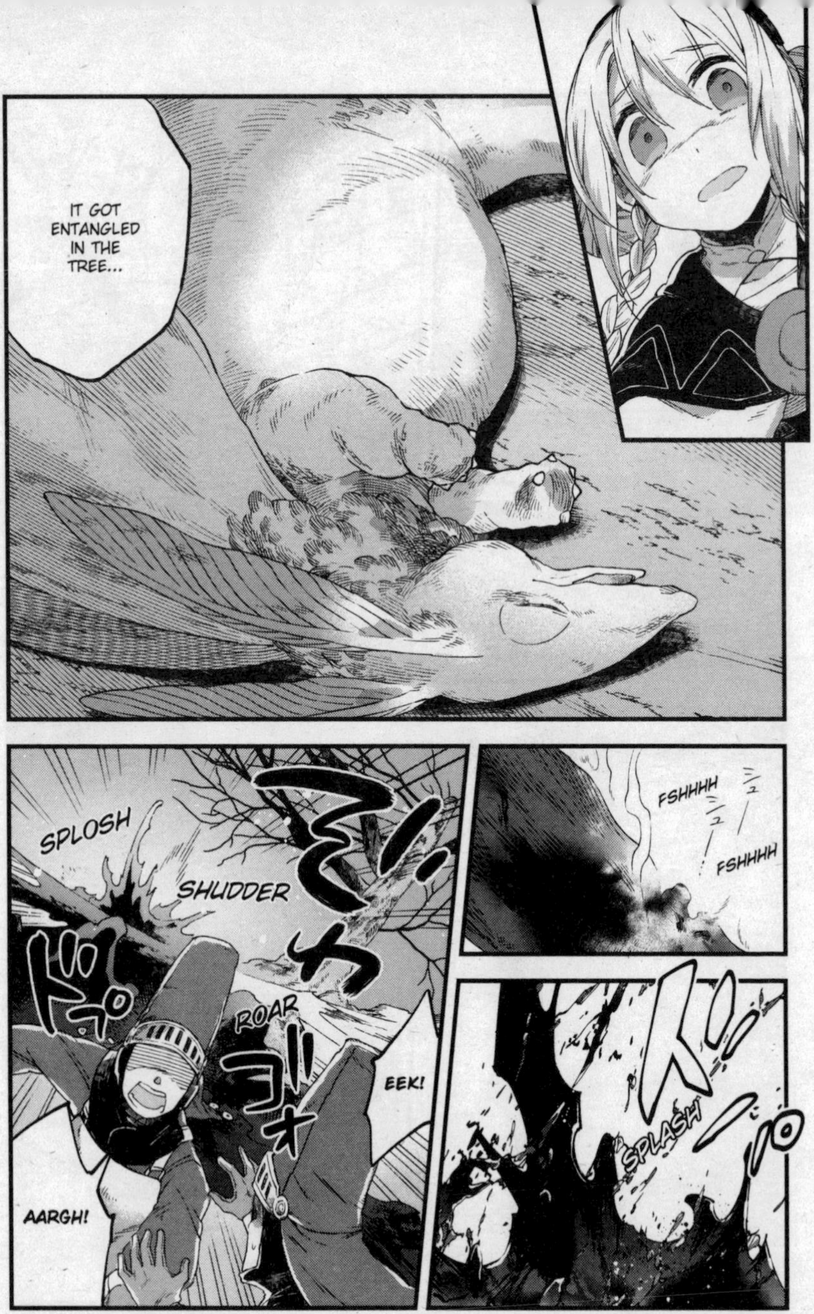
IT GOT ENTANGLED IN THE TREE...
FSHHHH
FSHHHH
SPLASH
SPLOSH
SHUDDER
ROAR
EEK!
AARGH!

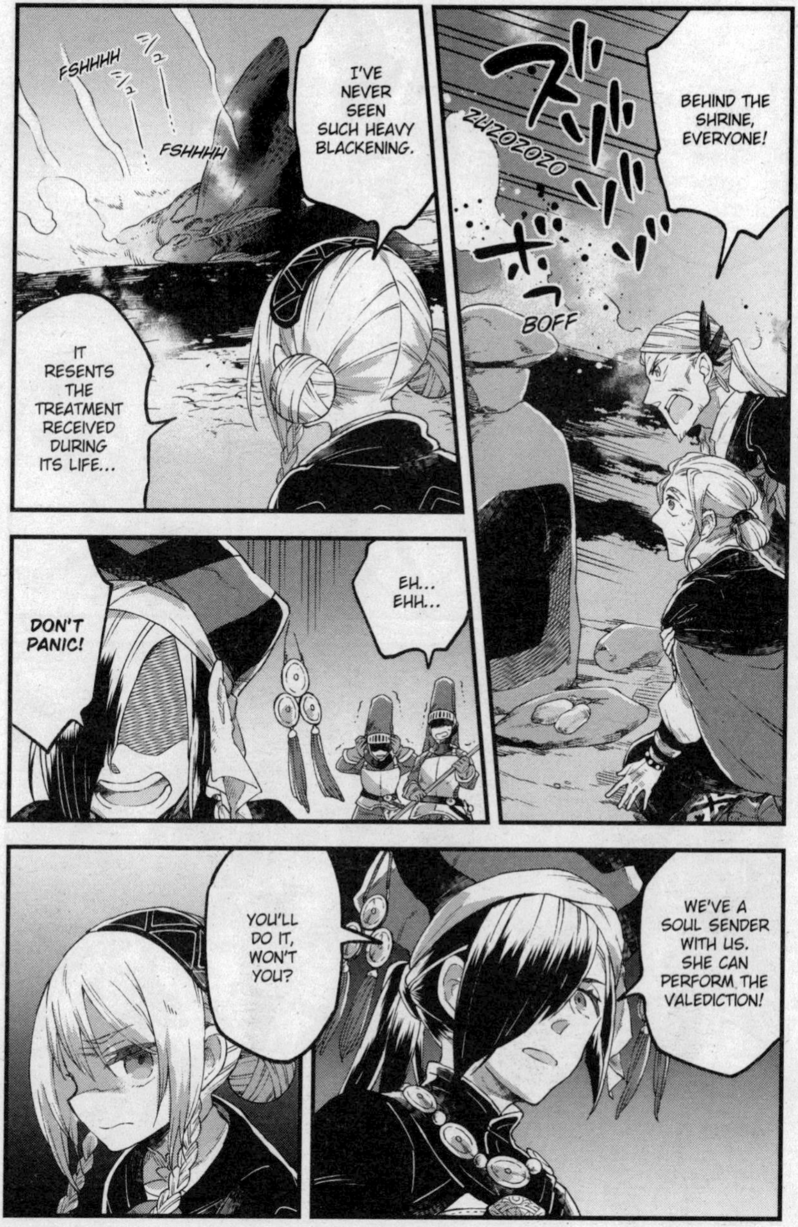
ZUZOZOZO
BEHIND THE SHRINE, EVERYONE!
BOFF
I'VE NEVER SEEN SUCH HEAVY BLACKENING.
FSHHHH
FSHHHH
IT RESENTS THE TREATMENT RECEIVED DURING ITS LIFE...
EH... EHH...
DON'T PANIC!
WE'VE A SOUL SENDER WITH US. SHE CAN PERFORM THE VALEDICTION!
YOU'LL DO IT, WON'T YOU?

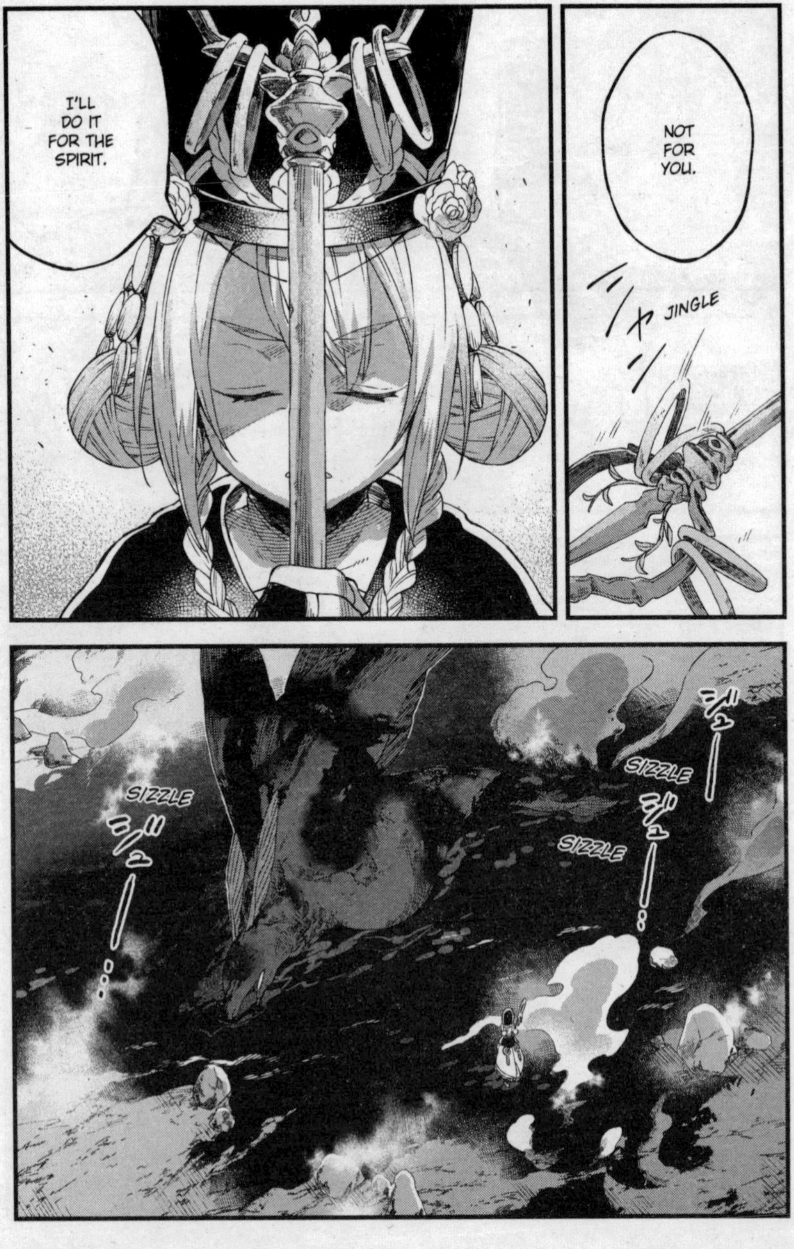
NOT FOR YOU.
JINGLE
I'LL DO IT FOR THE SPIRIT.
SIZZLE
SIZZLE
SIZZLE

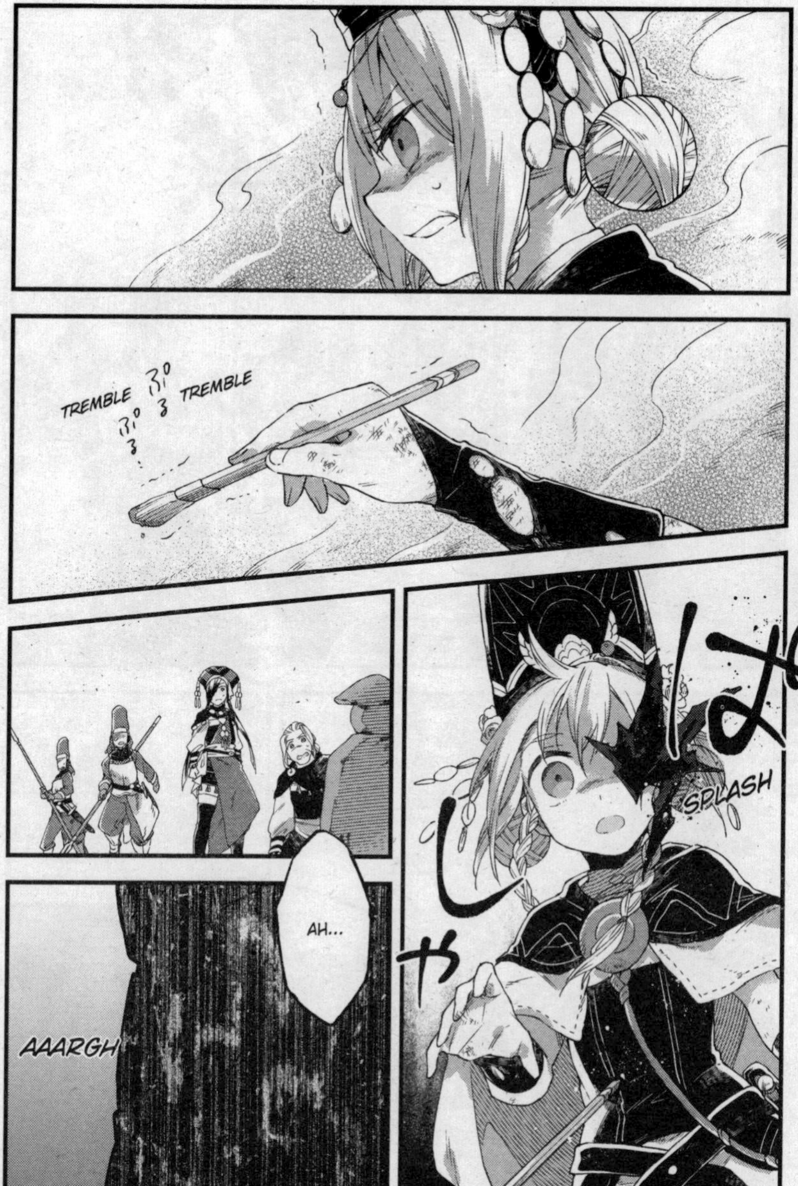
TREMBLE
ぷるぷる
TREMBLE
ばしゃ
SPLASH
AH...
AAARGH

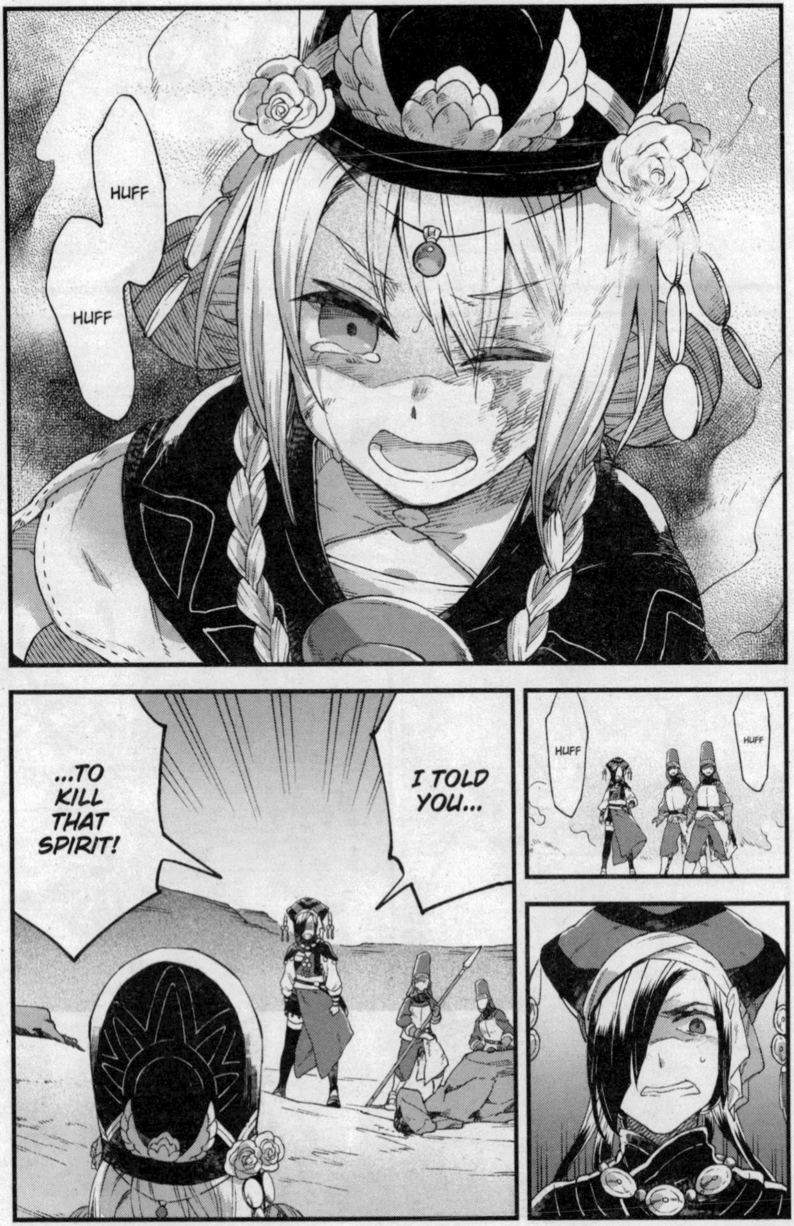
HUFF
HUFF
HUFF
HUFF
I TOLD YOU...
...TO KILL THAT SPIRIT!

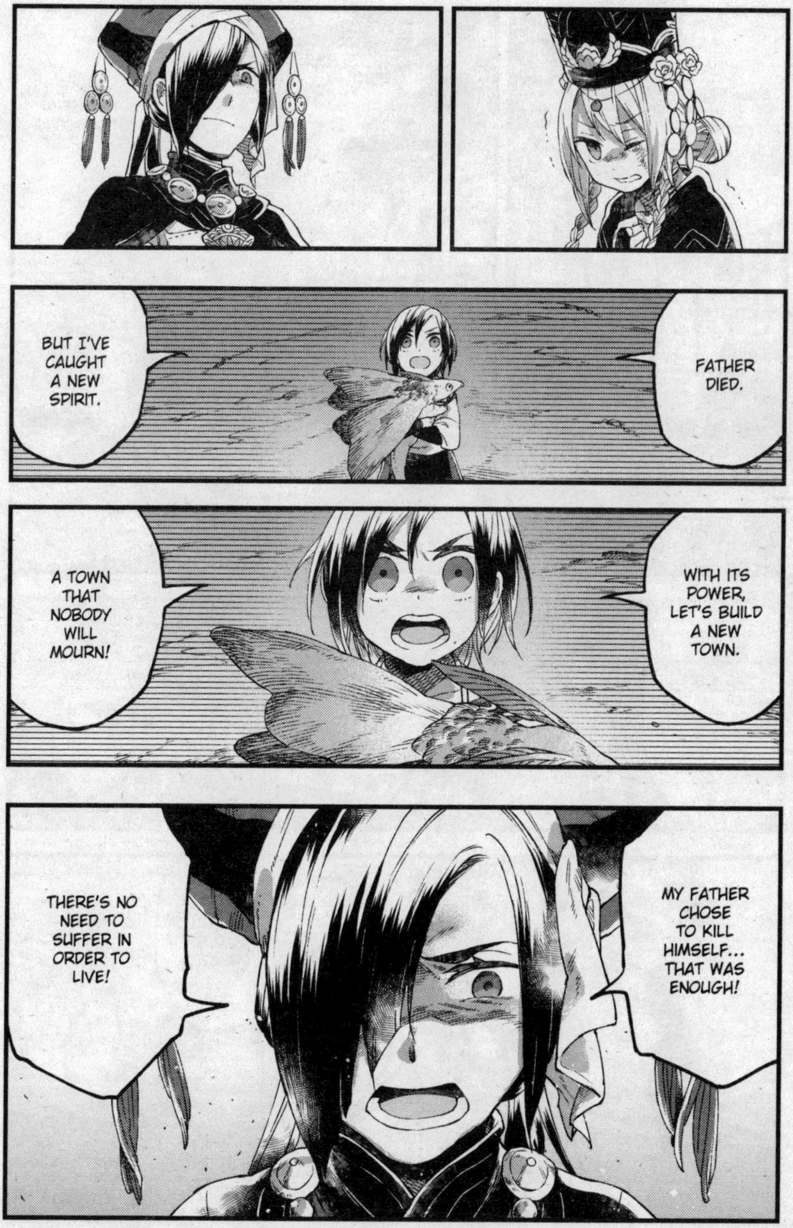
FATHER DIED.
BUT I'VE CAUGHT A NEW SPIRIT.
WITH ITS POWER, LET'S BUILD A NEW TOWN.
A TOWN THAT NOBODY WILL MOURN!
MY FATHER CHOSE TO KILL HIMSELF... THAT WAS ENOUGH!
THERE'S NO NEED TO SUFFER IN ORDER TO LIVE!

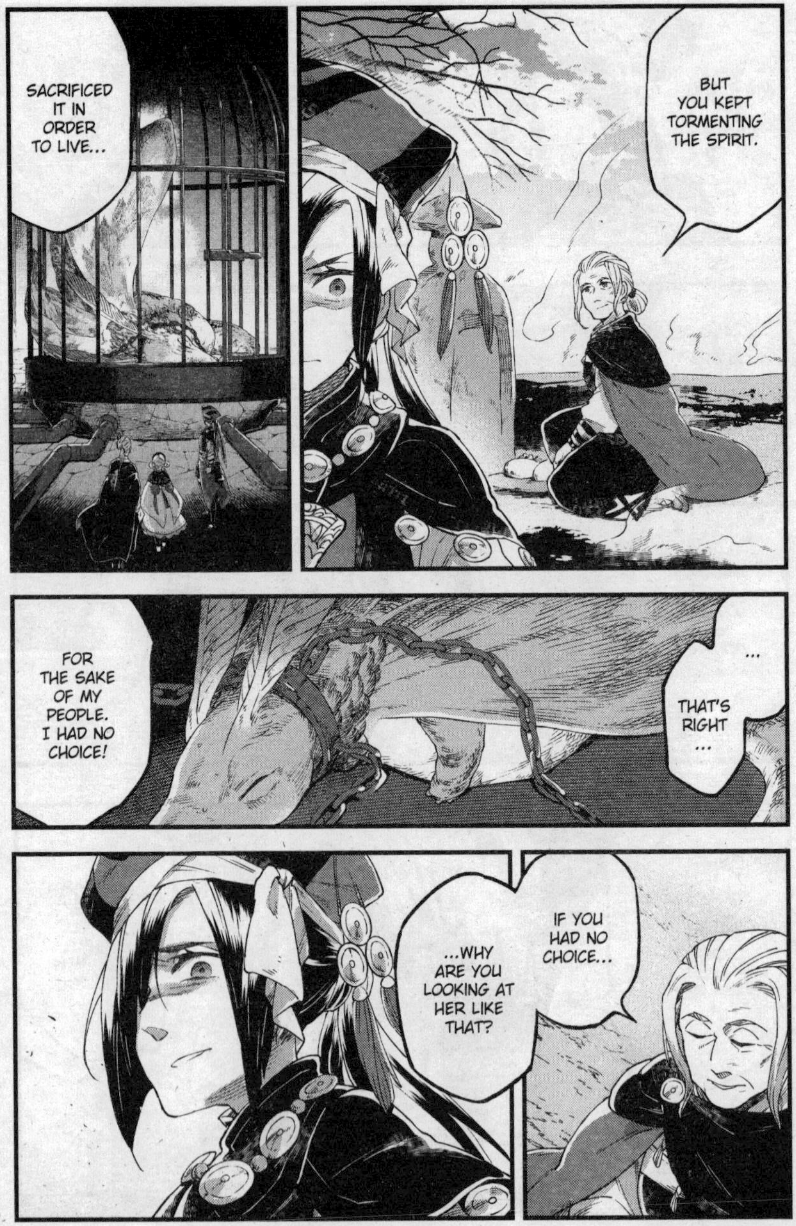
BUT YOU KEPT TORMENTING THE SPIRIT.
SACRIFICED IT IN ORDER TO LIVE...
... THAT'S RIGHT ...
FOR THE SAKE OF MY PEOPLE. I HAD NO CHOICE!
IF YOU HAD NO CHOICE...
...WHY ARE YOU LOOKING AT HER LIKE THAT?

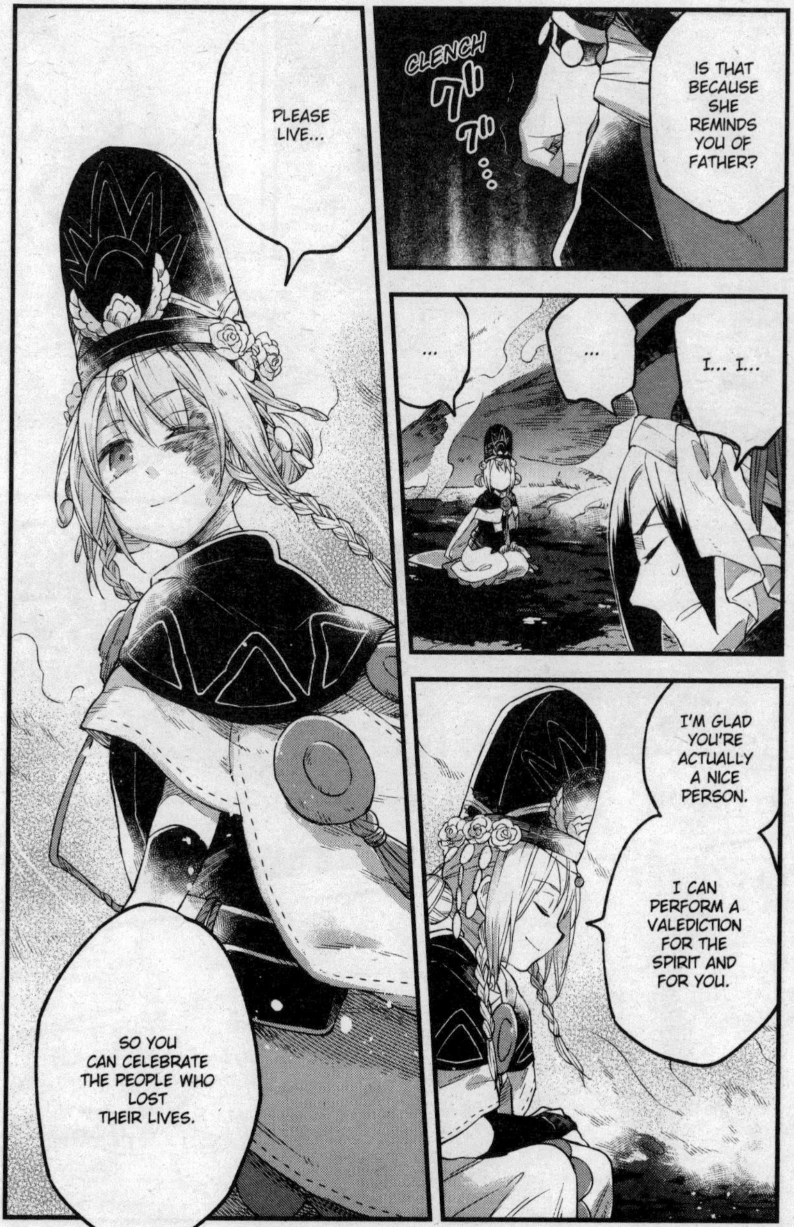
IS THAT BECAUSE SHE REMINDS YOU OF FATHER?
CLENCH
I... I...
...
...
I'M GLAD YOU'RE ACTUALLY A NICE PERSON.
I CAN PERFORM A VALEDICTION FOR THE SPIRIT AND FOR YOU.
PLEASE LIVE...
SO YOU CAN CELEBRATE THE PEOPLE WHO LOST THEIR LIVES.

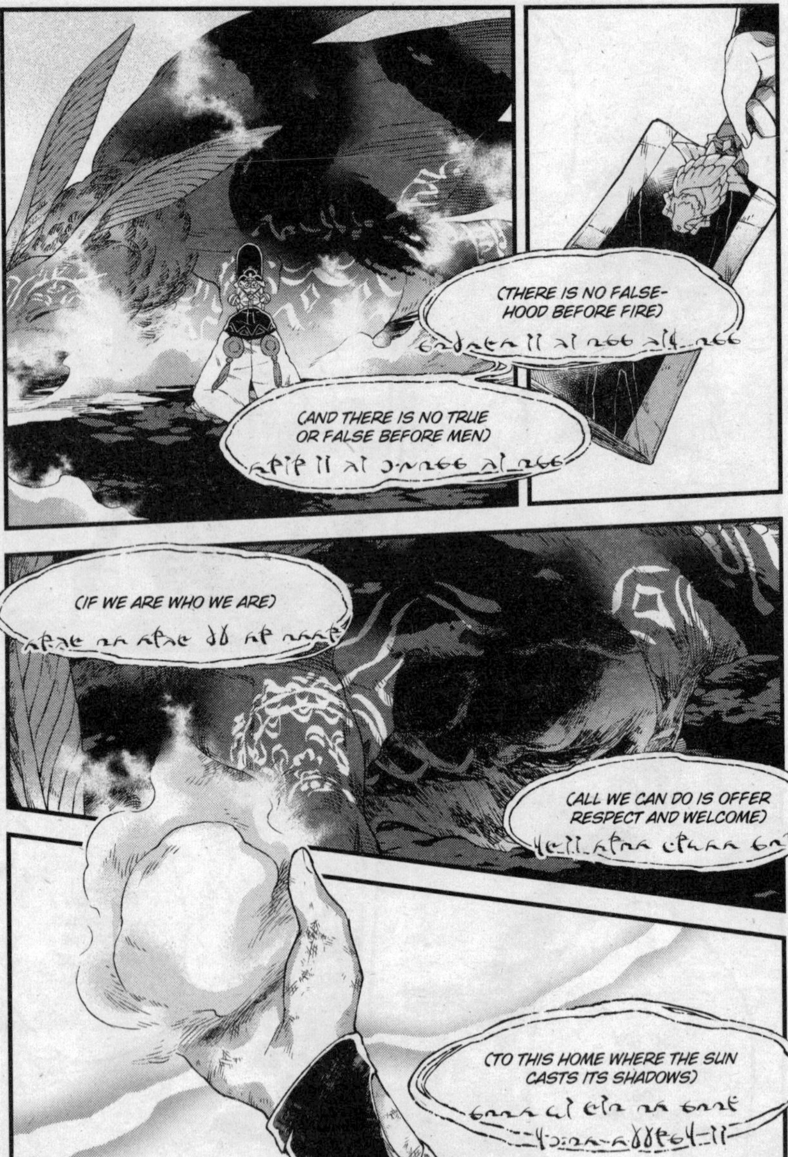
(THERE IS NO FALSEHOOD BEFORE FIRE)
(AND THERE IS NO TRUE OR FALSE BEFORE MEN)
(IF WE ARE WHO WE ARE)
(ALL WE CAN DO IS OFFER RESPECT AND WELCOME)
(TO THIS HOME WHERE THE SUN CASTS ITS SHADOWS)

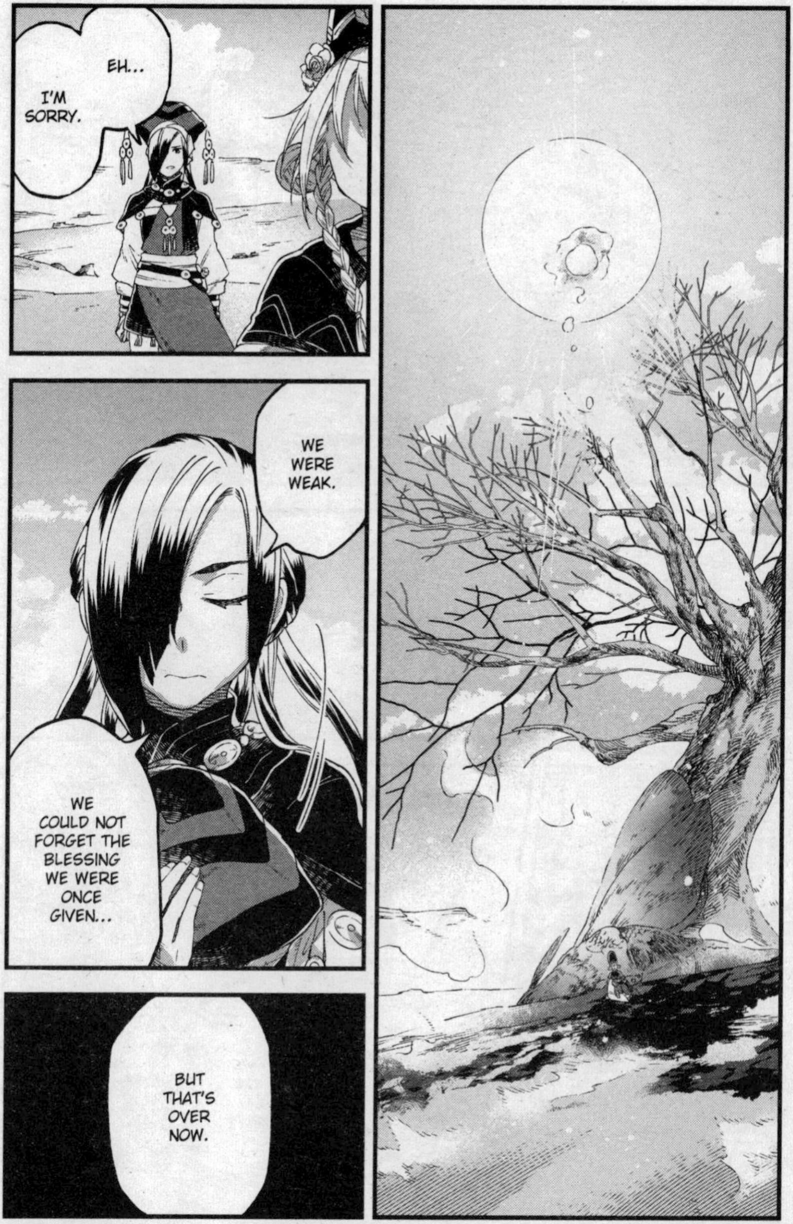
EH... I'M SORRY.
WE WERE WEAK.
WE COULD NOT FORGET THE BLESSING WE WERE ONCE GIVEN...
BUT THAT'S OVER NOW.

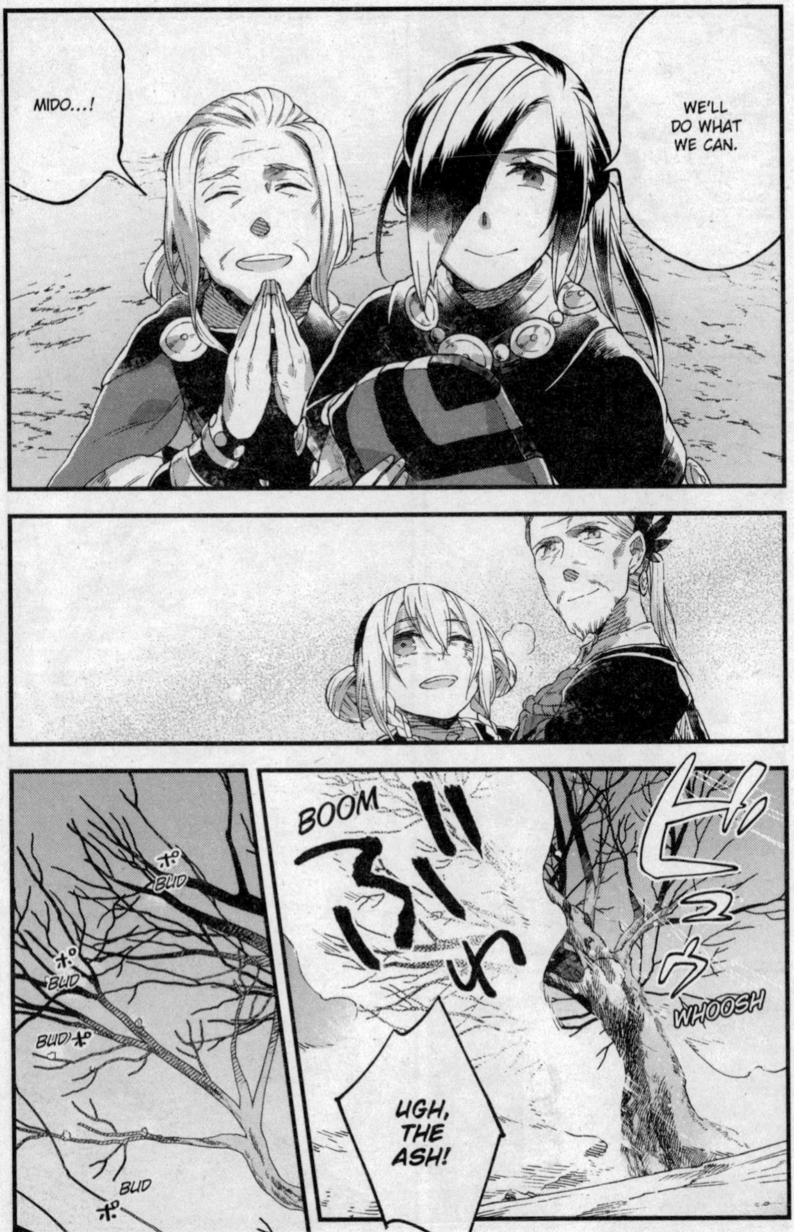
WE'LL DO WHAT WE CAN.
MIDO...!
WHOOSH
BOOM
UGH, THE ASH!
BUD
BUD
BUD
BUD

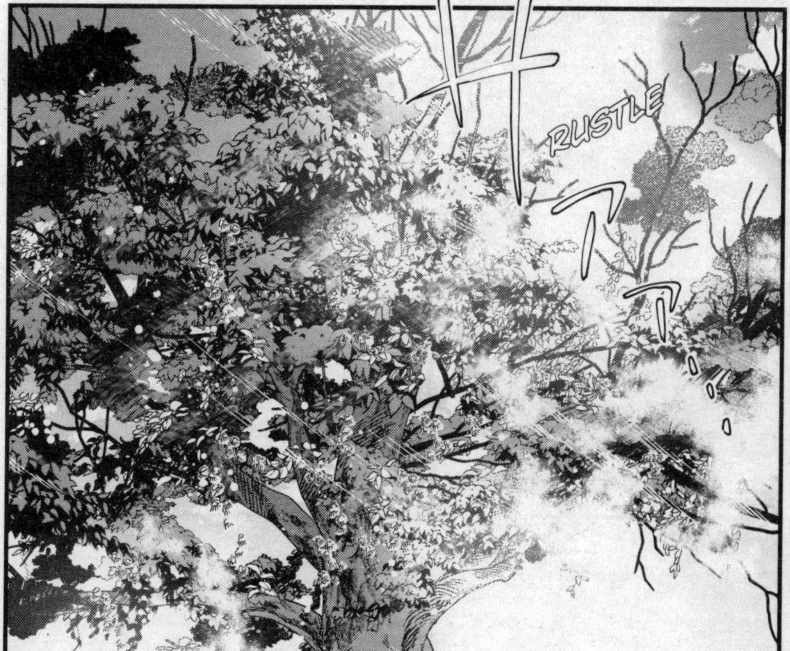
RUSTLE
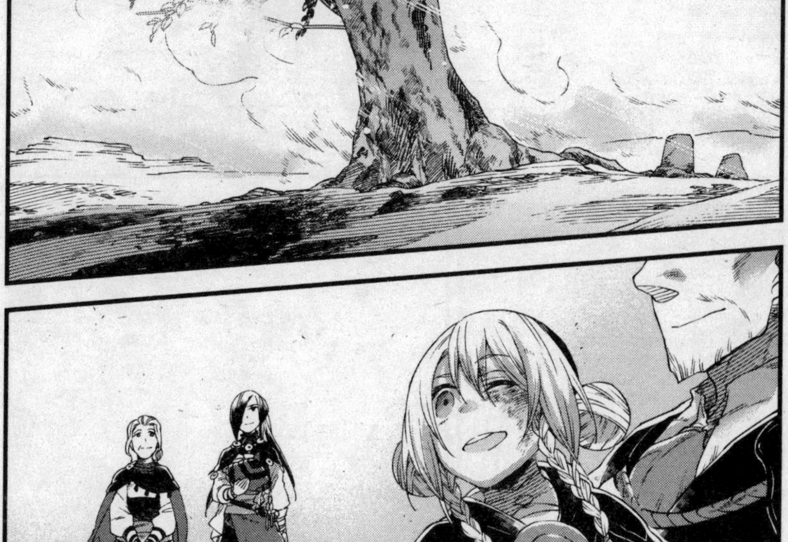

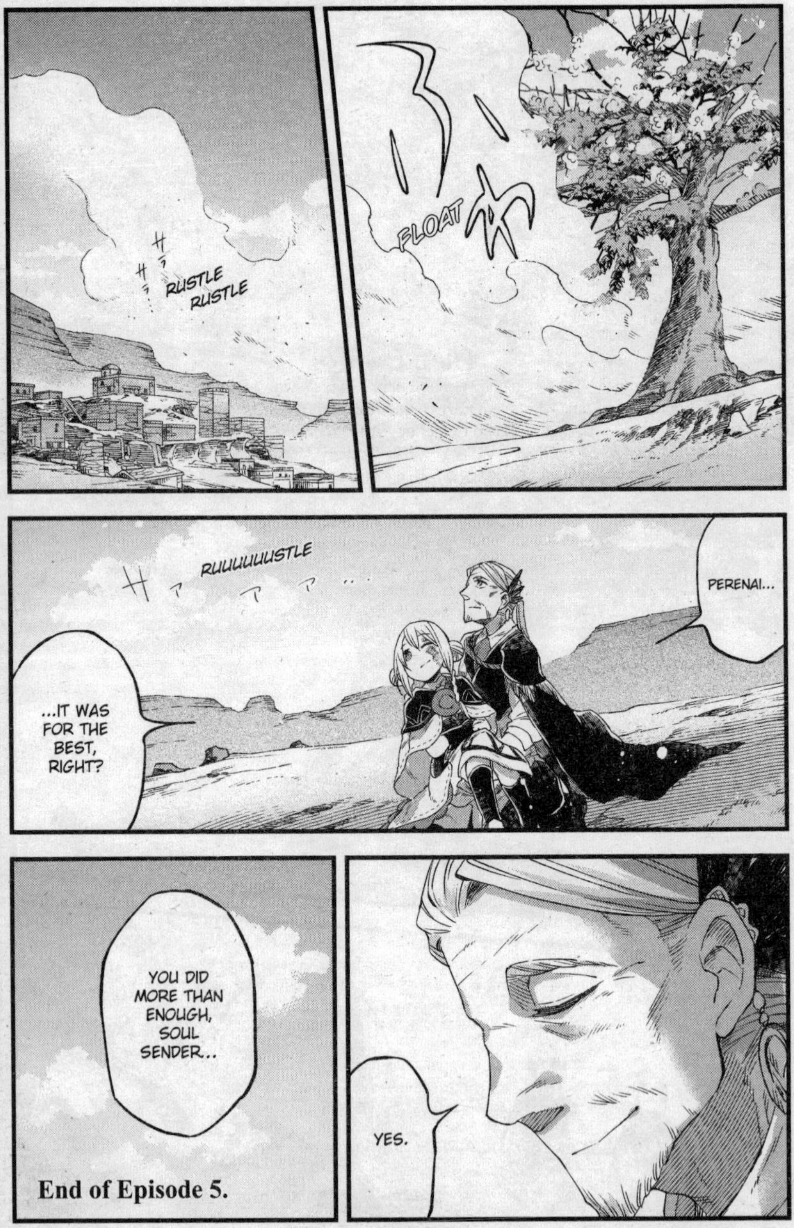
FLOAT
RUSTLE RUSTLE
PERENAI...
RUUUUUUSTLE
...IT WAS FOR THE BEST, RIGHT?
YES.
YOU DID MORE THAN ENOUGH, SOUL SENDER...
End of Episode 5.

Alpi – the Soul Sender.

Created by Rona
Translated by Motoko Tamamuro and Jonathan Clements
Lettered by Jonathan Stevenson

Titan Comics

Assistant Editor - Calum Collins / Group Editor - Jake Devine / Editor - Phoebe Hedges
Editorial Assistant - Ibraheem Kazi / Senior Creative Editor - David Manley-Leach
Designer - David Colderley / Art Director - Oz Browne
Production Controllers - Caterina Falqui & Kelly Fenlon / Production Manager - Jackie Flook
Sales & Circulation Manager - Steve Tothill / Marketing Coordinator - Lauren Noding
Publicity & Sales Coordinator - Alexandra Iciek / Publicity Manager - Will O'Mullane
Digital & Marketing Manager - Jo Teather / Head Of Rights - Jenny Boyce
Head of Creative & Business Development - Duncan Baizley
Publishing Director - Ricky Claydon / Publishing Director - John Dziewiatkowski
Group Operations Director - Alex Ruthen / Executive Vice President - Andrew Sumner
Publishers - Vivian Cheung & Nick Landau

Alpi - The Soul Sender 01

©2018 by RONA/COAMIX
Approved No.ZCW-147W
All Rights Reserved.
First Published in Japan in WEB ZENON by COAMIX, Inc., Tokyo
English translation rights arranged with COAMIX,Inc., Tokyo
through Tuttle-Mori Agency, Inc., Tokyo

This translation first published in 2023 by Titan Comics, a division of Titan Publishing Group, Ltd,
144 Southwark Street, London SE1 0UP, UK.
Titan Comics is a registered trademark of Titan Publishing Group Ltd.

10 9 8 7 6 5 4 3 2 1

First edition: October 2023
Printed in the UK
ISBN: 9781787741300

A CIP catalogue record for this title is available from the British Library.

STOP!

This manga is presented in its original right-to-left reading format. This is the back of the book!

Pages, panels, and speech balloons read from top right to bottom left, as shown above. SFX translations are placed adjacent to their original Japanese counterparts.